I0753898

LEISURE HOURS IN TOWN

A. K. H. Boyd.

LEISURE HOURS IN TOWN

BY THE AUTHOR OF

THE RECREATIONS OF A COUNTRY PARSON

BOSTON

TICKNOR AND FIELDS

1863

RIVERSIDE, CAMBRIDGE:
STEREOTYPED AND PRINTED BY H. O. HOUGHTON

CONTENTS.

CHAPTER IX.

CHAPTER X.

CHAPTER XI.

CHAPTER XII.

CHAPTER XIII.

CHAPTER XIV.

CHAPTER I.

CONCERNING THE PARSON'S LEISURE HOURS IN TOWN.

HIS is Friday evening. It has been a gloomy November day. And now, about nine o'clock, I hear the wind moaning as if there were to be a stormy night. But the fire is blazing, and the curtains are drawn: and here, in this little room, once the study of a wit and a poet, things are almost as quiet as if it were miles away from the great city in which it is. You might hear an occasional shout, from a street which is not far distant: and I am aware of a sound which appears to originate in the beating of carpets in the lane behind this row of houses. But the door-bell, which rings perpetually in the forenoon, and very frequently in the evening, is not likely to be rung any more to-night by any one whose business is with me: and no humble parishioner, interrupting the thread of one's thoughts, is likely to come now upon his little errand to his minister. This is indeed an hour of leisure: and oh, what a rest and relief such an hour is, to the man who has it only now and then!

Both my sermons for Sunday are ready; and they are in a drawer in this table on which I write. I have seen, I believe, every sick person in the congregation on some day during this week. As for the parish, *that* is by far too large and populous to be personally overtaken by any single clergyman; but I have the great comfort of being aided by a machinery of district visitation, which does not suffer one poor person in the parish to feel that he is forgotten in his parish church. I cannot, at this moment, think of any one matter of ministerial duty which demands instant attention: though of course I have the vague sense, which I suppose will never be absent, that there are many duties impending; many things which Monday morning at the latest will bring. Surely, then, if such are ever to come in a large town parish, here is one of my leisure hours.

When a country parson, leaving a little rustic cure, undertakes the charge of such a parish, if he be a man whose heart is in his work, he is quite certain greatly to overwork himself. It is indeed a total change, from the quiet of a country parish, where dwellings are dotted singly here and there, with great fields between them, to the town, where street after street of tall houses is filled with your parishioners, all entitled to some measure of your care and thought. And with that change, there comes a sudden acceleration of the wheels of life. You begin to live in a hurry. Your mind gets into a feverish state. You live under a constant feeling of pressure. You think, while you are doing anything, that something else is waiting to be done. It need not be said that such a feeling is, with most men, quite fatal to doing one's best: more particularly with the pen. And if you be of an anxious temperament, the time never comes in which you can sit down and rest, feeling that your work is done. You sit down sometimes and rest, through pure fatigue and exhaustion: but all the while you are thinking of something else which demands to be done, and which you are anxious to do. You will often wish for the precious power possessed by some men, of taking things easily: you may even sometimes sigh for the robust resolution of Lord Chancellor Thurlow. "I divide my work," he said, "into three parts. Part I do: part does itself: and part I leave undone." But many men could not for their lives resolve to do this last. They go with a hearty will at their work, till body and mind break down.

There is no work so hard, to a conscientious man, as that which he may make as easy or as hard as he chooses. It is a great blessing to have one's task set; and to be able to feel, when you have done it, that your work is done, and that you may rest with a clear conscience. But in the Church, *that* can never be. There is always something more that might be done. What clergyman can say that he has done for the good of his parish all that is possible for man to do; — that there is no new religious or benevolent agency which by energy yet more unsparing might be set in operation? It may here be said, that I do not in any degree approve the system of trying to dragoon people, whether poor or rich, into attention to their religious duties and interests, which is attempted by some good people whose zeal exceeds their discretion: and that I have no fancy for making a church, what with perpetual meetings, endless societies, and ever-recurring collections of money for this and that purpose, look like nothing so much as a great cotton-mill, with countless wheels whirring away, and dazing the brain by their ceaseless motion. It is fit to recognize the fact, that the poorest folk are responsible beings; and that intelligent artisans will not submit to be treated like children, even by people who wish to make them good children. And you know that a boy, who has learnt to swim by the aid of corks and bladders, is very apt to sink when that support is taken away. His power of swimming is not worth much. It seems to me to be even so with that form of religion, which can be kept alive only by a constant series of visits, exhortations, tracts, and week-day church-services. I venture to judge no man: but give me, say I, not the sickly exotic, but the hearty evergreen, that can bear frosts and winds. But the faithful clergyman, even trying to hold this principle in view, will find, in a large parish in a great city, work that would occupy him profitably, were each of his days as long as a week, and had he the strength of half a score of men. I firmly believe, that almost all the clergymen I know do day by day their very utmost to overtake that overwhelming duty. And now and then, there comes a special sense of the clergyman's weighty responsibility, and of the momentous consequences that may depend upon his exertions: and under that stimulus, resolving "to spend and be spent" in the work to which he has given himself, you will find him laboring in a fashion that endangers health and life.

Now, it is not right to do *that*. Even setting apart the consideration of the duty he owes his children, his duty to the Church is to work in that fashion in which he may hope to labor longest and most efficiently. And that fashion is not the breathless and feverish one. Yet nothing but constant watchfulness and firmness can prevent the town clergyman's life from growing one of chronic hurry and weariness. It is not merely his preaching, and his preparation for preaching: but the other calls of duty are innumerable. Pound after pound is added, till the camel labors along with weary foot: or even till the camel's back is broken. It is the rule in large towns, so far as I have known them, that the clergy shall be overwrought. Not that they are overdriven by the unreasonable expectations of their parishioners ; though that may sometimes be the case : but that they are spurred on by the exactions of their own conscience. Then, every now and then, you will find one making a stand against this over-pressure : feeling that he is breaking down ; and determining that he must have some leisure. You will find him beginning to take an hour's daily walk ; or resolutely setting himself to maintain some acquaintance with the literature of the day. You will find him resolving to see a little of his fellow-creatures, besides what he sees of them in the way of his duty ; and wondering if many men know what it is to feel, for days together, every word they speak an effort, and almost every step they walk. But all this is as when you determine to break yourself of the bad habit of walking too fast. You are walking along at five miles an hour. You pull up, and resolve you shall walk slowly. You set off at a moderate pace. But in a few minutes you cease to think of the rate at which you are progressing : and in a quarter of an hour you find of a sudden that you are going on at your old unreasonable speed again.

Going through your duty at this high pressure, you will, in a few months, find what will follow. Your brain gets fevered : your mind is confused : you cannot take a calm and deliberate view of any large subject : and by degrees your heart (I speak literally, not morally) tells you that this will not do. You seem almost to have lost the power of sleeping. And you find, that if you are to live and labor much longer in this world, you must do one of two things: either you must go back again to the country, or you must make a definitive arrangement that you shall have some appreciable amount of leisure in town. You may probably find, on looking back, that for a long time you have had none at all: except, indeed, in that autumnal holiday, which will not suffice to keep up for a whole year's work: and whose good effect you have probably used up within three weeks after its close. Yes, you must have leisure: a little of it every day: a half-holiday at least once a week. And I do not call it satisfactory leisure, when, at the close of a jading day, you sit down, wearied beyond talking, reading, or thinking: and feeling the presence even of your children too much for your shaken nerves. I call it leisure, when you can sit down in the evening, tired indeed, but not exhausted beyond chasing your little boy or girl about the lobby, and thinking of the soft green turf of quieter days. I call it leisure to sit down in your easy-chair by the fireside, and to feel that you may peacefully think, and dream if you please: that you may look vacantly into the fire: that you may read the new review or magazine by little bits: that you may give your mind total rest. And to this end, let us fix it in our remembrance, that all our Master requires of us is to do what we can: and that if after we have done our utmost, there still remains much more we would wish to do, we must train ourselves to look at it without disquiet, even as we train ourselves to be submissive in the presence of the inexplicable mysteries and the irremediable evils which are inherent in the present system of things. No doubt, it is hard to do this; but it is the clergyman's duty to do it. You have no more right to commit suicide by systematically overtasking your constitution, than by swifter and coarser means. Life is given to you as a trust to make the best of; and probably the worst you can make of it is to cut it short, or to embitter it by physical exhaustion and depression.

I dare say many clergymen with large parishes have known what it is to delight in a day of dreadful rain and hurricane: I mean a day when chimney-pots and slates are flying about the streets; and when no question can be raised, even by the most exacting moral sense, as to whether it is possible to go out or not. A forenoon of leisure comes so very seldom, that it is very precious and enjoyable when it comes. The leisure hours commonly attainable are in the evening. If you sit at your desk from ten o'clock in the morning till one or two in the afternoon: and if you then go out to your pastoral work till six: you may very fairly lay it down as a general rule, that at six the day's work shall be deemed over. In addition to this, it may be well to make the afternoon of Saturday a time of recreation. You will be much fitter for your Sunday work, which implies a good deal of physical fatigue as well as mental wear. And I begin to doubt if it be good or safe to begin the round of labor again on Monday after breakfast: and to think that possibly as much work would be done, and better done, if the forenoon of that day were given to recruiting one's energies after the Sunday duty. And I am not claiming these seasons of leisure for the clergymen, merely for Aristotle's reason: merely because "the end of work is to enjoy leisure:" merely because leisure is pleasant, and the hard-working parson has earned it fairly. I think not merely of the pleasure of the pastor, but of the profit of the flock. I do not think it expedient that a Christian congregation should get almost all its religious instruction from a fevered and overdriven mind. I have been struck, in listening to the preaching of one or two very able and very laborious friends, by a certain lack of calmness and sobriety of thought: by a something that reminded one of the atmosphere of a hot-house, and that seemed undefinably inconsistent with the realities of daily life. And it seemed to me that all this came of the fact, that they lived, worked, and wrote, in chronic excitement and hurry.

I trust that my non-clerical readers will pardon all this professional matter: it is a comfort to talk out one's mind even to friends whom one will never see. I dare say discerning folk will know, that the writer has been describing his own constant temptation; and that, however needful he may feel these seasons of rest to be, it is only now and then that he can train himself to take them. And he has found that nothing gives the mind more effectual rest, than change of employment. You have heard, doubtless, of that mill-horse, which all days of the week but Sunday was engaged in walking round and round a certain narrow circle. You may remember what was the Sunday's occupation of that sagacious creature. An unthinking person might have surmised that the horse, which had perpetually to walk on working days, would have chosen on its day of rest to lie still and do nothing. But the horse knew better. It spent Sunday in walking round and round, in the opposite direction from that in which it walked on week-days. It found rest, in short, not in idleness; but in variation of employment. I commend that horse. I have tried to do something analogous to what it did. These essays have been to me a pleasant change, from the writing of many sermons. And even in leisure hours, if it be (as

Sydney Smith said) "the nature of the animal to write," the pen will be taken up naturally and habitually.

I can say sincerely, that more important duties have never been postponed to the production of these chapters: and I please myself with the belief, that the hands into which this volume is likely to fall, will not be those of total strangers. You may perhaps find, my friendly reader, that these essays of an old friend, whom you knew in the days when he was a country parson, have somewhat changed their character, in consistence with his total change of life. But I have reason to cherish a quiet trust, that they have done good to some of my fellow-creatures. I suppose the like happens to all authors, who write in sincerity and in kindness of heart: but I cannot forget what numbers of men and women, otherwise unknown, from either side of the Atlantic, have cheered and encouraged the writer, sometimes in weary hours, by thanking him for some little good impression left by these pages upon heart and life. I have not been able to forego the great delight of trying to produce what might afford some pleasure and profit to friends far beyond the boundaries of my parish: nor have I been able to think that it was my duty to do so.

CHAPTER II.

CONCERNING VEAL:

A DISCOURSE OF IMMATURITY.

HE man who, in his progress through life, has listened with attention to the conversation of human beings; who has carefully read the writings of the best English authors; who has made himself well acquainted with the history and usages of his native land; and who has meditated much on all he has seen and read; must have been led to the firm conviction that by VEAL, those who speak the English language intend to denote the flesh of calves; and that by a calf is intended an immature ox or cow. A calf is a creature in a temporary and progressive stage of its being. It will not always be a calf; if it live long enough, it will assuredly cease to be a calf. And if impatient man, arresting the creature at that stage, should consign it to the hands of him whose business it is to convert the sentient animal into the impassive and unconscious meat, the nutriment which the creature will afford will be nothing more than immature beef. There may be many qualities of Veal; the calf which yields it may die at very different stages in its physical and moral development; but provided only it die as a calf — provided only that its

meat can fitly be styled Veal — *this* will be characteristic of it, that the meat shall be immature meat. It may be very good, very nutritious and palatable; some people may like it better than beef, and may feed upon it with the liveliest satisfaction; but when it is fairly and deliberately put to us, it must be admitted even by such as like Veal the best, that Veal is but an immature production of nature. I take Veal, therefore, as the emblem of IMMATURITY; of that which is now in a stage out of which it must grow; of that which, as time goes on, will grow older, will probably grow better, will certainly grow very different. *That* is what I mean by Veal.

And now, my reader and friend, you will discern the subject about which I trust we are to have some pleasant and not unprofitable thought together. You will readily believe that my subject is not that material Veal which may be beheld and purchased in the butcher's shops. I am not now to treat of its varied qualities, of the sustenance which it yields, of the price at which it may be procured, or of the laws according to which that price rises and falls. I am not going to take you to the green fields in which the creature which yielded the veal was fed, or to discourse of the blossoming hawthorn hedges from whose midst it was reft away. Neither shall I speak of the rustic life, the toils, cares, and fancies of the farm-house near which it spent its brief lifetime. The Veal of which I intend to speak is Moral Veal, or (to speak with entire accuracy), Veal Intellectual, Moral, and Æsthetical. By Veal I understand the immature productions of the human mind; immature compositions, immature opinions, feelings, and tastes. I wish to think of the work, the views, the fancies, the emotions, which are yielded by the human soul in its immature stages; while the calf (so to speak) is only growing into the ox; while the clever boy, with his absurd opinions and feverish feelings and fancies, is developing into the mature and sober-minded man. And if I could but rightly set out the thoughts which have at many different times occurred to me on this matter, if one could catch and fix the vague glimpses and passing intuitions of solid unchanging truth, if the subject on which one has thought long and felt deeply were always that on which one could write best, and could bring out to the sympathy of others what a man himself has felt, what an excellent essay this would be! But it will not be so; for as I try to grasp the thoughts I would set out, they melt away and elude me. It is like trying to catch and keep the rainbow hues you have seen the sunshine cast upon the spray of a waterfall, when you try to catch the tone, the thoughts, the feelings, the atmosphere of early youth.

There can be no question at all as to the fact, that clever young men and women, when their minds begin to open, when they begin to think for themselves, do pass through a stage of mental development which they by and by quite outgrow; and entertain opinions and beliefs, and feel emotions, on which afterwards they look back with no sympathy or approval. This is a fact as certain as that a calf grows into an ox, or that veal, if spared to grow, will become beef. But no analogy between the material and the moral must be pushed too far. There are points of difference between material and moral Veal. A calf knows it is a calf. It may think itself bigger and wiser than an ox, but it knows it is not an ox. And if it be a reasonable calf, modest, and free from prejudice, it is well aware that the joints it will yield after its demise, will be very different from those of the stately and well-consolidated ox which ruminates in the rich pasture near it. But the human boy often thinks he is a man, and even more than a man. He fancies that his mental stature is as big and as solid as it will ever become. He fancies that his mental productions — the poems and essays he writes, the political and social views he forms, the moods of feeling with which he regards things — are just what they may always be, just what they ought always to be. If spared in this world, and if he be one of those whom years make wiser, the day comes when he looks back with amazement and shame on those early mental productions. He discerns now how immature, absurd, and extravagant they were; in brief, how vealy. But at the time, he had not the least idea that they were so. He had entire confidence in himself; not a misgiving as to his own ability and wisdom. You, clever young student of eighteen years old, when you wrote your prize essay, fancied that in thought and style it was very like Macaulay; and not Macaulay in that stage of vealy brilliancy in which he wrote his essay on *Milton*, not Macaulay the fairest and most promising of calves, but Macaulay the stateliest and most beautiful of oxen. Well, read over your essay now at thirty, and tell us what you think of it. And you, clever, warm-hearted, enthusiastic young preacher of twenty-four, wrote your sermon; it was very ingenious, very brilliant in style, and you never thought, but that it would be felt by mature-minded Christian people as suiting their case, as true to their inmost experience. You could not see why you might not preach as well as a man of forty. And if people in middle age had complained that, eloquent as your preaching was, they found it suited them better and profited them more to listen to the plainer instructions of some good man with gray hair, you would not have understood their feeling; and you might perhaps have attributed it to many motives rather than the true one. But now, at five-and-thirty, find out the yellow manuscript, and read it carefully over; and I will venture to say, that if you were a really clever and eloquent young man, writing in an ambitious and rhetorical style, and prompted to do so by the spontaneous fervor of your heart and readiness of your imagination, you will feel now little sympathy even with the literary style of that early composition; you will see extravagance and bombast where once you saw only eloquence and graphic power. And as for the graver and more important matter of the thought of the discourse, I think you will be aware of a certain undefinable shallowness and crudity. Your growing experience has borne you beyond it. Somehow you feel it does not come home to you, and suit you as you would wish it should. It will not do. That old sermon you cannot preach now, till you have entirely recast and rewritten it. But you had no such notion when you wrote the sermon. You were satisfied with it. You thought it even better than the discourses of men as clever as yourself, and ten or fifteen years older. Your case was as though the youthful calf should walk beside the sturdy ox, and think itself rather bigger.

Let no clever young reader fancy from what has been said, that I am about to make an onslaught upon clever young men. I remember too distinctly how bitter and indeed ferocious I used to feel, about eleven or twelve years ago, when I have heard men of more than middle age and less than middling ability speak with contemptuous depreciation of the productions and doings of men considerably their juniors, and vastly their superiors; describing them as *boys*, and as *clever lads*, with looks of dark malignity. There are few more disgusting sights, than the envy and jealousy of their juniors, which may be seen in various malicious, commonplace old men; as there is hardly a more beautiful and pleasing sight than the old man hailing, and counselling, and encouraging the youthful genius which he knows far surpasses his own. And I, my young friend of two-and-twenty, who relatively to you, may be regarded as old, am going to assume no preposterous airs of superiority. I do not claim to be a bit wiser than you; all I claim is to be older. I have outgrown your stage; but I was once such as you, and all my sympathies are with you yet. But it is a difficulty in the way of the essayist, and, indeed, of all who set out opinions which they wish to be received and acted on by their fellow-creatures, that they seem, by the very act of offering advice to others, to claim to be wiser and better than those whom they advise. But in reality it is not so. The opinions of the essayist or of the preacher, if deserving of notice at all, are so because of their inherent truth, and not because he expresses them. Estimate them for yourself, and give them the weight which you think their due. And be sure of this, that the writer, if earnest and sincere, addressed all he said to himself as much as to any one else. This is the thing which redeems all didactic writing or speaking from the charge of offensive assumption and self-assertion. It is not for the preacher, whether of moral or religious truth, to address his fellows as outside sinners, worse than himself, and needing to be reminded of that of which he does not need to be reminded. No, the earnest preacher preaches to himself as much as to any in the congregation; it is from the picture ever before him in his own weak and wayward heart, that he learns to reach and describe the hearts of others, if indeed he do so at all. And it is the same with lesser things.

It is curious and it is instructive to remark how heartily men, as they grow towards middle age, despise themselves as they were a few years since. It is a bitter thing for a man to confess that he *is* a fool; but it costs little effort to declare that he *was* a fool, a good while ago. Indeed, a tacit compliment to his present self is involved in the latter confession; it suggests the reflection what progress he has made, and how vastly he has improved, since then. When a man informs us that he was a very silly fellow in the year 1851, it is assumed that he is not a very silly fellow in the year 1861. It is as when the merchant with ten thousand a year, sitting at his sumptuous table, and sipping his '41 claret, tells you how, when he came as a raw lad from the country, he used often to have to go without his dinner. He knows that the plate, the wine, the massively elegant apartment, the silent servants so alert yet so impassive, will appear to join in chorus with the obvious suggestion, "You see he has not to go without his dinner now!" Did you ever, when twenty years old, look back at the diary you kept when you were sixteen; or when twenty-five at the diary you kept when twenty; or at thirty, at the diary you kept when twenty-five? Was not your feeling a singular mixture of humiliation and self-complacency? What extravagant, silly stuff it seemed that you had thus written five years before! What Veal; and oh what a calf he must have been who wrote it! It is a difficult question, to which the answer cannot be elicited, Who is the greatest fool in this world? But every candid and sensible man of middle age, knows thoroughly well the answer to the question, Who was the greatest fool that he himself ever knew? And after all, it is your diary especially if you were wont to introduce into it poetical remarks and moral reflections, that will mainly help you to the humiliating conclusion. Other things, some of which I have already named, will point in the same direction. Look at the prize essays you wrote when you were a boy at school; look even at your earlier prize essays written at college (though of these last I have something to say hereafter); look at the letters you wrote home when away at school or even at college, especially if you were a clever boy, trying to write in a graphic and witty fashion; and if you have reached sense at last (which some, it may be remarked, never do), I think you will blush even through the unblushing front of manhood, and think what a terrific, unutterable, conceited, intolerable blockhead you were. It is not till people attain somewhat mature years that they can rightly understand the wonderful forbearance their parents must have shown in listening patiently to the frightful nonsense they talked and wrote. I have already spoken of sermons. If you go early into the Church, say at twenty-three or twenty-four, and write sermons regularly and diligently, you know what landmarks they will be of your mental progress. The first runnings of the stream are turbid, but it clears itself into sense and taste month by month and year by year. You wrote many sermons in your first year or two; you preached them with entire confidence in them, and they did really keep up the attention of the congregation in a remarkable way. You accumulate in a box a store of that valuable literature and theology, and when by and by you go to another parish, you have a comfortable feeling that you have a capital stock to go on with. You think that any Monday morning when you have the prospect of a very busy week, or when you feel very weary, you may resolve that you shall write no sermon that week, but just go and draw forth one from the box. I have already said what you will probably find, even if you draw forth a discourse which cost much labor. You cannot use it as it stands. Possibly it may be structural and essential Veal: the whole framework of thought may be immature. Possibly it may be Veal only in style; and by cutting out a turgid sentence here and there, and above all, by cutting out all the passages which you thought particularly eloquent, the discourse may do yet. But even then, you cannot give it with much confidence. Your mind can yield something better than that now. I imagine how a fine old orange-tree, that bears oranges with the thinnest possible skin and with no pips, juicy and rich, might feel that it has outgrown the fruit of its first years, when the skin was half an inch thick, the pips innumerable, and the eatable portion small and poor. It is with a feeling such as *that* that you read over your early sermon. Still, mingling with the sense of shame, there is a certain satisfaction. You have not been standing still; you have been getting on. And we always like to think *that.*

What is it that makes intellectual Veal? What are the things about a composition which stamp it as such? Well, it is a certain character in thought and style hard to define, but strongly felt by such as discern its presence at all. It is strongly felt by professors reading the compositions of their students, especially the compositions of the cleverest students. It is strongly felt by educated folk of middle age, in listening to the sermons of young pulpit orators, especially of such as think for themselves, of such as aim at a high standard of excellence, of such as have in them the makings of striking and eloquent preachers. Dull and stupid fellows never deviate into the extravagance and absurdity which I specially understand by Veal. They plod along in a humdrum manner: there is no poetry in their soul; none of those ambitious stirrings which lead the man who has in him the true spark of genius to try for grand things and incur severe and ignominious tumbles. A heavy dray-horse, walking along the road, may possibly advance at a very lagging pace, or may even stand still; but whatever he may do, he is not likely to jump violently over the hedge, or to gallop off at twenty-five miles an hour. It must be a thorough-bred who will go wrong in that grand fashion. And there are intellectual absurdities and extravagances which hold out hopeful promise of noble doings yet: the eagle, which will breast the hurricane yet, may meet various awkward tumbles before he learns the fashion in which to use those iron wings. But the substantial goose, which probably escapes those tumbles in trying to fly, will never do anything very magnificent in the way of flying. The man who in his early days writes in a very inflated and bombastic style, will gradually sober down into good sense and accurate taste, still retaining something of liveliness and eloquence. But expect little of the man who as a boy was always sensible, and never bombastic. *He* will grow awfully dry. *He* is sure to fall into the unpardonable sin of tiresomeness. The rule has exceptions; but the earliest productions of a man of real genius are almost always crude, flippant, and affectedly smart; or else turgid and extravagant in a high degree. Witness Mr. Disraeli; witness Sir E. B. Lytton; witness even Macaulay. The man who as a mere boy writes something very sound and sensible, will probably never become more than a dull, sensible, commonplace man. Many people can say, as they bethink themselves of their old college companions, that those who wrote with good sense and good taste at twenty, have mostly settled down into the dullest and baldest of prosers; while such as dealt in bombastic flourishes and absurd ambitiousness of style, have learned as time went on to prune their early luxuriances, while still retaining something of raciness, interest, and ornament.

I have been speaking very generally of the characteristics of Veal in composition. It is difficult to give any accurate description of it that shall go into minuter details. Of course it is easy to think of little external marks of the beast — that is, the calf. It is Veal in style when people, writing prose, think it a fine thing to write *o'er* instead of *over*, *ne'er* instead of *never*, *poesie* instead of *poetry*, and *methinks* under any circumstances whatsoever. References to the heart are generally of the nature of veal, also allusions to the mysterious throbbings and yearnings of our nature. The word *grand* has of late come to excite a strong suspicion of Veal; and when I read the other day in a certain poem something about a *great grand man*, I concluded that the writer of that poem is meanwhile a great grand calf. The only case in which the words may properly be used together is in speaking of your great grandfather. To talk about *mine* affections, meaning *my* affections, is Veal; and *mine bonnie love* was decided Veal, though it was written by Charlotte Brontë. To say *mayhap*, when you mean *perhaps*, is Veal. So is it also to talk of human *ken*, when you mean human *knowledge*. To speak of *something higher and holier* is invariably Veal: and it is usually Veal to speak of *something deeper*. *Wife mine* is Veal, though it stands in *The Caxtons*. I should rather like to see the man who in actual life is accustomed to address his spouse in that fashion. To say *Not, oh never*, shall we do so and so, is outrageous Veal. *Sylvan grove* or *sylvan vale* in ordinary conversation is Veal. The word *glorious* should be used with caution; when applied to trees, mountains, or the like, there is a strong suspicion of Veal about it. But one feels that in saying these things we are not getting at the essence of Veal. It is Veal in thought that is essential Veal, and *that* is very hard to define. Beyond extravagant language, beyond absurd fine things, it lies in a certain lack of reality and sobriety of sense and view — in a certain indefinable jejuneness in the mental fare provided, which makes mature men feel that somehow it does not satisfy their cravings. You know what I mean better than I can express it. You have seen and heard a young preacher, with a rosy face and an unlined brow, preaching about the cares and trials of life. Well, you just feel at once he knows nothing about them. You feel that all this is at second-hand. He is saying all this because he supposes it is the right thing to say. Give me the pilot to direct me who has sailed through the difficult channel many a time himself! Give me the friend to sympathize with me in sorrow, who has felt the like. There is a hollowness, a certain want, in the talk about much tribulation of the very cleverest man who has never felt any great sorrow at all. The great force and value of all teaching lie in the amount of personal experience which is embodied in it. You feel the difference between the production of a wonderfully clever boy and of a mature man when you read the first canto of *Childe Harold* and then read *Philip van Artevelde.* I do not say but that the boy's production may have a liveliness and interest beyond the man's. Veal is in certain respects superior to beef, though beef is best on the whole. I have heard vealy preachers whose sermons kept up breathless attention. From the first word to the last of a sermon which was unquestionable Veal, I have witnessed an entire congregation listen with that audible hush you know. It was very different indeed from the state of matters when a humdrum old gentleman was preaching, every word spoken by whom was the maturest sense, expressed in words to which the most fastidious taste could have taken no exception; but then the whole thing was sleepy; it was a terrible effort to attend. In the case of the Veal there was no effort at all. I defy you to help attending. But then you sat in pain. Every second sentence there was some outrageous offence against good taste; every third statement was absurd or overdrawn or almost profane. You felt occasional thrills of pure disgust and horror, and you were in terror what might come next. One thing which tended to carry all this off was the manifest confidence and earnestness of the speaker. *He* did not think it Veal that he was saying. And though great consternation was depicted on the faces of some of the better educated people in church, you could see that a very considerable part of the congregation did not think it Veal either. There can be no doubt, my middle-aged friend, if you could but give your early sermons now with the confidence and fire of the time when you wrote them, they would make a deep impression on many people yet. But it is simply impossible for you to give them; and if you should force yourself some rainy Sunday to preach one of them, you would give it with such a sense of its errors, and with such an absence of corresponding feeling, that it would fall very flat and dead. Your views are maturing: your taste is growing fastidious; the strong things you once said you could not bring yourself to say now. If you *could* preach those old sermons, there is no doubt they would go down with the mass of uncultivated folk, — go down better than your mature and reasonable ones. We have all known such cases as that of a young preacher who, at twenty-five, in his days of Veal, drew great crowds to the church at which he preached; and who at thirty-five, being a good deal tamed and sobered, and in the judgment of competent judges vastly improved, attracted no more than a respectable congregation. A very great and eloquent preacher lately lamented to me the uselessness of his store of early discourses. If he could but get rid of his present standard of what is right and good in thought and language, and preach them with the enchaining fire with which he preached them once! For many hearers remain immature, though the preacher has matured. Young people are growing up, and there are people whose taste never ripens beyond the enjoyment of Veal. There is a period in the mental development of those who will be ablest and maturest, at which vealy thought and language are accepted as the best. Veal will be highly appreciated by sympathetic calves; and the greatest men, with rare exceptions, are calves in youth, while many human beings are calves forever. And here I may remark, as something which has afforded me consolation on various occasions within the last year, that it seems unquestionable that sermons which are utterly revolting to people of taste and sense, have done much good to large masses of those people in whom common sense is most imperfectly developed, and in whom taste is not developed at all; and accordingly, wherever one is convinced of the sincerity of the individuals, however foolish and uneducated, who go about pouring forth those violent, exaggerated, and all but blasphemous discourses of which I have read accounts in the newspapers, one would humbly hope that a Power which works by many means, would bring about good even through an instrumentality which it is hard to contemplate without some measure of horror. The impression produced by most things in this world is relative to the minds on which the impression is produced. A coarse ballad, deficient in rhyme and rhythm, and only half decent, will keep up the attention of a rustic group to whom you might read from *In Memoriam* in vain. A waistcoat of glaring scarlet will be esteemed by a country bumpkin a garment every way preferable to one of aspect more subdued. A nigger melody will charm many a one who would yawn at Beethoven. You must have rough means to move rough people. The outrageous revival-orator may do good to people to whom Bishop Wilberforce or Dr. Caird might preach to no purpose; and if real good be done, by whatever means, all right-minded people should rejoice to hear of it.

And this leads to an important practical question, on which men at different periods of life will never agree.

When shall thought be regarded as mature? Is there a standard by which we can ascertain beyond question whether a composition be Veal or Beef? I sigh for fixity and assurance in matters æsthetical. It is vexatious that, what I think very good my friend Smith thinks very bad. It is vexatious that what strikes me as supreme and unapproachable excellence, strikes another person at least as competent to form an opinion, as poor. And I am angry with myself when I feel that I honestly regard as inflated commonplace and mystical jargon, what a man as old and (let us say) nearly as wise as myself thinks the utterance of a prophet. You know how, when you contemplate the purchase of a horse, you lead him up to the measuring-bar, and there ascertain the precise number of hands and inches which he stands. How have I longed for the means of subjecting the mental stature of human beings to an analogous process of measurement! Oh for some recognized and unerring gauge of mental calibre! It would be a grand thing if somewhere in a very conspicuous position — say on the site of the National Gallery at Charing-cross — there were a pillar erected, graduated by some new Fahrenheit, on which we could measure the height of a man's mind. How delightful it would be to drag up some pompous pretender who passes off at once upon himself and others as a profound and able man, and make him measure his height upon that pillar, and understand beyond all cavil what a pigmy he is! And how pleasant, too, it would be to bring up some man of unacknowledged genius, and make the world see the reach of *his* intellectual stature! The mass of educated people even are so incapable of forming an estimate of a man's ability, that it would be a blessing if men could be sent out into the world with the stamp upon them, telling what are their weight and value, plain for every one to see. But of course there are many ways in which a book, sermon, or essay, may be bad without being Vealy. It may be dull, stupid, illogical, and the like, and yet have nothing of boyishness about it. It may be insufferably bad, yet quite mature. Beef may be bad, and yet undoubtedly beef. And the question now is, not so much whether there be a standard of what is in a literary sense good or bad, as whether there be a standard of what is Veal and what is Beef. And there is a great difficulty here. Is a thing to be regarded as mature when it suits your present taste; when it is approved by your present deliberate judgment? For your taste is always changing: your standard is not the same for three successive years of your early youth. The Veal you now despise you thought Beef when you wrote it. And so, too, with the productions of other men. You cannot read now without amazement the books which used to enchant you as a child. I remember when I used to read Hervey's *Meditations* with great delight. That was when I was about five years old. A year or two later I greatly affected Macpherson's translation of Ossian. It is not so very long since I felt the liveliest interest in Tupper's *Proverbial Philosophy*. Let me confess that I retain a kindly feeling towards it yet; and that I am glad to see that some hundreds of thousands of readers appear to be still in the stage out of which I passed some years since. Yes, as you grow older your taste changes: it becomes more fastidious; and especially you come to have always less toleration for sentimental feeling and for flights of fancy. And besides this gradual and constant progression, which holds on uniformly year after year, there are changes in mood and taste sometimes from day to day and from hour to hour. The man who did a very silly thing thought it was a wise thing when he did it. He sees the matter differently in a little while. On the evening after the battle of Waterloo, the Duke of Wellington wrote a certain letter. History does not record its matter or style. But history does record that some years afterwards the Duke paid a hundred guineas to get it back again; and that on getting it he instantly burnt it, exclaiming that when he wrote it he must have been the greatest idiot on the face of the earth. Doubtless, if we had seen that letter, we should have heartily coincided in the sentiment of the hero. He *was* an idiot when he wrote it, but he did not think that he was one. I think, however, that there is a standard of sense and folly; and that there is a point at which Veal is Veal no more. But I do not believe that thought can justly be called mature only when it has become such as to suit the taste of some desperately dry old gentleman with as much feeling as a log of wood, and as much imagination as an oyster. I know how intolerant some dull old fogies are of youthful fire and fancy. I shall not be convinced that any discourse is puerile because it is pronounced such by the venerable Dr. Dryasdust. I remember that the venerable man has written many pages, possibly abundant in sound sense, but which no mortal could read, and to which no mortal could listen. I remember that though that not very amiable individual has outlived such wits as he once had, he has not outlived the unbecoming emotions of envy and jealousy; and he retains a strong tendency to evil-speaking and slandering. You told me, unamiable individual, how disgusted you were at hearing a friend of mine who is one of the best preachers in Britain, preach one of his finest sermons. Perhaps you really were disgusted: there is such a thing as casting pearls before swine, who will not appreciate them highly. But you went on to give an account of what the great preacher said; and though I know you are extremely stupid, you are not quite so stupid as to have actually fancied that the great preacher said what you reported that he said: you were well aware that you were grossly misrepresenting him. And when I find malice and insincerity in one respect I am ready to suspect them in another: and I venture to doubt whether you were disgusted. Possibly, you were only ferocious at finding yourself so unspeakably excelled. But even if you had been really disgusted; and even if you were a clever man; and even if you were above the suspicion of jealousy; I should not think that my friend's noble discourse was puerile because you thought it so. It is not when the warm feelings of earlier days are dried up into a cold, time-worn cynicism, that I think a man has become the best judge of the products of the human brain and heart. It is a noble thing when a man grows old, retaining something of youthful freshness and fervor. It is a fine thing to ripen without shrivelling: to reach the calmness of age, yet keep the warm heart and ready sympathy of youth. Show me such a man as *that*, and I shall be content to bow to *his* decision whether a thing be Veal or not. But as such men are not found very frequently, I should suggest it as an approximation to a safe criterion, that a thing may be regarded as mature when it is deliberately and dispassionately approved by an educated man of good ability, and above thirty years of age. No doubt a man of fifty may hold that fifty is the age of sound taste and sense: and a youth of twenty-three may maintain that he is as good a judge of human doings now as he will ever be. I do not claim to have proposed an infallible standard. I give you my present belief, being well aware that it is very likely to alter.

It is not desirable that one's taste should become too fastidious, or that natural feeling should be refined away. And a cynical young man is bad, but a cynical old one is a great deal worse. The cynical young man is probably shamming; he is a humbug, not a cynic. But the old man probably *is* a cynic, as heartless as he seems. And without thinking of cynicism, real or affected, let us remember that though the taste ought to be refined and daily refining, it ought not to be refined beyond being practically serviceable. Let things be good; but not too good to be workable. It is expedient that a cart for conveying coals should be of neat and decent appearance. Let the shafts be symmetrical, the boards well-planed, the whole strong yet not clumsy; and over the whole let the painter's skill induce a hue rosy as beauty's cheek, or dark-blue as her eye. All *that* is well; and while the cart will carry its coals satisfactorily, it will stand a good deal of rough usage, and it will please the eye of the rustic who sits in it on an empty sack, and whistles as it moves along. But it would be highly inexpedient to make that cart of walnut of the finest grain and marking, and to have it French-polished. It would be too fine to be of use; and its possessor would fear to scratch it; and would preserve it as a show, seeking some plainer vehicle to carry his coals. In like manner, do not refine too much either the products of the mind, or the sensibilities of the taste which is to appreciate them. I know an amiable professor very different from Dr. Dry-asdust. He was a country clergyman; a very interesting plain preacher. But when he got his chair, he had to preach a good deal in the college chapel; and by way of accommodating his discourses to an academic audience, he re-wrote them carefully; rubbed off all the salient points; cooled down whatever warmth was in them to frigid accuracy; toned down everything striking. The result was that his sermons became eminently classical and elegant; only they became impossible to attend to, and impossible to remember. And when you heard the good man preach, you sighed for the rough and striking heartiness of former days. And we have all heard of such a thing as taste refined to that painful sensitiveness, that it became a source of torment; that is, unfitted for common enjoyments and even for common duties. There was once a great man, let us say at Melipotamus, who never went to church. A clergyman once in speaking to a friend of the great man, lamented that the great man set so bad an example before his humbler neighbors. "How *can* that man go to church," was the reply; "his taste and his entire critical faculty, is sharpened to that degree, that in listening to any ordinary preacher, he feels outraged and shocked at every fourth sentence he hears, by its inelegance or its want of logic; and the entire sermon torments him by its unsymmetrical structure, its want of perspective in the presentment of details, and its general literary badness." I quite believe that there was a moderate proportion of truth in the excuse thus urged; and you will probably judge that it would have been better had the great man's mind not been brought to so painful a polish.

The mention of dried-up old gentlemen reminds one of a question which has sometimes perplexed me. Is it Vealy to feel or to show keen emotion? Is it a precious result and indication of the maturity of the human mind, to look as if you felt nothing at all? I have often looked with wonder, and with a moderate amount of veneration, at a few old gentlemen whom I know well, who are leading members of a certain legislative and judicial council, held in great respect in a country of which no more need be said. I have beheld these old gentlemen sitting apparently quite unmoved when discussions were going on in which I knew they felt a very deep interest, and when the tide of debate was setting strongly against their peculiar views. There they sat, impassive as a Red Indian at the stake. I think of a certain man, who, while a smart speech on the other side is being made, retains a countenance expressing actually nothing; he looks as if he heard nothing, felt nothing, cared for nothing. But when the other man sits down, he rises to reply. He speaks slowly at first, but every weighty word goes home and tells: he gathers warmth and rapidity as he goes on, and in a little you become aware that for a few hundred pounds a year, you may sometimes get a man who would have made an Attorney-General or a Lord Chancellor; you discern that under the appearance of almost stolidity, there was the sharpest attention watching every word of the argument of the other speaker, and ready to come down on every weak point in it; and the other speaker is (in a logical sense) pounded to jelly by a succession of straight-handed hits. Yes, it is a wonderful thing to find a combination of coolness and earnestness. But I am inclined to believe that the reason why some old gentlemen look as if they did not care, is that in fact they don't care. And there is no particular merit in looking cool while a question is being discussed, if you really do not mind a rush which way it may be decided. A keen, unvarying, engrossing regard for one's self, is a great safeguard against over-excitement in regard to all the questions of the day, political, social, and religious.

It is a curious but certain fact, that clever young men, at that period of their life when their own likings tend towards Veal, know quite well the difference between veal and beef; and are quite able, when necessary, to produce the latter. The tendency to boyishness of thought and style may be repressed, when you know you are writing for the perusal of readers with whom *that* will not go down. A student of twenty, who has in him great talent, no matter how undue a supremacy his imagination may meanwhile have, if he be set to producing an essay in Metaphysics to be read by professors of philosophy, will produce a composition singularly free from any trace of immaturity. For such a clever youth, though he may have a strong bent towards Veal, has in him an instinctive perception that it *is* Veal; and a keen sense of what will and will not do for the particular readers he has to please. Go, you essayist who carried off a host of university honors; and read over now the prize essays you wrote at twenty-one or twenty-two. I think the thing that will mainly strike you will be, how very mature these compositions are; how ingenious, how judicious, how free from extravagance, how quietly and accurately and even felicitously expressed. *They* are not Veal. And yet you know, that several years after you wrote them you were still writing a great deal which was Veal beyond all question. But then a clever youth can produce material to any given standard; and you wrote the essays not to suit your own taste, but to suit what you intuitively knew was the taste of the grave and even smoke-dried professors who were to read them and sit in judgment on them.

And though it is very fit and right that the academic standard should be an understood one, and quite different from the popular standard, still it is not enough that a young man should be able to write to a standard against which he in his heart rebels and protests. It is yet more important that you should get him to approve and adopt a standard which is accurate, if not severe. It is quite extraordinary what bombastic and immature sermons are preached in their first years in the Church by young clergymen who wrote many academic compositions in a style the most classical. It seems to be essential that a man of feeling and imagination should be allowed fairly to run himself out. The course apparently is, that the tree should send out its rank shoots, and then that you should prune them, rather than that by some repressive means you should prevent the rank shoots coming forth at all. The way to get a high-spirited horse to be content to stay peaceably in its stall, is to allow it to have a tearing gallop, and thus get out its superfluous nervous excitement and vital spirit. Let the boiler blow off its steam. All repression is dangerous. And some injudicious folk, instead of encouraging the highly-charged mind and heart to relieve themselves by blowing off in excited verse and extravagant bombast, would (so to speak) sit on the safety valve. Let the bursting spring flow! It will run turbid at first; but it will clear itself day by day. Let a young man write a vast deal: the more he writes, the sooner will the Veal be done with. But if a man write very little the bombast is not blown off; and it may remain till advanced years. It seems as if a certain quantity of fustian must be blown off before you reach the good material. I have heard a mercantile man of fifty read a paper he had written on a social subject. He had written very little save business letters all his life. And I assure you that his paper was bombastic to a degree that you would have said was barely tolerable in a youth of twenty. I have seldom listened to Veal so outrageous. You see he had not worked through it in his youth; and so here it was now. I have witnessed the like phenomenon in a man who went into the Church at five-and-forty. I heard him preach one of his earliest sermons, and I have hardly ever heard such boyish rodomontade. The imaginations of some men last out in liveliness longer than those of others; and the taste of some men never becomes perfect; and it is no doubt owing to these things that you find some men producing Veal so much later in life than others. You will find men who are very turgid and magniloquent at five-and-thirty, at forty, at fifty. But I attribute the phenomenon in no small measure to the fact that such men had not the opportunity of blowing off their steam in youth. Give a man at four-and-twenty two sermons to write a week, and he will very soon work through his Veal. It is probably because ladies write comparatively so little, that you find them writing at fifty poetry and prose of the most awfully romantic and sentimental strain.

We have been thinking, my friend, as you have doubtless observed, almost exclusively of intellectual and æsthetical immaturity, and of its products in composition, spoken or written. But combining with that immaturity, and going very much to affect the character of that Veal, there is moral immaturity, resulting in views, feelings, and conduct, which may be described as Moral Veal.

But indeed it is very difficult to distinguish between the different kinds of immaturity; and to say exactly what in the moods and doings of youth proceeds from each. It is safest to rest in the general proposition that, even as the calf yields Veal, so does the immature human mind yield immature productions. It is a stage which you outgrow, and therefore a stage of comparative immaturity, in which you read a vast deal of poetry, and repeat much poetry to yourself when alone, working yourself up thereby to an enthusiastic excitement. And very like a calf you look when some one suddenly enters the room in which you are wildly gesticulating or moodily laughing, and thinking yourself poetical and indeed sublime. The person probably takes you for a fool; and the best you can say for yourself is that you are not so great a fool as you seem to be. Vealy is the period of life in which you filled a great volume with the verses you loved; and in which you stored your memory, by frequent reading, with many thousands of lines. All that you outgrow. Fancy a man of fifty having his commonplace book of poetry! And it will be instructive to turn over the ancient volume, and to see how year by year the verses copied grew fewer, and finally ceased entirely. I do not say that all growth is progress; sometimes it is like that of the muscle which once advanced into manly vigor and usefulness, but is now ossifying into rigidity. It is well to have fancy and feeling under command: it is not well to have feeling and fancy dead. That season of life is vealy in which you are charmed by the melody of verse quite apart from its meaning. And there is a season in which that is so. And it is curious to remark what verses they are that have charmed many men. For they are often verses in which no one else could have discerned that singular fascination. You may remember how Robert Burns has recorded that in youth he was enchanted by the melody of two lines of Addison's: —

For though in dreadful whirls we hung,
High on the broken wave.

Sir Walter Scott felt the like fascination in youth (and he tells us it was not entirely gone even in age), in Mickle's stanza: —

The dews of summer night did fall;
The moon, sweet regent of the sky,
Silvered the walls of Cumnor Hall,
And many an oak that grew thereby.

Not a remarkable verse, I think. However, it at least presents a pleasant picture. But I remember well the enchantment which, when twelve years old, I felt in a verse by Mrs. Hemans, which I can now see presents an excessively disagreeable picture. I saw it not then; and when I used to repeat that verse, I know it was without the slightest perception of its meaning. You know the beautiful poem called the *Battle of Morgarten.* At least I remember it as beautiful; and I am not going to spoil my recollection by reading it now. Here is the verse: —

Oh! the sun in heaven fierce havoc viewed,
When the Austrian turned to fly:
And the brave, in the trampling multitude,
Had a fearful death to die!

As I write that verse (at which the critical reader will smile), I am aware that Veal has its hold of me yet. I see nothing of the miserable scene the poet describes; but I hear the waves murmuring on a distant beach, and I see the hills across the sea, the first sea I ever beheld; I see the school to which I went daily; I see the class-room and the place where I used to sit; I see the faces and hear the voices of my old companions, some dead, one sleeping in the middle of the great Atlantic, many scattered over distant parts of the world, almost all far away. Yes, I feel that I have not quite cast off the witchery of the *Battle of Morgarten*. Early associations can give to verse a charm and a hold upon one's heart which no literary excellence, however high, ever could. Look at the first hymns you learned to repeat, and which you used to say at your mother's knee; look at the psalms and hymns you remember hearing sung at church when you were a child: you know how impossible it is for you to estimate these upon their literary merits. They may be almost doggrel; but not Mr. Tennyson can touch you like them! The most effective eloquence is that which is mainly done by the mind to which it is addressed: it is *that* which touches chords which of themselves yield matchless music; it is *that* which wakens up trains of old remembrance, and which wafts around you the fragrance of the hawthorn that blossomed and withered many long years since. An English stranger would not think much of the hymns we sing in our Scotch churches: he could not know what many of them are to us. There is a magic about the words. I can discern, indeed, that some of them are mawkish in sentiment, faulty in rhyme, and on the whole what you would call extremely unfitted to be sung in public worship, if you were judging of them as new things: but a crowd of associations which are beautiful and touching gathers round the lines which have no great beauty or pathos in themselves.

You were in an extremely vealy condition when, having attained the age of fourteen, you sent some verses to the county newspaper, and with simple-hearted elation read them in the corner devoted to what was termed "Original Poetry." It is a pity you did not preserve the newspapers in which you first saw yourself in print, and experienced the peculiar sensation which accompanies that sight. No doubt your verses expressed the gloomiest views of life, and told of the bitter disappointments you had met in your long intercourse with mankind, and especially with womankind. And though you were in a flutter of anxiety and excitement to see whether or not your verses would be printed, your verses probably declared that you had used up life and seen through it; that your heart was no longer to be stirred by aught on earth; and that, in short, you cared nothing for anything. You could see nothing fine, then, in being good, cheerful, and happy; but you thought it a grand thing to be a gloomy man, of a very dark complexion, with blood on your conscience, upwards of six feet high, and accustomed to wander from land to land, like Childe Harold. You were extremely vealy when you used to fancy that you were sure to be a very great man; and to think how proud your relations would some day be of you, and how you would come back and excite a great commotion at the place where you used to be a schoolboy. And it is because the world has still left some impressionable spot in your hearts, my readers, that you still have so many fond associations with "the schoolboy spot, we ne'er forget, though we are there forgot." They were vealy days, though pleasant to remember, my old school companions, in which you used to go to the dancing-school (it was in a gloomy theatre, seldom entered by actors), in which you fell in love with several young ladies about eleven years old; and (being permitted occasionally to select your own partners) made frantic rushes to obtain the hand of one of the beauties of that small society. Those were the days in which you thought that when you grew up it would be a very fine thing to be a pirate, bandit, or corsair, rather than a clergyman, barrister, or the like; even a cheerful outlaw like Robin Hood did not come up to your views; you would rather have been a man like Captain Kyd, stained with various crimes of extreme atrocity, which would entirely preclude the possibility of returning to respectable society, and given to moody laughter in solitary moments. Oh, what truly asinine developments the human being must go through before arriving at the stage of common sense! You were very vealy, too, when you used to think it a fine thing to astonish people by expressing awful sentiments, such as that you thought Mahommedans better than Christians, that you would like to be dissected after death, that you did not care what you got for dinner, that you liked learning your lessons better than going out to play, that you would rather read Euclid than *Ivanhoe*, and the like. It may be remarked that this peculiar vealiness is not confined to youth; I have seen it appearing very strongly in men with gray hair. Another manifestation of vealiness, which appears both in age and youth, is the entertaining a strong belief that kings, noblemen, and baronets, are always in a condition of ecstatic happiness. I have known people pretty far advanced in life, who not only believed that monarchs must be perfectly happy, but that all who were permitted to continue in their presence would catch a considerable degree of the mysterious bliss which was their portion. I have heard a sane man, rather acute and clever in many things, seriously say, "If a man cannot be happy in the presence of his Sovereign, where can he be happy?"

And yet, absurd and foolish as is moral vealiness, there is something fine about it. Many of the old and dear associations most cherished in human hearts, are of the nature of Veal. It is sad to think that most of the romance of life is unquestionably so. All spooniness, all the preposterous idolization of some one who is just like anybody else, all love (in the narrow sense in which the word is understood by novel readers), you feel when you look back, are Veal. The young lad and the young girl, whom at a pic-nic party you have discerned stealing off under frivolous pretexts from the main body of guests, and sitting on the grass by the riverside, enraptured in the prosecution of a conversation which is intellectually of the emptiest, and fancying that they two make all the world, and investing that spot with remembrances which will continue till they are gray, are (it must in sober sadness be admitted) of the nature of calves. For it is beyond doubt that they are at a stage which they will outgrow, and on which they may possibly look back with something of shame. All these things, beautiful as they are, are no more than Veal. Yet they are fitting and excellent in their time. No, let us not call them veal, they are rather like lamb, which is excellent though immature. No doubt, youth is immaturity; and as you outgrow it you are growing better and wiser; still youth is a fine thing, and most people would be young again if they could. How cheerful and light-hearted is immaturity! How cheerful and lively are the little children even of silent and gloomy men! It is sad, and it is unnatural, when they are not so. I remember yet, when I was at school, with what interest and wonder I used to look at two or three boys, about twelve or thirteen years old, who were always dull, sullen, and unhappy-looking. In those days, as a general rule, you are never sorrowful without knowing the reason why. You are never conscious of the dull atmosphere, of the gloomy spirits, of after-time. The youthful machine, bodily and mental, plays smoothly; the young being is cheery. Even a kitten is very different from a grave old cat; and a young colt, from a horse sobered by the cares and toils of years. And you picture fine things to yourself in your youthful dreams. I remember a beautiful dwelling I used often to see, as if from the brow of a great hill. I see the rich valley below, with magnificent woods and glades, and a broad river reflecting the sunset; and in the midst of the valley, the vast Saracenic pile, with gilded minarets blazing in the golden light. I have since then seen many splendid habitations, but none in the least equal to that. I cannot even yet discard the idea that somewhere in this world there stands that noble palace, and that some day I shall find it out. You remember also the intense delight with which you read the books that charmed you then: how you carried off the poem or the tale to some solitary place, how you sat up far into the night to read it, how heartily you believed in all the story, and sympathized with the people it told of. I wish I could feel now the veneration for the man who has written a book which I used once to feel. Oh that one could read the old volumes with the old feeling! Perhaps you have some of them yet, and you remember the peculiar expression of the type in which they were printed: the pages look at you with the face of an old friend. If you were then of an observant nature, you will understand how much of the effect of any composition upon the human mind depends upon the printing, upon the placing of the points, even upon the position of the sentences on the page. A grand, high-flown, and sentimental climax ought always to conclude at the bottom of a page. It will look ridiculous if it ends four or five lines down from the top of the next page. Somehow there is a feeling as of the difference between the night before and the next morning. It is as though the crushed ball-dress and the dishevelled locks of the close of the evening re-appeared, the same, before breakfast. Let us have homely sense at the top of the page, pathos at the foot of it. What a force in the bad type of the shabby little *Childe Harold* you used to read so often! You turn it over in a grand illustrated edition, and it seems like another poem. Let it here be said, that occasionally you look with something like indignation on the volume which enchained you in your boyish days. For now you have burst the chain. And you have somewhat of the feeling of the prisoner towards the jailer who held him in unjust bondage. What right had that bombastic rubbish to touch and thrill you as it used to do? Well, remember that it suits successive generations at their enthusiastic stage. There are poets whose great admirers are for the most part under twenty years old; but probably almost every clever young person regards them at some period in his life as among the noblest of mortals. And it is no ignoble ambition to win the ardent appreciation of even immature tastes and hearts. Its brief endurance is compensated by its intensity. You sit by the fireside and read your leisurely *Times*, and you feel a tranquil enjoyment. You like it better than the *Sorrows of Werter*, but you do not like it a twentieth part as much as you once liked the *Sorrows of Werter*. You would be interested in meeting the man who wrote that brilliant and slashing leader; but you would not regard him with speechless awe, as something more than human. Yet, remembering all the weaknesses out of which men grow, and on which they look back with a smile or sigh, who does not feel that there is a charm which will not depart about early youth? Longfellow knew that he would reach the hearts of most men when he wrote such a verse as this: —

The green trees whispered low and mild;
  It was a sound of joy!
They were my playmates when a child,
And rocked me in their arms so wild;
Still they looked at me and smiled,
  As if I were a boy!

Such readers as are young men, will understand what has already been said as to the bitter indignation with which the writer, some years ago, listened to self-conceited elderly persons who put aside the arguments and the doings of younger men with the remark that these younger men were *boys*. There are few terms of reproach which I have heard uttered with looks of such deadly ferocity. And there are not many which excite feelings of greater wrath in the souls of clever young men. I remember how in those days I determined to write an essay, which should scorch up and finally destroy all these carping and malicious critics. It was to be called *A Chapter on Boys*. After an introduction of a sarcastic and magnificent character, setting out views substantially the same as those contained in the speech of Lord Chatham in reply to Walpole, which boys are taught to recite at school, that essay was to go on to show that a great part of English literature was written by very young men. Unfortunately, on proceeding to investigate the matter carefully, it appeared that the best part of English literature, even in the range of poetry, was in fact written by men of even more than middle age. So the essay was never finished, though a good deal of it was sketched out. Yesterday I took out the old manuscript; and after reading a bit of it, it appeared so remarkably vealy, that I put it with indignation into the fire. Still I observed various facts of interest as to great things done by young men, and some by young men who never lived to be old. Beaumont the dramatist died at twenty-nine. Christopher Marlowe wrote *Faustus* at twenty-five, and died at thirty. Sir Philip Sidney wrote his *Arcadia* at twenty-six. Otway wrote *The Orphan* at twenty-eight, and *Venice Preserved* at thirty. Thomson wrote the *Seasons* at twenty-seven. Bishop Berkeley had devised his Ideal System at twenty-nine; and Clarke at the same age published his great work on the *Being and Attributes of God.* Then there is Pitt, of course. But these cases are exceptional; and besides, men at twenty-eight and thirty are not in any way to be regarded as boys. What I wanted was proof of the great things that had been done by young fellows about two-and-twenty; and such proof was not to be found. A man is simply a boy grown up to his best; and of course what is done by men must be better than what is done by boys. Unless in very peculiar cases, a man at thirty will be every way superior to what he was at twenty; and at forty to what he was at thirty. Not indeed physically; let *that* be granted. Not always morally; but surely intellectually and æsthetically.

Yes, my readers, we have all been Calves. A great part of all our doings has been what the writer, in figurative language, has described as Veal. We have not said, written, or done very much on which we can now look back with entire approval. And we have said, written, and done a very great deal on which we cannot look back but with burning shame and confusion. Very many things which, when we did them, we thought remarkably good, and much better than the doings of ordinary men, we now discern, on calmly looking back, to have been extremely bad. That time, you know, my friend, when you talked in a very fluent and animated manner after dinner at a certain house, and thought you were making a great impression on the assembled guests, most of them entire strangers; you are now fully aware that you were only making a fool of yourself. And let this hint of one public manifestation of vealiness, suffice to suggest to each of us scores of similar cases. But though we feel, in our secret souls, what calves we have been, and though it is well for us that we should feel it deeply, and thus learn humility and caution, we do not like to be reminded of it by anybody else. Some people have a wonderful memory for the vealy sayings and doings of their friends. They may be very bad hands at remembering anything else; but they never forget the silly speeches and actions on which one would like to shut down the leaf. You may find people, a great part of whose conversation consists of repeating and exaggerating their neighbor's Veal; and though that Veal may be immature enough and silly enough, it will go hard but your friend Mr. Snarling will represent it as a good deal worse than the fact. You will find men who while at college were students of large ambition but slender abilities, revenging themselves in this fashion upon the clever men who beat them. It is easy, very easy, to remember foolish things that were said and done even by the senior wrangler or the man who takes a double first-class; and candid folk will think that such foolish things were not fair samples of the men; and will remember, too, that the men have grown out of these, have grown mature and wise, and for many a year past would not have said or done such things. But if you were to judge from the conversation of Mr. Limejuice (who wrote many prize essays, but through the malice and stupidity of the judges never got any prizes), you would conclude that every word uttered by his successful rivals was one that stamped them as essential fools, and calves which would never grow into oxen. I do not think it is a pleasing or magnanimous feature in any man's character, that he is ever eager to rake up these early follies. I would not be ready to throw in the teeth of a pretty butterfly that it was an ugly caterpillar once, unless I understood that the butterfly liked to remember the fact. I would not suggest to this fair sheet of paper on which I am writing, that not long ago it was dusty rags and afterwards dirty pulp. You cannot be an ox without previously having been a calf; you acquire taste and sense gradually; and in acquiring them you pass through stages in which you have very little of either. It is a poor burden for the memory, to collect and shovel into it the silly sayings and doings in youth of people who have become great and eminent. I read with much disgust a biography of Mr. Disraeli, which recorded, no doubt accurately, all the sore points in that statesman's history. I remember, with great approval, what Lord John Manners said in Parliament in reply to Mr. Bright, who had quoted a well-known and very silly passage from Lord John's early poetry. "I would rather," said Lord John, "have been the man who in his youth wrote those silly verses, than the man who in mature years would rake them up." And with even greater indignation I regard the individual who, when a man is doing creditably and Christianly the work of life, is ever ready to relate and aggravate the moral delinquencies of his schoolboy and student days, long since repented of and corrected. "Remember not," said a man who knew human nature well, "the sins of my youth." But there are men whose nature has a peculiar affinity for anything petty, mean, and bad. They fly upon it as a vulture on carrion. Their memory is of that cast, that you have only to make inquiry of them concerning any of their friends, to hear of something not at all to the friends' advantage. There are individuals, after listening to whom you think it would be a refreshing novelty, almost startling from its strangeness, to hear them say a word in favor of any human being whatsoever.

It is not a thing peculiar to immaturity; yet it may be remarked, that though it is an unpleasant thing to look back and see that you have said or done something very foolish, it is a still more unpleasant thing to be well aware at the time that you are saying or doing something very foolish. If a man be a fool at all, it is much to be desired that he should be a very great fool, for then he will not know when he is making a fool of himself. But it is painful not to have sense enough to know what you should do in order to be right, but to have sense enough to know that you are doing wrong. To know that you are talking like an ass, yet to feel that you cannot help it; that you must say something, and can think of nothing better to say; this is a suffering that comes with advanced civilization. This is a phenomenon frequently to be seen at public dinners in country towns, also at the entertainment which succeeds a wedding. Men at other times rational, seem to be stricken into idiocy when they rise to their feet on such occasions; and the painful fact is, that it is conscious idiocy. The man's words are asinine, and he knows they are asinine. His wits have entirely abandoned him: he is an idiot for the time. Have you sat next a man unused to speaking at a public dinner; have you seen him nervously rise and utter an incoherent, ungrammatical, and unintelligible sentence or two, and then sit down with a ghastly smile? Have you heard him say to his friend on the other side, in bitterness, "I have made a fool of myself!" And have you seen him sit moodily through the remainder of the feast, evidently ruminating on what he said, seeing now what he ought to have said, and trying to persuade himself that what he said was not so bad after all? Would you do a kindness to that miserable man? You have just heard his friend on the other side cordially agreeing with what he had said as to the badness of the appearance made by him. Enter into conversation with him; talk of his speech, congratulate him upon it; tell him you were extremely struck by the freshness and naturalness of what he said, that there is something delightful in hearing an unhackneyed speaker, that to speak with entire fluency looks professional — it is like a barrister or a clergyman. Thus you may lighten the mortification of a disappointed man; and what you say will receive considerable credence. It is wonderful how readily people believe anything they would like to be true.

I was walking this afternoon along a certain street, coming home from visiting certain sick persons, and wondering how I should conclude this essay, when, standing on the pavement on one side of the street, I saw a little boy of four years old, crying in great distress. Various individuals, who appeared to be Priests and Levites, looked as they passed at the child's distress, and passed on without doing anything to relieve it. I spoke to the little man, who was in great fear at being spoken to, but told me he had come away from his home and lost himself, and could not find his way back. I told him I would take him home if he could tell me where he lived: but he was frightened into utter helplessness, and could only tell that his name was Tom, and that he lived at the top of a stair. It was a poor neighborhood, in which many people live at the top of stairs, and the description was vague. I spoke to two humble, decent-looking women who were passing, thinking they might gain the little thing's confidence better than me; but the poor little man's great wish was just to get away from us, though when he got two yards off he could but stand and cry. You may be sure he was not left in his trouble, but that he was put safely in his father's hands. And as I was coming home, I thought that here was an illustration of something I have been thinking of all this afternoon. I thought I saw in the poor little child's desire to get away from those who wanted to help him, though not knowing where to go when left to himself, something analogous to what the immature human being is always disposed to. The whole teaching of our life is leading us away from our early delusions and follies, from all those things about us which have been spoken of under the similitude which need not be again repeated. Yet we push away the hand that would conduct us to soberer and better things, though when left alone we can but stand and vaguely gaze about us; and we speak hardly of the growing experience which makes us wiser, and which ought to make us happier too. Let us not forget that the teaching which takes something of the gloss from life is an instrument in the kindest Hand of all; and let us be humbly content if that kindest Hand shall lead us, even by rough means, to calm and enduring wisdom — wisdom by no means inconsistent with youthful freshness f feeling, and not necessarily fatal even to youthful gaiety of mood; — and at last to that Happy Place, where worn men regain the little child's heart, and old and young are blest together!

CHAPTER III.

CONCERNING THINGS SLOWLY LEARNT.

YOU will see in a little while what sort of things they are which I understand by *Things Slowly Learnt.* Some are facts, some are moral truths, some are practical lessons; but the great characteristic of all those which are to be thought of in this essay, is, that we have to learn them and act upon them in the face of a strong bias to think or act in an opposite way. It is not that they are so difficult in themselves; not that they are hard to be understood, or that they are supported by arguments whose force is not apparent to every mind. On the contrary, the things which I have especially in view are very simple, and for the most part quite unquestionable. But the difficulty of learning them lies in this: that, as regards them, the head seems to say one thing and the heart another. We see plainly enough what we ought to think or to do; but we feel an irresistible inclination to think or to do something else. It is about three or four of these things that we are going, my friend, to have a little quiet talk. We are going to confine our view to a single class, though possibly the most important class, in the innumerable multitude of Things Slowly Learnt.

The truth is, a great many things are slowly learnt.

I have lately had occasion to observe that the alphabet is one of these. I remember, too, in my own sorrowful experience, how the Multiplication Table was another. A good many years since, an eminent dancing-master undertook to teach a number of my schoolboy companions a graceful and easy deportment; but comparatively few of us can be said as yet to have thoroughly attained it. I know men who have been practising the art of extempore speaking for many years, but who have reached no perfection in it, and who, if one may judge from their confusion and hesitation when they attempt to speak, are not likely ever to reach even decent mediocrity in that wonderful accomplishment. Analogous statements might be made with truth, with regard to my friend Mr. Snarling's endeavors to produce magazine articles; likewise concerning his attempts to skate, and his efforts to ride on horseback unlike a tailor. Some folk learn with remarkable slowness that nature never intended them for wits. There have been men who have punned, ever more and more wretchedly, to the end of a long and highly respectable life. People submitted in silence to the infliction; no one liked to inform those reputable individuals that they had better cease to make fools of themselves. This, however, is part of a larger subject, which shall be treated hereafter. On the other hand, there are things which are very quickly learnt; which are learnt by a single lesson. One liberal tip, or even a few kind words heartily said, to a manly little schoolboy, will establish in his mind the rooted principle that the speaker of the words or the bestower of the tip is a jolly and noble specimen of humankind. Boys are great physiognomists: they read a man's nature at a glance. Well I remember how, when going to and from school, a long journey of four hundred miles, in days when such a journey implied travel by sea as well as by land, I used to know instantly the gentlemen or the railway officials to whom I might apply for advice or information. I think that this intuitive perception of character is blunted in after years. A man is often mistaken in his first impression of man or woman; a boy hardly ever. And a boy not only knows at once whether a human being is amiable or the reverse; he knows also whether the human being is wise or foolish. In particular, he knows at once whether the human being always means what he says, or says a great deal more than he means. Inferior animals learn some lessons quickly. A dog once thrashed for some offence, knows quite well not to repeat it. A horse turns for the first time down the avenue to a house where he is well fed and cared for; next week, or next month, you pass that gate, and though the horse has been long taught to submit his will to yours, you can easily see that he knows the place again, and that he would like to go back to the stable with which, in his poor, dull, narrow mind, there are pleasant associations. I would give a good deal to know what a horse is thinking about. There is something very curious and very touching about the limited intelligence and the imperfect knowledge of that immaterial principle, in which the immaterial does not imply the immortal. And yet, if we are to rest the doctrine of a future life in any degree upon the necessity of compensation of the sufferings and injustice of a present, I think the sight of the cab horses of any large town might plead for the admission of some quiet world of green grass and shady trees, where there should be no cold, starvation, over-work, or flogging. Some one has said that the most exquisite material scenery would look very cold and dead in the entire absence of irrational life. Trees suggest singing-birds; flowers and sunshine make us think of the drowsy bees. And it is curious to think how the future worlds of various creeds are described as not without their lowly population of animals inferior to man. We know what the "poor Indian" expects shall bear him company in his humble heaven; and possibly various readers may know some dogs who in certain important respects are very superior to certain men. You remember how, when a war-chief of the Western woods was laid by his tribe in his grave, his horse was led to the spot in the funeral procession, and at the instant when the earth was cast upon the dead warrior's dust, an arrow reached the noble creature's heart, that in the land of souls the man should find his old friend again. And though it has something of the grotesque, I think it has more of the pathetic, the aged huntsman of Mr. Assheton Smith desiring to be buried by his master, with two horses and a few couples of dogs, that they might all be ready to start together when they meet again far away.

This is a deviation; but *that* is of no consequence. It is of the essence of the present writer's essays to deviate from the track. Only we must not forget the thread of the discourse; and after our deviation we must go back to it. All this came of our remarking that some things are very quickly learnt; and that certain inferior classes of our fellow-creatures learn them quickly. But deeper and larger lessons are early learnt. Thoughtful children of a very few years old, have their own theory of human nature. Before studying the metaphysicians, and indeed while still imperfectly acquainted with their letters, young children have glimpses of the inherent selfishness of humanity. I was recently present when a small boy of three years old, together with his sister, aged five, was brought down to the dining-room at the period of dessert. The small boy climbed upon his mother's knee, and began by various indications to display his affection for her. A stranger remarked what an affectionate child he was. "Oh," said the little girl, "he suspects (by which she meant *expects*) that he is going to get something to eat!" Not Hobbes himself had reached a clearer perception or a firmer belief of the selfish system in moral philosophy. "He is always very affectionate," the youthful philosopher proceeded, "when he suspects he is going to get something good to eat!"

By *Things Slowly Learnt*, I mean not merely things which are in their nature such that it takes a long time to learn them; such as the Greek language, or the law of vendors and purchasers. These things indeed take long time and much trouble to learn; but once you have learnt them, you know them. Once you have come to understand the force of the second aorist, you do not find your heart whispering to you as you are lying awake at night, that what the grammar says about the second aorist is all nonsense; you do not feel an inveterate disposition, gaining force day by day, to think concerning the second aorist just the opposite of what the grammar says. By *Things Slowly Learnt*, I understand things which it is very hard to learn at the first, because strong as the reasons which support them are, you find it so hard to make up your mind to them. I understand things which you can quite easily (when it is fairly put to you) see to be true; but which it seems as if it would change the very world you live in to accept. I understand things you discern to be true, but which you have all your life been accustomed to think false; and which you are extremely anxious to think false. And by *Things Slowly Learnt* I understand things which are not merely very hard to learn at the first; but which it is not enough to learn for once, ever so well. I understand things which, when you have made the bitter effort, and admitted them to be true and certain, you put into your mind to keep (so to speak); and hardly a day has passed when a soft quiet hand seems to begin to crumble them down and to wear them away to nothing. You write the principle which was so hard to receive, upon the tablet of your memory; and day by day a gentle hand comes over it with a bit of india-rubber, till the inscription loses its clear sharpness, grows blurred and indistinct, and finally quite disappears. Nor is the gentle hand content even then; but it begins, very faintly at first, to trace letters which bear a very different meaning. Then it deepens and darkens them day by day, week by week, till at a month's or a year's end the tablet of memory bears in great, sharp, legible letters, just the opposite thing to that which you had originally written down there. These are my *Things Slowly Learnt.* Things you learn at first in the face of a strong bias against them; things when once taught you gradually forget, till you come back again to your old way of thinking. Such things, of course, lie within the realm to which extends the influence of feeling and prejudice. They are things in the accepting of which both head and heart are concerned. Once convince a man that two and two make four, and he learns the truth without excitement, and he never doubts it again. But prove to a man that he is of much less importance than he has been accustomed to think; or prove to a woman that her children are very much like those of other folk; or prove to the inhabitant of a country parish that Britain has hundreds of parishes which in soil, and climate, and productions, are just as good as his own; or prove to the great man of a little country town that there are scores of towns in this world where the walks are as pleasant, the streets as well paved, and the population as healthy and as well conducted; and in each such case you will find it very hard to convince the individual at the time, and you will find that in a very short space the individual has succeeded in entirely escaping from the disagreeable conviction. You may possibly find, if you endeavor to instil such belief into minds of but moderate cultivation, that your arguments will be met less by force of reason than by roaring of voice and excitement of manner; you may find that the person you address will endeavor to change the issue you are arguing, to other issues, wholly irrelevant, touching your own antecedents, character, or even personal appearance; and you may afterwards be informed by good-natured friends, that the upshot of your discussion had been to leave on the mind of your acquaintance the firm conviction that you yourself are intellectually a blockhead, and morally a villain. And even when dealing with human beings who have reached that crowning result of a fine training, that they shall have got beyond thinking a man their "enemy because he tells them the truth," you may find that you have rendered a service like that rendered by the surgeon's amputating knife — salutary, yet very painful — and leaving forever a sad association with your thought and your name. For among the things we slowly learn, are truths and lessons which it goes terribly against the grain to learn at first;

which must be driven into us time after time; and which perhaps are never learnt completely.

One thing very slowly learnt by most human beings, is, that they are of no earthly consequence beyond a very small circle indeed; and that really nobody is thinking or talking about them. Almost all commonplace men and women in this world have a vague but deeply-rooted belief that they are quite different from anybody else, and of course quite superior to everybody else. It may be in only one respect they fancy they are this, but that one respect is quite sufficient. I believe that if a grocer or silk-mercer in a little town has a hundred customers, each separate customer lives on under the impression that the grocer or the silk-mercer is prepared to give to him or her certain advantages in buying and selling which will not be accorded to the other ninety-nine customers. "Say it is for Mrs. Brown," is Mrs. Brown's direction to her servant when sending for some sugar; "say it is for Mrs. Brown, and he will give it a little better." The grocer, keenly alive to the weaknesses of his fellow-creatures, encourages this notion. "This tea," he says, "would be four-and-sixpence a pound *to any one else*, but *to you* it is only four-and-threepence." Judging from my own observation, I should say that retail dealers trade a good deal upon this singular fact in the constitution of the human mind, that it is inexpressibly bitter to most people to believe that they stand on the ordinary level of humanity; that, in the main, they are just like their neighbors. Mrs. Brown would be filled with unutterable wrath if it were represented to her that the grocer treats her precisely as he does Mrs. Smith, who lives on one side of her, and Mrs. Snooks, who lives on the other. She would be still more angry if you asked her what earthly reason there is why she should in any way be distinguished beyond Mrs. Snooks and Mrs. Smith. She takes for granted she is quite different from them: quite superior to them. Human beings do not like to be classed, at least with the class to which in fact they belong. To be classed at all is painful to an average mortal, who firmly believes that there never was such a being in this world. I remember one of the cleverest friends I have — one who assuredly cannot be classed intellectually, except in a very small and elevated class — telling me how mortified he was, when a very clever boy of sixteen, at being classed at all. He had told a literary lady that he admired Tennyson. "Yes," said the lady, "I am not surprised at that: there is a class of young men who like Tennyson at your age." It went like a dart to my friend's heart. *Class of young men*, indeed! Was it for *this* that I outstripped all competitors at school, that I have been fancying myself an unique phenomenon in nature, *different* at least from every other being that lives, that I should be spoken of as one of *a class of young men!* Now, in my friend's half-playful reminiscence, I see the exemplification of a great fact in human nature. Most human beings fancy themselves, and all their belongings, to be quite different from all other beings, and the belongings of all other beings. I heard an old lady, whose son is a rifleman, and just like all the other volunteers of his corps, lately declare that on the occasion of a certain grand Review her Tom looked so entirely different from all the rest. No doubt he did to her, poor old lady, for he was her own. But the irritating thing was, that the old lady wished it to be admitted that Tom's superiority was an actual fact, equally patent to the eyes of all mankind. Yes, my friend: it is a thing very slowly learnt by most men, that they are very much like other people. You see the principle which underlies what you hear so often said by human beings, young and old, when urging you to do something which it is against your general rule to do. "Oh, but you might do it *for me!*" Why for you more than for any one else, would be the answer of severe logic. Bu a kindly man would not take that ground: for doubtles the *Me*, however little to every one else, is to each unit in human-kind the centre of all the world.

Arising out of this mistaken notion of their own difference from all other men, is the fancy entertained by many, that they occupy a much greater space in the thoughts of others than they really do. Most folk think mainly about themselves and their own affairs. Even a matter which "everybody is talking about," is really talked about by each for a very small portion of the twenty-four hours. And a name which is "in everybody's mouth," is not in each separate mouth for more than a few minutes at a time. And during those few minutes, it is talked of with an interest very faint when compared with that you feel for yourself. You fancy it a terrible thing when you yourself have to do something which you would think nothing about if done by anybody else. A lady grows sick, and has to go out of church during the sermon. Well, you remark it; possibly indeed you don't; and you say, Mrs. Thomson went out of church to-day; she must be ill; and there the matter ends. But a day or two later you see Mrs. Thomson, and find her quite in a fever at the awful fact. It was a dreadful trial, walking out, and facing all the congregation: they must have thought it so strange; she would not run the risk of it again for any inducement. The fact is just this: Mrs. Thompson thinks a great deal of the thing, because it happened to herself. It did not happen to the other people, and so they hardly think of it at all. But nine in every ten of them, in Mrs. Thomson's place, would have Mrs. Thomson's feeling; for it is a thing which you, my reader, slowly learn, that people think very little about you.

Yes, it is a thing slowly learnt: by many not learnt at all. How many persons you meet walking along the street who evidently think that everybody is looking at them! How few persons can walk through an exhibition of pictures at which are assembled the grand people of the town and all their own grand acquaintances, in a fashion thoroughly free from self-consciousness! I mean without thinking of themselves at all, or of how they look; but in an unaffected manner, observing the objects and beings around them. Men who have attained recently to a moderate eminence, are sometimes, if of small minds, much affected by this disagreeable frailty. Small literary men, and preachers with no great head or heart, have within my own observation suffered from it severely. I have witnessed a poet, whose writings I have never read, walking along a certain street. I call him a poet to avoid periphrasis. The whole get-up of the man, his dress, his hair, his hat, the style in which he walked, showed unmistakably that he fancied that everybody was looking at him, and that he was the admired of all admirers. In fact, nobody was looking at him at all. Some time since I beheld a portrait of a very, very small literary man. It was easy to discern from it that the small author lives in the belief that wherever he goes he is the object of universal observation. The intense self-consciousness and self-conceit apparent in that portrait were, in the words of Mr. Squeers, "more easier conceived than described." The face was a very commonplace and rather good-looking one: the author, notwithstanding his most strenuous exertions, evidently could make nothing of the features to distinguish him from other men. But the length of his hair was very great; and oh, what genius he plainly fancied glowed in those eyes! I never in my life witnessed such an extraordinary glare. I do not believe that any human being ever lived whose eyes habitually wore that expression: only by a violent effort could the expression be produced; and then for a very short time, without serious injury to the optic nerves. The eyes were made as large as possible; and the thing after which the poor fellow had been struggling was that peculiar look which may be conceived to penetrate through the beholder, and pierce his inmost thoughts. I never beheld the living original, but if I saw him I should like in a kind way to pat him on the head, and tell him that *that* sort of expression would produce a great effect on the gallery of a minor theatre. The other day I was at a public meeting. A great crowd of people was assembled in a large hall: the platform at one end of it remained unoccupied till the moment when the business of the meeting was to begin. It was an interesting sight for any philosophic observer seated in the body of the hall to look at the men who by and by walked in procession on to the platform, and to observe the different ways in which they walked in. There were several very great and distinguished men: every one of these walked on to the platform and took his seat in the most simple and unaffected way, as if quite unconscious of the many eyes that were looking at them with interest and curiosity.

There were many highly respectable and sensible men, whom nobody cared particularly to see, and who took their places in a perfectly natural manner, as though well aware of the fact. But there were one or two small men, struggling for notoriety; and I declare it was pitiful to behold their entrance. I remarked one in particular, who evidently thought that the eyes of the whole meeting were fixed upon himself; and that as he walked in everybody was turning to his neighbor, and saying with agitation, "See, that's Snooks!" His whole gait and deportment testified that he felt that two or three thousand eyes were burning him up: you saw it in the way he walked to his place, in the way he sat down, in the way he then looked about him. If any one had tried to get up three cheers for Snooks, Snooks would not have known that he was being made a fool of. He would have accepted the incense of fame as justly his due. There once was a man who entered the Edinburgh theatre at the same instant with Sir Walter Scott. The audience cheered lustily; and while Sir Walter modestly took his seat, as though unaware that those cheers were to welcome the Great Magician, the other man advanced with dignity to the front of the box, and bowed in acknowledgment of the popular applause. This of course was but a little outburst of the great tide of vain self-estimation which the man had cherished within his breast for years. Let it be said here, that an affected unconsciousness of the presence of a multitude of people is as offensive an exhibition of self-consciousness as any that is possible. Entire naturalness, and a just sense of a man's personal insignificance, will produce the right deportment. It is very irritating to see some clergymen walk into church to begin the service. They come in, with eyes affectedly cast down, and go to their place without ever looking up, and rise and begin without one glance at the congregation. To stare about them as some clergymen do, in a free and easy manner, befits not the solemnity of the place and the worship; but the other is the worse thing. In a few cases it proceeds from modesty: in the majority from intolerable self-conceit. The man who keeps his eyes downcast in that affected manner fancies that everybody is looking at him. There is an insufferable self-consciousness about him; and he is much more keenly aware of the presence of other people than the man who does what is natural, and looks at the people to whom he is speaking. It is not natural nor rational to speak to one human being with your eyes fixed on the ground; and neither is it natural or rational to speak to a thousand. And I think that the preacher who feels in his heart that he is neither wiser nor better than his fellow-sinners to whom he is to preach, and that the advices he addresses to them are addressed quite as solemnly to himself, will assume no conceited airs of elevation above them, but will unconsciously wear the demeanor of any sincere worshipper, somewhat deepened in solemnity by the remembrance of his heavy personal responsibility in leading the congregation's worship; but assuredly and entirely free from the vulgar conceit which may be fostered in a vulgar mind by the reflection, "Now everybody is looking at me!" I have seen, I regret to say, various distinguished preachers whose pulpit demeanor was made to me inexpressibly offensive by this taint of self-consciousness. And I have seen some, with half the talent, who made upon me an impression a thousand-fold deeper than ever was made by the most brilliant eloquence; because the simple earnestness of their manner said to every heart, "Now, I am not thinking in the least about myself, or about what you may think of me: my sole desire is to impress on your hearts these truths I speak, which I believe will concern us all forever!" I have heard great preachers, after hearing whom you could walk home quite at your ease, praising warmly the eloquence and the logic of the sermon. I have heard others (infinitely greater in my poor judgment), after hearing whom you would have felt it profanation to criticize the literary merits of their sermon, high as those were: but you walked home thinking of the lesson and not of the teacher; solemnly revolving the truths you had heard; and asking the best of all help to enable you to remember them and act upon them.

There are various ways in which self-consciousness disagreeably evinces its existence; and there is not one perhaps more disagreeable than the affected avoidance of what is generally regarded as egotism. Depend upon it, my reader, that the straightforward and natural writer who frankly uses the first person singular, and says, "I think thus and thus," "I have seen so and so," is thinking of himself and his own personality a mighty deal less than the man who is always employing awkward and roundabout forms of expression to avoid the use of the obnoxious *I*. Every such periphrasis testifies unmistakably that the man was thinking of himself; but the simple, natural writer, warm with his subject, eager to press his views upon his readers, uses the *I* without a thought of self, just because it is the shortest, most direct, and most natural way of expressing himself. The recollection of his own personality probably never once crossed his mind during the composition of the paragraph from which an ill-set critic might pick out a score of *I's*. To say "It is submitted" instead of "I think," "It has been observed" instead of "I have seen," "the present writer" instead of "I," is much the more really egotistical. Try to write an essay without using that vowel which some men think the very shibboleth of egotism, and the remembrance of yourself will be in the background of your mind all the time you are writing. It will be always intruding and pushing in its face, and you will be able to give only half your mind to your subject. But frankly and naturally use the "I," and the remembrance of yourself vanishes. You are grappling with the subject; you are thinking of it and of nothing else. You use the readiest and most unaffected mode of speech to set out your thoughts of it. You have written *I* a dozen times, but you have not thought of yourself once.

You may see the self-consciousness of some men strongly manifested in their handwriting. The handwriting of some men is essentially affected; more especially their signature. It seems to be a very searching test whether a man is a conceited person or an unaffected person, to be required to furnish his autograph to be printed underneath his published portrait. I have fancied I could form a theory of a man's whole character from reading, in such a situation, merely the words "Very faithfully yours, Eusebius Snooks." You could see that Mr. Snooks was acting when he wrote that signature. He was thinking of the impression it would produce on those who saw it. It was not the thing which a man would produce who simply wished to write his name legibly in as short a time and with as little needless trouble as possible. Let me say with sorrow that I have known even venerable bishops who were not superior to this irritating weakness. Some men aim at an aristocratic hand; some deal in vulgar flourishes. These are the men who have reached no farther than that stage at which they are proud of the dexterity with which they handle their pen. Some strive after an affectedly simple and student-like hand; some at a dashing and military style. But there may be as much self-consciousness evinced by handwriting as by anything else. Any clergyman who performs a good many marriages will be impressed by the fact that very few among the humbler classes can sign their name in an unaffected way. I am not thinking of the poor bride who shakily traces her name, or of the simple bumpkin who slowly writes his, making no secret of the difficulty with which he does it. These are natural and pleasing. You would like to help and encourage them. But it is irritating when some forward fellow, after evincing his marked contempt for the slow and cramped performances of his friends, jauntily takes up the pen and dashes off his signature at a tremendous rate and with the air of an exploit, evidently expecting the admiration of his rustic friends, and laying a foundation for remarking to them on his way home that the parson could not touch him at penmanship. I have observed with a little malicious satisfaction that such persons, arising in their pride from the place where they wrote, generally smear their signature with their coat-sleeve, and reduce it to a state of comparative illegibility. I like to see the smirking, impudent creature a little taken down.

But it is endless to try to reckon up the fashions in which people show that they have not learnt the lesson of their own unimportance. Did you ever stop in the street and talk for a few minutes to some old bachelor? If so, I dare say you have remarked a curious phenomenon. You have found that all of a sudden the mind of the old gentleman, usually reasonable enough, appeared stricken into a state approaching idiocy, and that the sentence which he had begun in a rational and intelligible way was ending in a maze of wandering words, signifying nothing in particular. You had been looking in another direction, but in sudden alarm you look straight at the old gentleman to see what on earth is the matter; and you discern that his eyes are fixed on some passer-by, possibly a young lady, perhaps no more than a magistrate or the like, who is by this time a good many yards off, with the eyes still following, and slowly revolving on their axis so as to follow without the head being turned round. It is this spectacle which has drawn off your friend's attention; and you notice his whole figure twisted into an ungainly form, intended to be dignified or easy, and assumed because he fancied that the passer-by was looking at him. Oh the pettiness of human nature! Then you will find people afraid that they have given offence by saying or doing things which the party they suppose offended had really never observed that they had said or done. There are people who fancy that in church everybody is looking at them, when in truth no mortal is taking the trouble to do so. It is an amusing though irritating sight to behold a weak-minded lady walking into church and taking her seat under this delusion. You remember the affected air, the downcast eyes, the demeanor intended to imply a modest shrinking from notice, but through which there shines the real desire, "Oh, for any sake, look at me!" There are people whose voice is utterly inaudible in church six feet off, who will tell you that a whole congregation of a thousand or fifteen hundred people was listening to their singing

Such folk will tell you that they went to a church where the singing was left too much to the choir, and began to sing as usual, on which the entire congregation looked round to see who it was that was singing, and ultimately proceeded to sing lustily too. I do not remember a more disgusting exhibition of vulgar self-conceit than I saw a few months ago at Westminster Abbey. It was a week-day afternoon service, and the congregation was small. Immediately before me there sat an insolent boor, who evidently did not belong to the Church of England. He had walked in when the prayers were half over, having with difficulty been made to take off his hat, and his manifest wish was to testify his contempt for the whole place and service. Accordingly he persisted in sitting, in a lounging attitude, when the people stood, and in standing up and staring about with an air of curiosity while they knelt. He was very anxious to convey that he was not listening to the prayers; but rather inconsistently he now and then uttered an audible grunt of disapproval. No one can enjoy the choral service more than I do, and the music that afternoon was very fine; but I could not enjoy it or join in it as I wished for the disgust I felt at the animal before me, and for my burning desire to see him turned out of the sacred place he was profaning. But the thing which chiefly struck me about the individual was not his vulgar and impudent profanity; it was his intolerable self-conceit. He plainly thought that every eye under the noble old roof was watching all his movements. I could see that he would go home and boast of what he had done, and tell his friends that all the clergy, choristers, and congregation had been awe-stricken by him, and that possibly word had by this time been conveyed to Lambeth or Fulham of the weakened influence and approaching downfall of the Church of England. I knew that the very thing he wished was that some one should rebuke his conduct, otherwise I should certainly have told him either to behave with decency or to be gone.

I have sometimes witnessed a curious manifestation of this vain sense of self-importance. Did you ever, my reader, chance upon such a spectacle as this: a very commonplace man, and even a very great blockhead, standing in a drawing-room where a large party of people is assembled, with a grin of self-complacent superiority upon his unmeaning face? I am sure you understand the thing I mean. I mean a look which conveyed that, in virtue of some hidden store of genius or power, he could survey with a calm, cynical loftiness the little conversation and interests of ordinary mortals. You know the kind of interest with which a human being would survey the distant approaches to reason of an intelligent dog, or a colony of ants. I have seen this expression on the face of one or two of the greatest blockheads I ever knew. I have seen such a one wear it while clever men were carrying on a conversation in which he could not have joined to have saved his life. Yet you could see that (who can tell how?) the poor creature had somehow persuaded himself that he occupied a position from which he could look down upon his fellow-men in general. Or was it rather that the poor creature knew he was a fool, and fancied that thus he could disguise the fact? I dare say there was a mixture of both feelings.

You may see many indications of vain self-importance in the fact that various persons, old ladies for the most part, are so ready to give opinions which are not wanted, on matters of which they are not competent to judge.

Clever young curates suffer much annoyance from these people: they are always anxious to instruct the young curates how to preach. I remember well, ten years ago, when I was a curate (which in Scotland we call an *assistant*) myself, what advices I used to receive (quite unsought by me) from well-meaning but densely stupid old ladies. I did not think the advices worth much, even then; and now, by longer experience, I can discern that they were utterly idiotic. Yet they were given with entire confidence. No thought ever entered the head of these well-meaning but stupid individuals, that possibly they were not competent to give advice on such subjects. And it is vexatious to think that people so stupid may do serious harm to a young clergyman by head-shakings and sly innuendos as to his orthodoxy or his gravity of deportment. In the long run they will do no harm, but at the first start they may do a good deal of mischief. Not long since, such a person complained to me that a talented young preacher had taught unsound doctrine. She cited his words. I showed her that the words were taken *verbatim* from the *Confession of Faith*, which is our Scotch Thirty-nine Articles. I think it not unlikely that she would go on telling her tattling story just the same. I remember hearing a stupid old lady say, as though her opinion were quite decisive of the question, that no clergyman ought to have so much as a thousand a year; for if he had, he would be sure to neglect his duty. You remember what Dr. Johnson said to a woman who expressed some opinion or other upon a matter she did not understand. "Madam," said the moralist, "before expressing your opinion, you should consider what your opinion is worth." But this shaft would have glanced harmlessly from off the panoply of the stupid and self-complacent old lady of whom I am thinking. It was a fundamental axiom with her that her opinion was entirely infallible. Some people would feel as though the very world were crumbling away under their feet, if they realized the fact that they could go wrong.

Let it here be said, that this vain belief of their own importance which most people cherish, is not at all a source of unmixed happiness. It will work either way. When my friend, Mr. Snarling, got his beautiful poem printed in the county newspaper, it no doubt pleased him to think, as he walked along the street, that every one was pointing him out as the eminent literary man who was the pride of the district; and that the whole town was ringing with that magnificent effusion. Mr. Tennyson, it is certain, felt that his crown was being reft away. But on the other hand, there is no commoner form of morbid misery than that of the poor nervous man or woman who fancies that he or she is the subject of universal unkindly remark. You will find people, still sane for practical purposes, who think that the whole neighborhood is conspiring against them, when in fact nobody is thinking of them.

All these pages have been spent in discussing a single thing slowly learnt: the remaining matters to be considered in this essay must be treated briefly.

Another thing slowly learnt is that we have no reason or right to be angry with people because they think poorly of us. This is a truth which most people find it very hard to accept, and at which, probably, very few arrive without pretty long thought and experience. Most people are angry when they are informed that some one has said that their ability is small, or that their proficiency in any art is limited. Mrs. Malaprop was very indignant when she found that some of her friends had spoken lightly of her parts of speech. Mr. Snarling was wroth when he learned that Mr. Jollikin thought him no great preacher. Miss Brown was so on hearing that Mr. Smith did not admire her singing; and Mr. Smith on learning that Miss Brown did not admire his horsemanship. Some authors feel angry on reading an unfavorable review of their book. The present writer has been treated very, very kindly by the critics; far more so than he ever deserved; yet he remembers showing a notice of him which was intended to extinguish him for all coming time, to a warm-hearted friend, who read it with gathering wrath, and vehemently starting up at its close, exclaimed (we knew who wrote the notice) "Now, I shall go straight and kick that fellow!" Now all this is very natural; but assuredly it is quite wrong. You understand, of course, that I am thinking of unfavorable opinions of you, honestly held, and expressed without malice. I do not mean to say that you would choose for your special friend or companion one who thought meanly of your ability or your sense; it would not be pleasant to have him always by you; and the very fact of his presence would tend to keep you from doing justice to yourself. For it is true, that when with people who think you very clever and wise, you really are a good deal cleverer and wiser than usual; while with people who think you stupid and silly, you find yourself under a malign influence which tends to make you actually so for the time. If you want a man to gain any good quality, the way is to give him credit for possessing it. If he has but little, give him credit for all he has, at least; and you will find him daily get more. You know how Arnold made boys truthful; it was by giving them credit for truth. Oh that we all fitly understood that the same grand principle should be extended to all good qualities, intellectual and moral! Diligently instil into a boy that he is a stupid, idle, bad-hearted blockhead, and you are very likely to make him all *that.* And so you can see that it is not judicious to choose for a special friend and associate one who thinks poorly of one's sense or one's parts. Indeed, if such a one honestly thinks poorly of you, and has any moral earnestness, you could not get him for a special friend if you wished it. Let us choose for our companions (if such can be found) those who think well and kindly of us, even though we may know within ourselves that they think too kindly and too well. For that favorable estimation will bring out and foster all that is good in us. There is between this and the unfavorable judgment all the difference between the warm, genial sunshine, that draws forth the flowers and encourages them to open their leaves, and the nipping frost or the blighting east-wind that represses and disheartens all vegetable life. But though thus you would not choose for your special companion one who thinks poorly of you, and though you might not even wish to see him very often, you have no reason to have any angry feeling towards him. He cannot help his opinion. His opinion is determined by his lights. His opinion, possibly, founds on those æsthetic considerations as to which people will never think alike, with which there is no reasoning, and for which there is no accounting. God has made him so that he dislikes your book, or at least cannot heartily appreciate it; and that is not his fault. And, holding his opinion, he is quite entitled to express it. It may not be polite to express it to yourself. By common consent it is understood that you are never, except in cases of absolute necessity, to say to any man that which is disagreeable to him. And if you go, and, without any call to do so, express to a man himself that you think poorly of him, he may justly complain, not of your unfavorable opinion of him, but of the malice which is implied in your needlessly informing him of it. But if any one expresses such an unfavorable opinion of you in your absence, and some one comes and repeats it to you, be angry with the person who repeats the opinion to you, not with the person who expressed it. For what you do not know will cause you no pain. And all sensible folk, aware how estimates of any mortal must differ, will, in the long run, attach nearly the just weight to any opinion, favorable or unfavorable.

Yes, my friend, utterly put down the natural tendency in your heart to be angry with the man who thinks poorly of you. For you have, in sober reason, no right to be angry with him. It is more pleasant, and indeed more profitable, to live among those who think highly of you. It makes you better. You actually grow into what you get credit for. Oh how much better a clergyman preaches to his own congregation, who listen with kindly and sympathetic attention to all he says, and always think too well of him, than to a set of critical strangers, eager to find faults and to pick holes! And how heartily and pleasantly the essayist covers his pages, which are to go into a magazine whose readers have come to know him well, and to bear with all his ways! If every one thought him a dull and stupid person, he could not write at all. Indeed, he would bow to the general belief, and accept the truth that he is dull and stupid. But further, my reader, let us be reasonable when it is pleasant; and let us sometimes be irrational when *that* is pleasant too. It is natural to have a very kindly feeling to those who think well of us. Now, though, in severe truth, we have no more reason for wishing to shake hands with the man who thinks well of us, than for wishing to shake the man who thinks ill of us; yet let us yield heartily to the former pleasant impulse. It is not reasonable, but it is all right. You cannot help liking people who estimate you favorably, and say a good word of you. No doubt we might slowly learn not to like them more than anybody else; but we need not take the trouble to learn *that* lesson. Let us all, my readers, be glad if we can reach that cheerful position of mind at which various authors have arrived, that we shall be extremely gratified when we find ourselves favorably reviewed, and not in the least angry when we find ourselves reviewed unfavorably; that we shall have a very kindly feeling towards such as think well of us, and no unkind feeling whatever to those who think ill of us. Thus, whenever we have written an article in a magazine, at the beginning of the month shall we look with equal minds at the newspaper notices of it; we shall be soothed and exhilarated when we find ourselves described as sages, and we shall be amused and interested when we find ourselves shown up as little better than geese.

Of course, it makes a difference in the feeling with which you ought to regard any unfavorable opinion of you, whether spoken or written, if the unfavorable opinion which is expressed be plainly not honestly held, and be maliciously expressed. You may occasionally hear a judgment expressed of a young girl's music or dancing, of a gentleman's horses, of a preacher's sermons, of an author's books, which is manifestly dictated by personal spite and jealousy, and which is expressed with the intention of doing mischief and giving pain to the person of whom the judgment is expressed. You will occasionally find such judgments supported by wilful misrepresentation, and even by pure invention. In such a case as this, the essential thing is not the unfavorable opinion; it is the malice which leads to its entertainment and expression. And the conduct of the offending party should be regarded with that feeling which, on calm thought, you discern to be the right feeling with which to regard malice, accompanied by falsehood. Then is it well to be angry here? I think not. You may see that it is not safe to have any communication with a person who will abuse and misrepresent you; it is not safe, and it is not pleasant. But don't be angry. It is not worth while. That old lady, indeed, told all her friends that you said, in your book, something she knew quite well you did not say. Mr. Snarling did the like. But the offences of such people are not worth powder and shot; and besides this, my friend, if you saw the case from their point of view, you might see that they have something to say for themselves. You failed to call for the old lady so often as she wished you should. You did not ask Mr. Snarling to dinner. These are bad reasons for pitching into you; but still they are reasons; and Mr. Snarling and the old lady, by long brooding over them, may have come to think that they are very just and weighty reasons. And did you never, my friend, speak rather unkindly of these two persons? Did you never give a ludicrous account of their goings-on, or even an ill-set account, which some kind friend was sure to repeat to them? Ah, my reader; don't be too hard on Snarling; possibly you have yourself done something very like what he is doing now.

Forgive, as you need to be forgiven! And try to attain that quite attainable temper, in which you will read or listen to the most malignant attack upon you, with curiosity and amusement, and with no angry feeling at all. I suppose great people attain to this. I mean cabinet ministers and the like, who are daily flayed in print somewhere or other. They come to take it all quite easily. And if they were pure angels, somebody would attack them. Most people, even those who differ from him, know that if this world has a humble, conscientious, pious man in it, that man is the present Archbishop of Canterbury. Yet last night I read in a certain powerful journal, that the great characteristics of that good man, are cowardice, trickery, and simple rascality! Honest Mr. Bumpkin, kind-hearted Miss Goodbody, do you fancy that *you* can escape?

Then we ought to try to fix it in our mind, that in all matters into which taste enters at all, the most honest and the most able men may hopelessly, diametrically, differ. Original idiosyncrasy has so much to say here; and training has also so much. One cultivated and honest man has an enthusiastic and most real love and enjoyment of Gothic architecture, and an absolute hatred for that of the classic revival; another man equally cultivated and honest, has tastes which are the logical contradictory of these. No one can doubt the ability of Byron, or of Sheridan; yet each of them thought very little of Shakspeare. The question is, *what suits you?* You may have the strongest conviction that you ought to like an author; you may be ashamed to confess that you don't like him; and yet you may feel that you detest him. For myself, I confess with shame, and I know the reason is in myself, I cannot for my life see anything to admire in the writings of Mr. Carlyle. His style, both of thought and language, is to me insufferably irritating. I tried to read the *Sartor Resartus*, and could not do it. So if all people who have learned to read English were like me, Mr. Carlyle would have no readers. Happily the majority, in most cases, possesses the normal taste. At least there is no further appeal than to the deliberate judgment of the majority of educated men. I confess, further, that I would rather read Mr. Helps than Milton: I do not say that I think Mr. Helps the greater man, but that I feel he suits me better. I value the *Autocrat of the Breakfast-table* more highly than all the writings of Shelley put together. It is a curious thing to read various reviews of the same book; particularly if it be one of those books which, if you like at all, you will like very much, and which if you don't like you will absolutely hate. It is curious to find opinions flatly contradictory of one another set forth in those reviews by very able, cultivated, and unprejudiced men. There is no newspaper published in Britain which contains abler writing than the *Edinburgh Scotsman*. And of course no one need say anything as to the literary merits of the *Times*. Well, one day within the last few months, the *Times* and the *Scotsman* each published a somewhat elaborate review of a certain book. The reviews were flatly opposed to one another; they had no common ground at all; one said the book was extremely good, and the other that it was extremely bad. You must just make up your mind that in matters of taste there can be no unvarying standard of truth. In æsthetic matters, truth is quite relative. What is bad to you, is good to me perhaps.

If you, my reader, are a wise and kind-hearted person (as I have no doubt whatever but you are), I think you would like very much to meet and converse with any person who has formed a bad opinion of you. You would take great pleasure in overcoming such a one's prejudice against you; and if the person were an honest and worthy person, you would be almost certain to do so. Very few folk are able to retain any bitter feeling towards a man they have actually talked with, unless the bitter feeling be one which is just. And a very great proportion of all the unfavorable opinions which men entertain of their fellow-men found on some misconception. You take up somehow an impression that such a one is a conceited, stuck-up person: you come to know him, and you find he is the frankest and most unaffected of men. You had a belief that such another was a cynical, heartless being, till you met him one day coming down a long black stair in a poor part of the town from a bare chamber in which is a little sick child, with two large tears running down his face; and when you enter the poor apartment you learn certain facts as to his quiet benevolence which compel you suddenly to construct a new theory of that man's character. It is only people who are radically and essentially bad whom you can really dislike after you come to know them. And the human beings who are thus essentially bad are very few. Something of the original Image lingers yet in almost every human soul. And in many a homely, commonplace person, what with vestiges of the old, and a blessed planting-in of something new, there is a vast deal of it. And every human being, conscious of honest intention and of a kind heart, may well wish that the man who dislikes and abuses him could just know him.

But there are human beings whom, if you are wise, you would not wish to know you too well. I mean the human beings (if such there should be) who think very highly of you; who imagine you very clever and very amiable. Keep out of the way of such! Let them see as little of you as possible. For when they come to know you well, they are quite sure to be disenchanted. The enthusiastic ideal which young people form of any one they admire is smashed by the rude presence of facts. I have got somewhat beyond the stage of feeling enthusiastic admiration, yet there are two or three living men whom I should be sorry to see. I know I should never admire them so much any more. I never saw Mr. Dickens: I don't want to see him. Let us leave Yarrow unvisited: our sweet ideal is fairer than the fairest fact. No hero is a hero to his valet: and it may be questioned whether any clergyman is a saint to his beadle. Yet the hero may be a true hero, and the clergyman a very excellent man: but no human being can bear too close inspection. I remember hearing a clever and enthusiastic young lady complain of what she had suffered on meeting a certain great bishop at dinner. No doubt he was dignified, pleasant, clever; but the mysterious halo was no longer round his head. Here is a sad circumstance in the lot of a very eminent man: I mean such a man as Mr. Tennyson or Professor Longfellow. As an elephant walks through a field, crushing the crop at every step, so do these men advance through life, smashing, every time they dine out, the enthusiastic fancies of several romantic young people.

This was to have been a short essay. But you see it is already long; and I have treated only two of the four Things Slowly Learnt which I had noted down. The other two must be very briefly stated.

The first of the two things is a practical lesson. It is

this: to allow for human folly, laziness, carelessness, and the like, just as you allow for the properties of matter, such as weight, friction, and the like, without being surprised or angry at them. You know that if a man is lifting a piece of lead he does not think of getting into a rage because it is heavy; or if a man is dragging a tree along the ground he does not get into a rage because it plows deeply into the earth as it comes. He is not surprised at these things. They are nothing new. It is just what he counted on. But you will find that the same man, if his servants are lazy, careless, and forgetful; or if his friends are petted, wrong-headed, and impracticable; will not only get quite angry, but will get freshly angry at each new action which proves that his friends or servants possess these characteristics. Would it not be better to make up your mind that such things are characteristic of humanity, and so that you must look for them in dealing with human beings? And would it not be better, too, to regard each new proof of laziness, not as a new thing to be angry with, but merely as a piece of the one great fact that your servant is lazy, with which you get angry once for all, and have done with it? If your servant makes twenty blunders a day, do not regard them as twenty separate facts at which to get angry twenty several times. Regard them just as twenty proofs of the one fact, that your servant is a blunderer; and be angry just once, and no more. Or if some one you know gives twenty indications in a day that he or she (let us say she) is of a petted temper, regard these merely as twenty proofs of one lamentable fact, and not as twenty different facts to be separately lamented. You accept the fact that the person is petted and ill-tempered: you regret it and blame it once for all. And after this once you take as of course all new manifestations of pettedness and ill-temper. And you are no more surprised at them, or angry with them, than you are at lead for being heavy, or at down for being light. It is their nature, and you calculate on it, and allow for it.

Then the second of the two remaining things is this — that you have no right to complain if you are postponed to greater people, or if you are treated with less consideration than you would be if you were a greater person. Uneducated people are very slow to learn this most obvious lesson. I remember hearing of a proud old lady, who was proprietor of a small landed estate in Scotland. She had many relations, some greater, some less. The greater she much affected, the less she wholly ignored. But they did not ignore *her;* and one morning an individual arrived at her mansion-house, bearing a large box on his back. He was a travelling peddler; and he sent up word to the old lady that he was her cousin, and hoped she would buy something from him. The old lady indignantly refused to see him, and sent orders that he should forthwith quit the house. The peddler went; but on reaching the court-yard, he turned to the inhospitable dwelling, and in a loud voice exclaimed, in the ears of every mortal in the house, "Ay, if I had come in my carriage-and-four, ye wad have been proud to have ta'en me in!" The peddler fancied that he was hurling at his relative a scathing sarcasm: he did not see that he was simply stating a perfectly unquestionable fact. No doubt earthly, if he had come in a carriage-and-four, he would have got a hearty welcome, and he would have found his claim of kindred eagerly allowed. But he thought he was saying a bitter and cutting thing, and (strange to say) the old lady fancied she was listening to a bitter and cutting thing. He was merely expressing a certain and innocuous truth. But though all mortals know that in this world big people meet greater respect than small (and quite right too), most mortals seem to find the principle a very unpleasant one when it comes home to themselves. And we learn but slowly to acquiesce in seeing ourselves plainly subordinated to other people. Poor Oliver Goldsmith was very angry when at the club one night he was stopped in the middle of a story by a Dutchman, who had noticed that the Great Bear was rolling about in preparation for speaking, and who exclaimed to Goldsmith, "Stop, stop; Toctor Shonson is going to speak!" Once I arrived at a certain railway station. Two old ladies were waiting to go by the same train. I knew them well, and they expressed their delight that we were going the same way. "Let us go in the same carriage," said the younger, in earnest tones; "and will you be so very kind as to see about our luggage?" After a few minutes of the lively talk of the period and district, the train came up. I feel the tremor of the platform yet. I handed my friends into a carriage, and then saw their baggage placed in the van. It was a station at which trains stop for a few minutes for refreshments. So I went to the door of the carriage into which I had put them, and waited a little before taking my seat. I expected that my friends would proceed with the conversation which had been interrupted; but to my astonishment I found that I had become wholly invisible to them. They did not see me or speak to me at all. In the carriage with them was a living peer, of wide estates and great rank, whom they knew. And so thoroughly did he engross their eyes and thoughts and words, that they had become unaware of my presence, or even my existence. The stronger sensation rendered them unconscious of the weaker. Do you think I felt angry? No, I did not. I felt very much amused. I recognized a slight manifestation of a grand principle. It was a straw showing how a current sets, but for which Britain would not be the country it is. I took my seat in another carriage, and placidly read my *Times*. There was one lady in that carriage. I think she inferred, from the smiles which occasionally for the first few miles overspread my countenance without apparent cause, that my mind was slightly disordered.

These are the two things already mentioned. But you cannot understand, friendly reader, what an effort it has cost me to treat them so briefly. The experienced critic will discern at a glance that the author could easily have made a great many pages out of the material you have here in very few. The author takes his stand upon this—that there are few people who can beat out thought so thin, or say so little in such a great number of words. I remember how a dear friend, once the editor of a certain well-known magazine (whom all who knew him well miss more and more as days and weeks go on, and never will cease to miss), used to remark this fact in various warm-hearted and playful letters, with wonder not unmixed with indignation. And I remember how a very great prelate (who could compress all I have said into a page and a half) once comforted me by telling me that for the consumption of many minds it was desirable that thought should be very greatly diluted; that quantity as well as quality is needful in the dietetics both of the body and the mind. With this soothing reflection I close the present essay.

Annotations on the foregoing Chapter.

By the Archbishop of Dublin.

(1.) The Indian Brahmin who purchased, for a great price, an elaborate microscope which had shown him that he swallowed multitudes of minute animalculæ in every draught of water, dashed it to pieces, saying it should never inflict that misery upon others it had upon him.

(2.) E. S. (now Lord St. L.), is the son of a hairdresser, said to have been very eminent in his own way. A gentleman asked the man who was cutting his hair whether he remembered anything of him. "Oh, yes; I remember him very well when I was an apprentice. Wonderful man! Had half-a-guinea for cutting hair! Nobody like him since!" "Well," said the other, "his *son* is a very eminent man too in *his* way." "Oh, is he, sir?" "Yes; the first lawyer in England." "Oh, is he, sir — *I never heard of him.*"

(3.) A gentleman who was fond of attending at the Lord Mayor of London's, to hear the trials and petitions and memorials that were going on, heard a memorial sent in by some Chimney-Sweepers, who complained of an interference which encroached on their annual May-Day festival, on which they dress themselves up and go round to receive contributions from their customers. They complained that their place had been usurped by certain *Dustmen* and other *low fellows pretending to be Chimney-Sweepers!*

CHAPTER IV.

GONE.

EDGAR ALLAN POE thought the most touching of all words, *Nevermore;* which, in American fashion, he made one word. American writers do the like with *Forever*, I think with bad effect. Ellesmere, in that most beautiful story of *Gretchen*, tells of a sermon he heard in Germany, in which "that pathetic word *verloren* (lost) occurred many times." Every one knows what Dr. Johnson wrote about *The Last.* It is, of course, a question of individual associations, and how it may strike different minds; but I stand up for the unrivalled reach and pathos of the short word GONE.

There is not very much difference, you see, between the three words. All are on the suburbs of the same idea. All convey the idea of a state of matters which existed for a time, and which is now over. All suggest that the inmost longing of most human hearts is less for a future, untried happiness than for a return, a resurrection, beautified and unalloyed with care, of what has already been. Somehow, we are ready to feel as if we were safest and surest with *that.*

It is curious, that the saddest and most touching of human thoughts, when we run it up to its simplest form, is of so homely a thing as a material object existing in a certain space, and then removing from that space to another. *That* is the essential idea of *Gone.*

Yet, in the commonest way, there is something touching in that: something touching in the sight of vacant space, once filled by almost anything. You feel a blankness in the landscape when a tree is gone that you have known all your life. You are conscious of a vague sense of something lacking when even a post is pulled up that you remember always in the centre of a certain field. You feel this yet more when some familiar piece of furniture is taken away from a room which you know well. Here that clumsy easy-chair used to stand: and it is gone. You feel yourself an interloper, standing in the space where it stood so long. It touches you still more to look at the empty chair which you remember so often filled by one who will never fill it more. You stand in a large railway station: you have come to see a train depart. There is a great bustle on the platform, and there is a great quantity of human life, and of the interests and cares of human life, in those twelve or fourteen carriages, and filling that little space between the rails. You stand by and watch the warm interiors of the carriages, looking so large, and so full, and as if they had so much in them. There are people of every kind of aspect, children and old folk, multitudes of railway rugs, of carpet-bags, of portmanteaus, of parcels, of newspapers, of books, of magazines. At length you hear the last bell; then comes that silent, steady pull, which is always striking, though seen ever so often. The train glides away: it is gone. You stand, and look vacantly at the place where it was. How little the space looks; how blank the air! There are the two rails, just four feet eight and a half inches apart: how close together they look! You can hardly think that there was so much of life, and of the interests of life, in so little room. You feel the power upon the average human being of the simple, commonplace fact, that something has been here, and is gone.

Then I go away in thought, to a certain pier: a pair of wooden piles, running two hundred yards into the sea, at a quiet spot on a lovely coast, where various steam-vessels call on a summer day. You stand at the seaward end of the pier, where it broadens into a considerable platform: and you look down on the deck of a steamer lying alongside. What a bustle: what a hive of human beings, and their children, and their baggage, their hopes, fears, and schemes, fills that space upon the water of a hundred and fifty feet long and twenty-five wide! And what a deafening noise, too, of escaping steam fills the air! Men with baggage dash up against you; women shrilly vociferate above the roar of the steam; it is a fragment of the vitality and hurry of the great city carried for a little to the quiet country-place. But the last rope is thrown off; the paddles turn; the steamer moves — it is gone. There is the blank water, churned now into foam, but in a few minutes transparent green, showing the wooden piles, encrusted with shells, and with weeds that wave about below the surface. There you stand, and look vaguely, and think vaguely. It is a curious feeling. It is a feeling you do not understand except by experience. And to a thoughtful person a thing does not become commonplace because it is repeated hundreds of thousands of times. There is something strange and something touching about even a steamboat going away from a pier at which a dozen call every day.

But you sit upon the pier, you saunter upon the beach,

you read the newspapers; you enjoy the sense of rest. The day wears away, and in the evening the steamboat comes back again. It has travelled scores of miles, and carried many persons through many scenes, while you were resting and idling through these hours; and the feeling you had when it was gone is effaced by its return. The going away is neutralized by the coming back. And to understand the full force of *Gone* in such a case, you must see a ship go, and see its vacant space when it is gone, when it goes away for a long time, and takes some with it who go forever. Perhaps you know by experience what a choking sensation there is in looking at an emigrant vessel clearing out, even though you have no personal interest in any one on board. I have seen such a ship depart on her long voyage. I remember the confusion and hurry that attended her departure: the crowded deck, thronged with old and young; gray-headed men bidding farewell to their native land; and little children who would carry but dim remembrances of Britain to the distant Australian shore. And who that has witnessed such a scene can forget how, when the canvas was spread at length, and the last rope cast off, the outburst of sobs and weeping arose as the great ship solemnly passed away? You could see that many who parted there, had not understood what parting means till they were in the act of going. You could see that the old parents who were willing, they thought, to part from their boy, because they thought his chances in life were so much better in the new country, had not quite felt what parting from him was, till he was gone.

Have you ever been one of a large gay party who have made an excursion to some beautiful scene, and had a picnic festival? Not that such festivals are much to be approved; at least to spots of very noble scenery. The noble scenery is vulgarized by them. There is an inconsistency in seeking out a spot which ought to awe-strike, merely to make it a theatre for eating and drinking, for stupid joking and laughter. No; let small-talk be manufactured somewhere else. And the influence of the lonely place is lost, its spirit is unfelt, unless you go alone, or go with very few, and these not boisterously merry. But let us accept the picnic as a fact. It has been, and the party has been very large and very lively. But go back to the place after the party is gone; go back a minute after for something forgotten; go back a month or a year after. What a little spot it is that you occupied, and how blank it looks! The place remains, but the people are gone; and we so lean to our kind, that the place alone occupies but a very little part in our recollection of any passage in our history in which there were both scenery and human life. Or go back after several years to the house where you and your brothers and sisters were children together, and you will wonder to find how small and how blank it will look. It will touch you, and perhaps deeply; but still you will discern that not places, but persons, are the true objects of human affection; and you will think what a small space of material ground may be the scene of what are to you great human events and interests. It is so with matters on a grander scale. How little a space was ancient Greece — how little a space the Holy Land! Strip these of their history and their associations, and they are insignificant. And history and associations are invisible; and at the first glimpse of the place without them the place looks poor. Let the little child die that was the light and hope of a great dwelling, and you will understand the truth of the poet's reflection on the loss of his: "'Twas strange that such a little thing, Should leave a blank so large!"

There is no place perhaps where you have such a feeling of blankness when life has gone from it as in a church. It is less so, if the church be a very grand one, which compels you to attend to itself a good deal, even while the congregation is assembled. But if the church be a simple one, and the congregation a very large one, crowding the simple church, you hardly know it again when the congregation is gone. You could not believe that such a vast number of human beings could have been gathered in it. The place is unchanged, yet it is quite different. It is a curious feeling to look at the empty pulpit where a very great preacher once was accustomed to preach. It is especially so if it be thirty years since he used to preach there; more so, if it be many centuries. I have often looked at the pulpit whence Chalmers preached in the zenith of his fame; you can no more bring up again the excited throng that surrounded it, and the rush of the great orator's eloquence, than when standing under a great oak in December you can call up plainly what it looked in June. And far less, standing under the dome of St. Sophia, could one recall as a present reality, or as anything but a dreamy fancy, the aspect and the eloquence of Chrysostom, ages since gone.

The feeling of *blankness*, which is the essential thing contained in the idea suggested by the word Gone, is one that touches us very nearly. It seems to get closer to us than even positive evil or suffering present with us. *That* fixes our attention: it arouses us; and unless we be very weak indeed, awakens something of resistance. But in the other case, the mind is not stimulated:

it is receptive, not active; and we muse and feel, vacantly, in the thought of something gone. You are, let us suppose, a country parson; you take your wife and children over to your railway-station, and you see them away to the seaside, whither you are not to follow for a fortnight: then you come back from the railway-station, and you reach home. The house is quite changed. How startlingly quiet it is! You go to the nursery, usually a noisy place: you feel the silence. There are the pictures on the walls: there the little chairs: there some flowers, still quite fresh, lying upon a table, laid down by little hands. Gone! There is something sad in it, even with the certainty of soon meeting again, — that is, so far as there is certainty in this world. You can imagine, distantly, what it would be if the little things were gone, not to return. *That* is the GONE consummate. All who have heard it know the unutterable sadness of the farewell of the Highland emigrant leaving his native hills. You would not laugh at the bagpipes, if you heard their wild wailing tones, blending with broken voices joining in that *Macrimmon's Lament*, whose perpetual refrain is just the statement of that consummate Gone. I shall not write the Gaelic words, because you could not pronounce them; but the refrain is this: *We return, we return, we return no more!* Yes; Gone for ever! And all to make room for deer! There was a man whose little boy died. The father bore up wonderfully. But on the funeral day, after the little child was laid down to his long rest, the father went out to walk in the garden. There, in a corner, was the small wheelbarrow with its wooden spade; and the foot-prints in the earth left by the little feet that were gone! You do not think the less of the strong man that at the sight he wept aloud: wept, as Some One Else had wept before him. You may remember that little poem of Longfellow's, in which he tells of a man, still young, who once had a wife and child: but wife and child were dead. There is no pathos like that of homely fact, which we may witness every day. They were gone; and after those years in their company, he was left alone. He walked about the world, with no one to care for him now, as they had cared. The life with them would seem like a dream, even if it had lasted for years. And all the sadder that so much of life might yet have to come. I do not mind about an old bachelor, in his solitary room. I think of the kind-hearted man, sitting in the evening in his chair by the fireside: once, when he sat down there, little pattering feet were about him and their little owners climbed upon his knee. Now, he may sit long enough, and no one will interrupt him. He may read his newspaper undisturbed. He may write his sermon, and no sly knock come to the door: no little dog walk in, with much barking quite unlike that of common dogs, and ask for a penny. Gone! I remember, long ago, reading a poem called the *Scottish Widow's Lament*, written by some nameless poet. The widow had a husband and two little children, but one bleak winter they all went together: —

I ettle whiles to spin,
  But wee, wee patterin' feet,
Come runnin' out and in,
  And then I just maun greet.
I ken it's fancy a'
  And faster flows the tear,
That my a' dwined awa',
  Sin' the fa' o' the year.

You have said good-bye to a dear friend who has

stayed a few days with you, and whom you will not see again for long: and you have, for a while, felt the house very blank without him. Did you ever think how the house would seem, without yourself? Have you fancied yourself gone; and the place, blank of that figure you know? *When I am gone;* let us not say these words unless seriously; they express what is, to each of us the most serious of all facts. *The May Queen* has few lines which touch me more than these: —

> For lying broad awake I thought of you and Effie dear;
> I saw you sitting in the house, and I no longer here.

Lord Macaulay, a few years before he died, had something presented to him at a great public meeting in Scotland; something which pleased him much. "I shall treasure it," he said, "as long as I live; and *after I am gone*" — There the great man's voice faltered, and the sentence remained unfinished. Yet the thought at which Macaulay broke down, may touch many a lesser man more. For when we are gone, my friends, we may leave behind us those who cannot well spare us. It is not for one's own sake, that the Gone, so linked with one's own name, touches so much. We have had enough of this world before very long; and (as Uncle Tom expressed it) "heaven is better than Kentuck." But we can think of some, for whose sake we may wish to put off our going as long as may be. "Our minister," said a Scotch rustic, "aye preaches aboot goin' to heaven; but he'll never go to heaven as long as he can get stoppin' at Drumsleekie."

No doubt, that fit of toothache may be gone; or that unwelcome guest who stayed with you three weeks whether you would or not; as well as the thing or the friend you most value. And there is the auctioneer's *Going, going*, as well as this July sun going down in glory. But I defy you to vulgarize the word. The water which makes the Atlantic will always be a sublime sight, though you may have a little of it in a dirty puddle. And though the stupid bore who comes when you are busy, and wastes your time, may tell you when you happily get rid of him, that he will often come back again to see you (ignorant that you instantly direct your servant never to admit him more), even *that* cannot detract from the beauty of Mr. Tennyson's lines, in which the dying girl, as she is going, tells her mother that after she is gone, she will (if it may be) often come back: —

> If I can I'll come again, mother, from out my resting-place;
> Though you'll not see me, mother, I shall look upon your face:
> Though I cannot speak a word, I shall hearken what you say,
> And be often, often with you, when you think I'm far away.

CHAPTER V.

CONCERNING PEOPLE OF WHOM MORE MIGHT HAVE BEEN MADE.

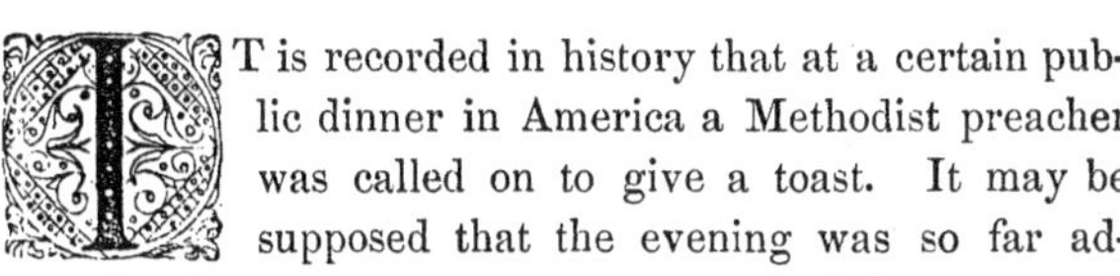T is recorded in history that at a certain public dinner in America a Methodist preacher was called on to give a toast. It may be supposed that the evening was so far advanced, that every person present had been toasted already, and also all the friends of every one present. It thus happened that the Methodist preacher was in considerable perplexity as to the question, what being, or class of beings, should form the subject of his toast. But the good man was a person of large sympathies; and some happy link of association recalled to his mind certain words with which he had a professional familiarity, and which set forth a subject of a most comprehensive character. Arising from his seat, the Methodist preacher said that, without troubling the assembled company with any preliminary observations, he begged to propose the health of ALL PEOPLE THAT ON EARTH DO DWELL.

Not unnaturally, I have thought of that Methodist preacher and his toast as I begin to write this essay. For though its subject was suggested to me by various little things of very small concern to mankind in general, though of great interest to one or two individual beings,

I now discern that the subject of this essay is in truth as comprehensive as the subject of that toast. I have something to say *Concerning People of whom More might have been Made:* I see now that the class which I have named includes every human being. More might have been made, in some respect, possibly in many respects, of *All people that on earth do dwell.* Physically, intellectually, morally, spiritually, more might have been made of all. Wise and diligent training on the part of others; self-denial, industry, tact, decision, promptitude, on the part of the man himself; might have made something far better than he now is of every man that breathes. No one is made the most of. There have been human beings who have been made the most of as regards some one thing; who have had some single power developed to the utmost; but no one is made the most of, all round; no one is even made the most of as regards the two or three most important things of all. And indeed it is curious to observe that the things in which human beings seem to have attained to absolute perfection, have for the most part been things comparatively frivolous; accomplishments which certainly were not worth the labor and the time which it must have cost to master them. Thus, M. Blondin has probably made as much of himself as can be made of mortal, in the respect of walking on a rope stretched at a great height from the ground. Hazlitt makes mention of a man who had cultivated to the very highest degree the art of playing at rackets; and who accordingly played at rackets incomparably better than any one else ever did. A wealthy gentleman, lately deceased, by putting his whole mind to the pursuit, esteemed himself to have reached entire perfection in the matter of killing otters. Various individuals have probably developed the power of turning somersets, of picking pockets, of playing on the piano, jew's-harp, banjo, and penny trumpet, of mental calculation in arithmetic, of insinuating evil about their neighbors without directly asserting anything, — to a measure as great as is possible to man. Long practice and great concentration of mind upon these things, have sufficed to produce what might seem to tremble on the verge of perfection: what unquestionably leaves the attainments of ordinary people at an inconceivable distance behind. But I do not call it making the most of a man, to develop, even to perfection, the power of turning somersets and playing at rackets. I call it making the most of a man, when you make the best of his best powers and qualities; when you take those things about him which are the worthiest and most admirable, and cultivate these up to their highest attainable degree. And it is in this sense that the statement is to be understood, that no one is made the most of. Even in the best, we see no more than the rudiments of good qualities which might have been developed into a great deal more; and in very many human beings, proper management might have brought out qualities essentially different from those which these beings now possess. It is not merely that they are rough diamonds, which might have been polished into blazing ones; not merely that they are thoroughbred colts drawing coal-carts, which with fair training would have been new Eclipses: it is that they are vinegar which might have been wine, poison which might have been food, wild-cats which might have been harmless lambs, soured miserable wretches who might have been happy and useful, almost devils who might have been but a little lower than the angels. Oh the unutterable sadness that is in the thought of what might have been!

Not always, indeed. Sometimes, as we look back, it is with deep thankfulness that we see the point at which we were (we cannot say how) inclined to take the right turning, when we were all but resolved to take that which we can now see would have landed us in wreck and ruin. And it is fit that we should correct any morbid tendency to brood upon the fancy of how much better we might have been, by remembering also how much worse we might have been. Sometimes the present state of matters, good or bad, is the result of long training; of influences that were at work through many years; and that produced their effect so gradually that we never remarked the steps of the process, till some day we waken up to a sense of the fact, and find ourselves perhaps a great deal better, probably a great deal worse, than we had been vaguely imagining. But the case is not unfrequently otherwise. Sometimes one testing time decided whether we should go to the left or to the right. There are in the moral world things analogous to the sudden accident which makes a man blind or lame for life: in an instant there is wrought a permanent deterioration. Perhaps a few minutes before man or woman took the step which can never be retraced, which must banish them forever from all they hold dear, and compel them to seek in some new country far away a place where to hide their shame and misery, they had just as little thought of taking that miserable step as you, my reader, have of taking one like it. And perhaps there are human beings in this world, held in the highest esteem, and with not a speck on their snow-white reputation, who know within themselves that they have barely escaped the gulf; that the moment has been in which all their future lot was trembling in the balance; and that a grain's weight more in the scale of evil, and by this time they might have been reckoned among the most degraded and abandoned of the race. But probably the first deviation, either to right or left, is in most cases a very small one. You know, my friend, what is meant by the *points* upon a railway. By moving a lever, the rails upon which the train is advancing are, at a certain place, broadened or narrowed by about the eighth of an inch. That little movement decides whether the train shall go north or south. Twenty carriages have come so far together; but here is a junction station, and the train is to be divided. The first ten carriages deviate from the main line by a fraction of an inch at first; but in a few minutes the two portions of the train are flying on, miles apart. You cannot see the one from the other, save by distant puffs of white steam through the clumps of trees. Perhaps already a high hill has intervened, and each train is on its solitary way — one to end its course, after some hours, amid the roar and smoke and bare ugliness of some huge manufacturing town; and the other to come through green fields to the quaint, quiet, dreamy-looking little city, whose place is marked, across the plain, by the noble spire of the gray cathedral rising into the summer blue. We come to such points in our journey through life: railway-points (as it were), which decide not merely our lot in life, but even what kind of folk we shall be, morally and intellectually. A hair's-breadth may make the deviation at first. Two situations are offered you at once: you think there is hardly anything to choose between them. It does not matter which you accept; and perhaps some slight and fanciful consideration is allowed to turn the scale. But now you look back, and you can see that *there* was the turning-point in your life; it was because you went there to the right, and not to the left, that you are now a great English prelate and not a humble Scotch professor. Was there not a time in a certain great man's life, at which the lines of rail diverged, and at which the question was settled, should he be a minister of the Scotch Kirk, or should he be Lord High Chancellor of Great Britain? I can imagine a stage in the history of a lad in a counting-house, at which the little angle of rail may be pushed in or pushed back that shall send the train to one of two places five hundred miles asunder; it may depend upon whether he shall take or not take that half-crown, whether, thirty years after, he shall be taking the chair, a rubicund baronet, at a missionary society meeting, and receive the commendations of philanthropic peers and earnest bishops; or be laboring in chains at Norfolk Island, a brutalized, cursing, hardened, scourge-scarred, despairing wretch, without a hope for this life or the other. Oh, how much may turn upon a little thing! Because the railway train in which you were coming to a certain place was stopped by a snow-storm, the whole character of your life may have been changed. Because some one was in the drawing-room when you went to see Miss Smith on a certain day, resolved to put to her a certain question, you missed the tide, you lost your chance, you went away to Australia and never saw her more. It fell upon a day that a ship, coming from Melbourne, was weathering a rocky point on an iron-bound coast, and was driven close upon that perilous shore. They tried to put her about; it was the last chance. It was a moment of awful risk and decision. If the wind catches the sails, now shivering as the ship comes up, on the right side, then all on board are safe. If the wind catches the sails on the other side, then all on board must perish. And so it all depends upon which surface of certain square yards of canvas the uncertain breeze shall strike, whether John Smith, who is coming home from the diggings with twenty thousand pounds, shall go down and never be heard of again by his poor mother and sisters away in Scotland; or whether he shall get safely back, a rich man, to gladden their hearts, and buy a pretty little place, and improve the house on it into the pleasantest picture; and purchase, and ride, and drive various horses; and be seen on market days sauntering in the High-street of the county town; and get married, and run about the lawn before his door, chasing his little children; and become a decent elder of the Church; and live quietly and happily for many years. Yes: from what precise point of the compass the next flaw of wind should come, would decide the question between the long homely life in Scotland, and a nameless burial deep in a foreign sea.

It seems to me to be one of the main characteristics of human beings, not that they actually are much, but that they are something of which much may be made. There are untold potentialities in human nature. The tree cut down, concerning which its heathen owner debated whether he should make it into a god or into a three-legged stool, was positively nothing in its capacity of coming to different ends and developments, when we compare it with each human being born into this world. Man is not so much a thing already, as he is the germ of something. He is (so to speak) material formed to the hand of circumstances. He is essentially a germ, either of good or evil. And he is not like the seed of a plant, in whose development the tether allows no wider range than that between the more or less successful manifestation of its inherent nature. Give a young tree fair play: good soil and abundant air; tend it carefully, in short, and you will have a noble tree. Treat the young tree unfairly: give it a bad soil, deprive it of needful air and light, and it will grow up a stunted and poor tree. But in the case of the human being, there is more than this difference in degree. There may be a difference in kind. The human being may grow up to be (as it were) a fair and healthful fruit tree, or to be a poisonous one. There is something positively awful about the potentialities that are in human nature. The Archbishop of Canterbury might have grown up under influences which would have made him a bloodthirsty pirate or a sneaking pickpocket. The pirate or the pickpocket, taken at the right time, and trained in the right way, might have been made a pious exemplary man. You remember that good divine, two hundred years since, who, standing in the market-place of a certain town, and seeing a poor wretch led by him to the gallows, said, "There goes myself, but for the grace of God." Of course, it is needful that human laws should hold all men as equally responsible. The punishment of such an offence is such an infliction, no matter who committed the offence. At least the mitigating circumstances which human laws can take into account must be all of a very plain and intelligible character. It would not do to recognize anything like a graduated scale of responsibility. A very bad training in youth would be in a certain limited sense regarded as lessening the guilt of any wrong thing done; and you may remember accordingly how that magnanimous monarch, Charles II., urged to the Scotch lords, in extenuation of the wrong things he had done, that his father had given him a very bad education. But though human laws and judges may vainly and clumsily endeavor to fix each wrong-doer's place in the scale of responsibility; and though they must, in a rough way, do what is rough justice in five cases out of six; still we may well believe that in the view of the Supreme Judge the responsibilities of men are most delicately graduated to their opportunities. There is One who will appreciate with entire accuracy the amount of guilt that is in each wrong deed of each wrongdoer, and mercifully allow for such as never had a chance of being anything but wrongdoers. And it will not matter whether it was from original constitution or from unhappy training that these poor creatures never had that chance. I was lately quite astonished to learn that some sincere but stupid American divines have fallen foul of the eloquent author of *Elsie Venner*, and accused him of fearful heresy, because he declared his confident belief that "God would never make a man with a crooked spine and then punish him for not standing upright." Why, that statement of the *Autocrat* appears to me at least as certain as that two and two make four. It may indeed contain some recondite and malignant reference which the stupid American divines know, and which I do not: it may be a mystic Shibboleth indicating far more than it asserts; as at one time in Scotland it was esteemed as proof that a clergyman preached unsound doctrine if he made use of the Lord's Prayer. But, understanding it simply as meaning that the Judge of all the earth will do right, it appears to me an axiom beyond all question. And I take it as putting in a compact form the spirit of what I have been arguing for — to wit, that though human law must of necessity hold all rational beings as alike responsible, yet in the eye of God the difference may be immense. The graceful vase that stands in the drawing-room under a glass shade, and never goes to the well, has no great right to despise the rough pitcher that goes often and is broken at last. It is fearful to think what malleable material we are in the hands of circumstances. And a certain Authority, considerably wiser and incomparably more charitable than the American divines already mentioned, has recognized the fact when He taught us to pray, "Lead us not into temptation!" We shall think, in a little while, of certain influences which may make or mar the human being; but it may be said here, that I firmly believe that happiness is one of the best of disciplines. As a general rule, if people were happier, they would be better. When you see a poor cabman on a winter day, soaked with rain, and fevered with gin, violently thrashing the wretched horse he is driving, and perhaps howling at it, you may be sure that it is just because the poor cabman is so miserable that he is doing all that. It is a sudden glimpse, perhaps, of his bare home and hungry children, and of the dreary future which lies before himself and them, that was the true cause of those two or three furious lashes you saw him deal upon the unhappy screw's ribs. Whenever I read any article in a review, which is manifestly malignant, and intended not to improve an author but to give him pain, I cannot help immediately wondering what may have been the matter with the man who wrote the malignant article. Something must have been making him very unhappy, I think. I do not allude to playful attacks upon a man, made in pure thoughtlessness and buoyancy of spirit; but to attacks which indicate a settled, deliberate, calculating rancor. Never be angry with the man who makes such an attack; you ought to be sorry for him. It is out of great misery that malignity for the most part proceeds. To give the ordinary mortal a fair chance, let him be reasonably successful and happy. Do not worry a man into nervous irritability, and he will be amiable. Do not dip a man in water, and he will not be wet.

Of course, my friend, I know who is to you the most interesting of all beings; and whose history is the most interesting of all histories. *You* are to yourself the centre of this world, and of all the interests of this world. And this is quite right. There is no selfishness about all this, except that selfishness which forms an essential element in personality; that selfishness which must go with the fact of one's having a self. You cannot help looking at all things as they appear from your own point of view; and things press themselves upon your attention and your feeling as they affect yourself. And apart from anything like egotism, or like vain self-conceit, it is probable that you may know that a great deal depends upon your exertion and your life. There are those at home who would fare but poorly if you were just now to die. There are those who must rise with you if you rise, and sink with you if you sink. Does it sometimes suddenly strike you, what a little object you are, to have so much depending on you? Vaguely, in your thinking and feeling, you add your circumstances and your lot to your personality; and these make up an object of considerable extension. You do so with other people as well as with yourself. You have all their belongings as a background to the picture of them which you have in your mind; and they look very little when you see them in fact, because you see them without these belongings. I remember when a boy, how disappointed I was at first seeing the Archbishop of Canterbury. It was Archbishop Howley.

There he was, a slender pale old gentleman, sitting in an arm-chair at a public meeting. I was chiefly disappointed, because there was *so little* of him. There was just the human being. There was no background of grand accessories. The idea of the Primate of England which I had in some confused manner in my mind, included a vision of the venerable towers of Lambeth, — of a long array of solemn predecessors, from Thomas A'Becket downwards, — of great historical occasions on which the Archbishop of Canterbury had been a prominent figure; and in some way I fancied, vaguely, that you would see the primate surrounded by all these things. You remember the highlander in *Waverley* who was much mortified when his chief came to meet an English guest, unattended by any retinue; and who exclaimed in consternation and sorrow, "He has come without his tail!" Even such was my early feeling. You understand, later, that associations are not visible; and that they do not add to a man's extension in space. But (to go back) you do, as regards yourself, what you do as regards greater men; you add your lot to your personality, and thus you make up a bigger object. And when you see yourself in your tailor's shop, in a large mirror (one of a series) wherein you see your figure all round, reflected several times, your feeling will probably be, what a little thing you are! If you are a wise man, you will go away somewhat humbled, and possibly somewhat the better for the sight. You have, to a certain extent, done what Burns thought it would do all men much good to do; you have "seen yourself as others see you." And even to do so physically, is a step towards a juster and humbler estimate of yourself in more important things. It may here be said as a further illustration of the principle set forth, that people who stay very much at home, feel their stature, bodily and mental, much lessened when they go far away from home, and spend a little time among strange scenes and people. For, going thus away from home, you take only yourself. It is but a small part of your extension that goes. You go ; but you leave behind your house, your study, your children, your servants, your horses, your garden. And not only do you leave them behind; but they grow misty and unsubstantial when you are far away from them. And somehow you feel that when you make the acquaintance of a new friend some hundreds of miles off, who never saw your home and your family, you present yourself before him, only a twentieth part or so of what you feel yourself to be when you have all your belongings about you. Do you not feel all that? And do you not feel, that if you were to go away to Australia for ever, almost as the English coast turned blue and then invisible on the horizon, your life in England would first turn cloud-like, and then melt away ?

But without further discussing the philosophy of how it comes to be, I return to the statement that you yourself, as you live in your home, are to yourself the centre of this world ; and that you feel the force of any great principle most deeply, when you feel it in your own case. And though every worthy mortal must be often taken out of himself, especially by seeing the deep sorrows and great failures of other men, still, in thinking of people of whom more might have been made, it touches you most to discern that you are one of these. It is a very sad thing to think of yourself, and to see how much more might have been made of you. Sit down by the fire in winter ; or go out now in summer and sit down under a tree; and look back on the moral discipline you have gone through; look back on what you have done and suffered. Oh how much better and happier you might have been! And how very near you have often been to what would have made you so much happier and better! If you had taken the other turning when you took the wrong one, after much perplexity; if you had refrained from saying such a hasty word; if you had not thoughtlessly made such a man your enemy! Such a little thing may have changed the entire complexion of your life. Ah, it was because the points were turned the wrong way at that junction, that you are now running along a line of railway through wild moorlands, leaving the warm champaign below ever more hopelessly behind. Hastily, or pettedly, or despairingly, you took the wrong turning; or you might have been dwelling now amid verdant fields and silver waters in the country of contentment and success. Many men and women, in the temporary bitterness of some disappointment, have hastily made marriages which will embitter all their future life; or which at least make it certain that in this world they will never know a joyous heart any more. Men have died as almost briefless barristers, toiling into old age in heartless wrangling, who had their chance of high places on the bench; but ambitiously resolved to wait for something higher; and so missed the tide. Men in the church have taken the wrong path at some critical time; and doomed themselves to all the pangs of disappointed ambition. But I think a sincere man in the church has a great advantage over almost all ordinary disappointed men. He has less temptation, reading affairs by the light of after-time, to look back with bitterness on any mistake he may have made. For if he be the man I mean, he took the decisive step not without seeking the best of guidance; and the whole training of his mind has fitted him for seeing a higher Hand in the allotment of human conditions. And if a man acted for the best, according to the light he had; and if he truly believes that God puts all in their places in life: he may look back without bitterness upon what may appear the most grievous mistakes. I must be suffered to add, that if he is able heartily to hold certain great truths, and to rest on certain sure promises, hardly any conceivable earthly lot should stamp him a soured or disappointed man. If it be a sober truth, that "all things shall work together for good" to a certain order of mankind; and if the deepest sorrows in this world may serve to prepare us for a better; why, then, I think that one might hold by a certain ancient philosopher (and something more), who said "I have learned, in whatsoever state I am, therewith to be content!"

You see, reader, that in thinking of *People of whom more might have been made*, we are limiting the scope of the subject. I am not thinking how more might have been made of us originally. No doubt the potter had power over the clay. Give a larger brain, of finer quality, and the commonplace man might have been a Milton. A little change in the chemical composition of the gray matter of that little organ which is unquestionably connected with the mind's working as no other organ of the body is, and oh, what a different order of thought would have rolled off from your pen when you sat down and tried to write your best! If we are to believe Robert Burns, some people have been made more of than was originally intended. A certain poem records how that which, in his homely phrase, he calls "stuff to mak' a swine," was ultimately converted into a very poor specimen of a human being. The poet had no irreverent intention, I dare say; but I am not about to go into the field of speculation which is opened up by his words. I know indeed that in the hands of the Creator each of us might have been made a different man. The pounds of material which were fashioned into Shakespeare might have made a bumpkin with little thought beyond pigs and turnips; or, by some slight difference beyond man's skill to trace, might have made an idiot. A little infusion of energy into the mental constitution might have made the mild, pensive day-dreamer who is wandering listlessly by the river-side, sometimes chancing upon noble thoughts, which he does not carry out into action, and does not even write down on paper, into an active worker, with Arnold's keen look, who would have carved out a great career for himself, and exercised a real influence over the views and conduct of numbers of other men. A very little alteration in feature might have made a plain face into a beautiful one, and some slight change in the position or the contractibility of certain of the muscles might have made the most awkward of manners and gaits into the most dignified and graceful. All *that* we all understand. But my present subject is the making which is in circumstances after our natural disposition is fixed — the training, coming from a hundred quarters, which forms the material supplied by nature into the character which each of us actually bears. And setting apart the case of great genius, whose bent towards the thing in which it will excel is so strong that it will find its own field by inevitable selection, and whose strength is such that no unfavorable circumstances can hold it down, almost any ordinary human being may be formed into almost any development. I know a huge massive beam of rough iron, which supports a great weight. Whenever I pass it, I cannot help giving it a pat with my hand, and saying to it, "You might have been hair-springs for watches." I know an odd-looking little man attached to a certain railway-station, whose business it is when a train comes in to go round it with a large box of a yellow concoction, and supply grease to the wheels. I have often looked out of the carriage-window at that odd little man, and thought to myself, "Now you might have been a chief justice." And indeed I can say from personal observation, that the stuff ultimately converted into cabinet ministers does not at an early stage at all appreciably differ from that which never becomes more than country parsons. There is a great gulf between the human being who gratefully receives a shilling, and touches his cap as he receives it, and the human being whose income is paid in yearly or half-yearly sums, and to whom a pecuniary tip would appear as an insult; yet of course that great gulf is the result of training alone. John Smith the laborer, with twelve shillings a week, and the bishop with eight thousand a year, had, by original constitution, precisely the same kind of feeling towards that much-sought yet much-abused reality which provides the means of life. Who shall reckon up by what millions of slight touches from the hand of circumstance, extending over many years, the one man is gradually formed into the giving of the shilling, and the other man into the receiving of it with that touch of his hat? Who shall read back the forming influences at work since the days in the cradle, that gradually formed one man into sitting down to dinner, and another man into waiting behind his chair? I think it would be occa sionally a comfort if one could believe, as American planters profess to believe about their slaves, that there is an original and essential difference between men; for truly the difference in their positions is often so tremendous that it is painful to think that it is the selfsame clay and the selfsame common mind that are promoted to dignity and degraded to servitude. And if *you* sometimes feel *that*, *you* in whose favor the arrangement tends, what do you suppose your servants sometimes think upon the subject? It was no wonder that the millions of Russia were ready to grovel before their Czar, while they believed that he was "an emanation from the Deity." But in countries where it is quite understood that every man is just as much an emanation from the Deity as any other, you will not long have that sort of thing. You remember Goldsmith's noble lines, which Dr. Johnson never could read without tears, concerning the English character. It is not true that it is just because the humble but intelligent Englishman understands distinctly that we are all of us *people of whom more might have been made*, that he has "learnt to venerate himself as man!" And, thinking of influences which form the character, there is a sad reflection which has often occurred to me. It is, that circumstances often develop a character which it is hard to contemplate without anger and disgust. And yet in many such cases it is rather pity that is due. The more disgusting the character formed in some men, the more you should pity them. Yet it is hard to do *that*. You easily pity the man whom circumstances have made poor and miserable; how much more you should pity the man whom circumstances have made bad. You pity the man from whom some terrible accident has taken a limb or a hand; but how much more should you pity the man from whom the influences of years have taken a conscience and a heart! And something is to be said for even the most unamiable and worst of the race. No doubt it is mainly their own fault that they are so bad; but still it is hard work to be always rowing against wind and tide, and some people could be good only by doing *that* ceaselessly. I am not thinking now of pirates and pickpockets. But take the case of a sour, backbiting, malicious, wrong-headed, lying old woman, who gives her life to saying disagreeable things and making mischief between friends. There are not many mortals with whom one is less disposed to have patience. But yet, if you knew all, you would not be so severe in what you think and say of her. You do not know the physical irritability of nerve and weakness of constitution which that poor creature may have inherited; you do not know the singular twist of mind which she may have got from nature and from bad and unkind treatment in youth; you do not know the bitterness of heart she has felt at the polite snubbings and ladylike tortures which in excellent society are often the share of the poor and the dependent. If you knew all these things, you would bear more patiently with my friend Miss Limejuice; though I confess that sometimes you would find it uncommonly hard to do so.

As I wrote that last paragraph, I began dimly to fancy that somewhere I had seen the idea which is its subject treated by an abler hand by far than mine. The idea, you may be sure, was not suggested to me by books, but by what I have seen of men and women. But it is a pleasant thing to find that a thought which at the time is strongly impressing one's self, has impressed other men. And a modest person, who knows very nearly what his humble mark is, will be quite pleased to find that another man has not only anticipated his thoughts, but has expressed them much better than he could have done. Yes, let me turn to that incomparable essay of John Foster, *On a Man's writing Memoirs of Himself.* Here it is: —

Make the supposition that any given number of persons, a hundred, for instance, taken promiscuously, should be able to write memoirs of themselves so clear and perfect as to explain, to your discernment at least, the entire process by which their minds have attained their present state, recounting all the most impressive circumstances. If they should read these memoirs to you in succession, while your benevolence and the moral principles according to which you felt and estimated, were kept at the highest pitch, you would often, during the disclosure, regret to observe how many things may be the causes of irretrievable mischief. Why is the path of life, you would say, so haunted as if with evil spirits of every diversity of noxious agency, some of which may patiently accompany, or others of which may suddenly cross, the unfortunate wanderer? And you would regret to observe into how many forms of intellectual and moral perversion the human mind readily yields itself to be modified.

. . . .

I compassionate you, would, in a very benevolent hour, be your language to the wealthy, unfeeling *tyrant of a family and a neighborhood*, who seeks in the overawed timidity and unretaliated injuries of the unfortunate beings within his power, the gratification that should have been sought in their affections. Unless you had brought into the world some extraordinary refractoriness to the influence of evil, the process that you have undergone could not easily fail of being efficacious. If your parents idolized their own importance in their son so much, that they never opposed your inclinations themselves, nor permitted it to be done by any subject to their authority; if the humble companion, sometimes summoned to the honor of amusing you, bore your caprices and insolence with the meekness without which he had lost his enviable privilege; if you could despoil the garden of some nameless dependent neighbor of the carefully reared flowers, and torment his little dog or cat, without his daring to punish you or to appeal to your infatuated parents; if aged men addressed you in a submissive tone, and with the appellation of "Sir," and their aged wives uttered their wonder at your condescension, and pushed their grandchildren away from around the fire for your sake, if you happened, though with the strut of pertness, and your hat on your head, to enter one of their cottages, perhaps to express your contempt of the homely dwelling, furniture, and fare; if, in maturer life, you associated with vile persons, who would forego the contest of equality to be your allies in trampling on inferiors; and if, both then and since, you have been suffered to deem your wealth the compendium or equivalent of every ability and every good quality — it would indeed be immensely strange if you had not become, in due time, the miscreant, who may thank the power of the laws in civilized society that he is not assaulted with clubs and stones; to whom one could cordially wish the opportunity and the consequences of attempting his tyranny among some such people as those *submissive* sons of nature in the forests of North America; and whose dependents and domestic relatives may be almost forgiven when they shall one day rejoice at his funeral.

What do you think of *that*, my reader, as a specimen of embittered eloquence and nervous pith? It is something to read massive and energetic sense, in days wherein mystical twaddle, and subtlety which hopelessly defies all logic, are sometimes thought extremely fine, if they are set out in a style which is refined into mere effeminacy.

I cherish a very strong conviction (as has been said) that, at least in the case of educated people, happiness is a grand discipline for bringing out what is amiable and excellent. You understand, of course, what I mean by happiness. We all know, of course, that light heartedness is not very familiar to grown-up people, who are doing the work of life — who feel its many cares, and who do not forget the many risks which hang over it. I am not thinking of the kind of thing which is suggested to the minds of children, when they read, at the end of a tale, concerning its heroine and hero, that "they lived happily ever after." No; we don't look for that. By happiness, I mean freedom from terrible anxiety and from pervading depression of spirits: the consciousness that we are filling our place in life with decent success and approbation: religious principle and character: fair physical health throughout the family; and moderate good temper and good sense. And I hold, with Sydney Smith, and with that keen practical philosopher, Becky Sharpe, that happiness and success tend very greatly to make people passably good. Well, I see an answer to the statement, as I do to most statements; but, at least, the beam is never subjected to the strain which would break it. I have seen the gradual working of what I call happiness and success in ameliorating character. I have known a man who, by necessity, by the pressure of poverty, was driven to write for the magazines: a kind of work for which he had no special talent or liking, and which he had never intended to attempt. There was no more miserable, nervous, anxious, disappointed being on earth than he was when he began his writing for the press. And sure enough his articles were bitter and ill-set to a high degree. They were thoroughly ill-natured and bad. They were not devoid of a certain cleverness; but they were the sour products of a soured nature. But that man gradually got into comfortable circumstances: and with equal step with his lot the tone of his writings mended; till as a writer he became conspicuous for the healthful, cheerful, and kindly nature of all he produced. I remember seeing a portrait of an eminent author, taken a good many years ago, at a time when he was struggling into notice, and when he was being very severely handled by the critics. That portrait was really truculent of aspect. It was sour, and even ferocious-looking. Years afterwards I saw that author, at a time when he had attained vast success, and was universally recognized as a great man. How improved that face! All the savage lines were gone: the bitter look was gone: the great man looked quite genial and amiable. And I came to know that he really was all he looked. Bitter judgments of men, imputations of evil motives, disbelief in anything noble or generous, a disposition to repeat tales to the prejudice of others, envy, hatred, malice, and all uncharitableness, — all these things may possibly come out of a bad heart; but they certainly came out of a miserable one. The happier any human being is, the better and more kindly he thinks of all. It is the man who is always worried, whose means are uncertain, whose home is uncomfortable, whose nerves are rasped by some kind friend who daily repeats and enlarges upon everything disagreeable for him to hear: it is he who thinks hardly of the character and prospects of humankind, and who believes in the essential and unimprovable badness of the race.

This is not a treatise on the formation of character: it pretends to nothing like completeness. If this essay were to extend to a volume of about three hundred and eighty pages, I might be able to set out and discuss, in something like a full and orderly fashion, the influences under which human beings grow up, and the way in which to make the best of the best of these influences, and to evade or neutralize the worst. And if, after great thought and labor, I had produced such a volume, I am well aware that nobody would read it. So I prefer to briefly glance at a few aspects of a great subject just as they present themselves, leaving the complete discussion of it to solid individuals with more leisure at their command.

Physically, no man is made the most of. Look at an acrobat or a boxer: *there* is what your limbs might have been made for strength and agility. *That* is the potential which is in human nature in these respects. I never witnessed a prize-fight, and assuredly I never will witness one : but I am told that when the champions appear in the ring, stripped for the combat (however bestial and blackguard-looking their countenances may be), the clearness and beauty of their skin testify that by skilful physical discipline a great deal more may be made of that human hide than is usually made of it. Then if you wish to see what may be made of the human muscles as regards rapid dexterity, look at the Wizard of the North or at an Indian juggler. I am very far indeed from saying or thinking that this peculiar pre-eminence is worth the pains it must cost to acquire it. Not that I have a word to say against the man who maintains his children by bringing some one faculty of the body to absolute perfection : I am ready even to admit that it is a very right and fit thing that one man in five or six millions should devote his life to showing the very utmost that can be made of the human fingers, or the human muscular system as a whole : it is fit that a rare man here and there should cultivate some accomplishment to a perfection that looks magical, just as it is fit that a man here and there should live in a house that cost a million of pounds to build, and round which a wide tract of country shows what may be made of trees and fields where unlimited wealth and exquisite taste have done their best to improve nature to the fairest forms of which it is capable. But even if it were possible, it would not be desirable that all human beings should live in dwellings like Hamilton Palace or Arundel Castle ; and it would serve no good end at all, certainly no end worth the cost, to have all educated men muscular as Tom Sayers, or swift of hand as Robert Houdin. Practical efficiency is what is wanted for the business of this world, not absolute perfection: life is too short to allow any but exceptional individuals, few and far between, to acquire the power of playing at rackets as well as rackets can possibly be played. We are obliged to have a great number of irons in the fire: it is needful that we should do decently well a great number of things; and we must not devote ourselves to one thing to the exclusion of all the rest. And accordingly, though we may desire to be reasonably muscular and reasonably active, it will not disturb us to think that in both these respects we are people of whom more might have been made. It may here be said that probably there is hardly an influence which tends so powerfully to produce extreme self-complacency as the conviction that as regards some one physical accomplishment, one is a person of whom more could not have been made. It is a proud thing to think that you stand decidedly ahead of all mankind: that Eclipse is first and the rest nowhere; even in the matter of keeping up six balls at once, or of noting and remembering twenty different objects in a shop window as you walk past it at five miles an hour. I do not think I ever beheld a human being whose aspect was of such unutterable pride, as a man I lately saw playing the drum as one of a certain splendid military band. He was playing in a piece in which the drum music was very conspicuous; and even an unskilled observer could remark that his playing was absolute perfection. He had the thorough mastery of his instrument. He did the most difficult things not only with admirable precision, but without the least appearance of effort. He was a great tall fellow: and it was really a fine sight to see him standing very upright, and immovable save as to his arms, looking fixedly into distance, and his bosom swelling with the lofty belief that out of four or five thousand persons who were present, there was not one who, to save his life, could have done what he was doing so easily.

So much of physical dexterity. As for physical grace, it will be admitted that in that respect more might be made of most human beings. It is not merely that they are ugly and awkward naturally, but that they are ugly and awkward artificially. Sir Bulwer Lytton in his earlier writings was accustomed to maintain that just as it is a man's duty to cultivate his mental powers, so is it his duty to cultivate his bodily appearance. And doubtless, all the gifts of nature are talents committed to us to be improved; they are things intrusted to us to make the best of. It may be difficult to fix the point at which the care of personal appearance in man or woman becomes excessive. It does so unquestionably when it engrosses the mind to the neglect of more important things. But I suppose that all reasonable people now believe that scrupulous attention to personal cleanliness, freshness, and neatness, is a Christian duty. The days are past almost everywhere in which piety was held as associated with dirt. Nobody would mention now as a proof how saintly a human being was, that (for the love of God) he had never washed his face or brushed his hair for thirty years. And even scrupulous neatness need bring with it no suspicion of puppyism. The most trim and tidy of old men was good John Wesley; and he conveyed to the minds of all who saw him the notion of a man whose treasure was laid up beyond this world, quite as much as if he had dressed in such a fashion as to make himself an object of ridicule, or as if he had forsworn the use of soap.

Some people fancy that slovenliness of attire indicates a mind above petty details. I have seen an eminent preacher ascend the pulpit, with his bands hanging over his right shoulder, his gown apparently put on by being dropped upon him from the vestry ceiling, and his hair apparently unbrushed for several weeks. There was no suspicion of affectation about that good man; yet I regarded his untidiness as a defect and not as an excellence. He gave a most eloquent sermon; yet I thought it would have been well had the lofty mind that treated so admirably some of the grandest realities of life and of immortality, been able to address itself a little to the care of lesser things. I confess that when I heard the Bishop of Oxford preach, I thought the effect of his sermon was increased by the decorous and careful fashion in which he was arrayed in his robes. And it is to be admitted that the grace of the human aspect may be in no small measure enhanced by bestowing a little pains upon it. You, youthful matron, when you take your little children to have their photographs taken, and when their nurse in contemplation of that event attired them in their most tasteful dresses, and arranged their hair in its prettiest curls, you know that the little things looked a great deal better than they do on common days. It is pure nonsense to say that beauty when unadorned is adorned the most. For that is as much as to say that a pretty young woman, in the matter of physical appearance, is a person of whom no more can be made. Now taste and skill can make more of almost anything. And you will set down Thomson's lines as flatly opposed to fact, when your lively young cousin walks into your room to let you see her before she goes out to an evening party; and when you compare that radiant vision, in her robes of misty texture, and with hair arranged in folds the most complicated — wreathed, and satin shoed — with the homely figure that took a walk with you that afternoon, russet-gowned, tartan-plaided, and shod with serviceable boots for tramping through country mud. One does not think of loveliness in the case of men, because they have not got any: but their aspect, such as it is, is mainly made by their tailors. And it is a lamentable thought, how very ill the clothes of most men are made. I think that the art of draping the male human body has been brought to much less excellence by the mass of those who practise it, than any other of the useful and ornamental arts. Tailors, even in great cities, are generally extremely bad. Or it may be that the providing of the human frame with decent and well-fitting garments is so very difficult a thing, that (save by a great genius here and there) it can be no more than approximated to. As for tailors in little country villages, their power of distorting and disfiguring is wonderful. When I used to be a country clergyman, I remember how, when I went to the funeral of some simple rustic, I was filled with surprise to see the tall, strapping, fine young country lads, arrayed in their black suits. What awkward figures they looked in those unwonted garments! How different from their easy, natural appearance in their every-day fustian! Here you would see a young fellow, with a coat whose huge collar covered half his head when you looked at him from behind; a very common thing was to have sleeves which entirely concealed the hands; and the wrinkled and baggy aspect of the whole suits could be imagined only by such as have seen them. It may be remarked here, that those strong country lads were in another respect people of whom more might have been physically made. Oh for a drill-sergeant to teach them to stand upright, and to turn out their toes; and to get rid of that slouching, hulking gait which gives such a look of clumsiness and stupidity! If you could but have the well-developed muscles and the fresh complexion of the country, with the smartness and alertness of the town! You have there the rough material of which a vast deal may be made; you have the water-worn pebble which will take on a beautiful polish. Take from the moorland cottage the shepherd-lad of sixteen; send him to a Scotch college for four years; let him be tutor in a good family for a year or two; and (if he be an observant fellow) you will find in him the quiet, self-possessed air and the easy address of the gentleman who has seen the world. And it is curious to see one brother of a family thus educated and polished into refinement, while the other three or four, remaining in their father's simple lot, retain its rough manners and its unsophisticated feelings. Well, look at the man who has been made a gentleman, probably by the hard labor and sore self-denial of the others; and see in him what each of the others might have been! Look with respect on the diamond which needed only to be polished. Reverence the undeveloped potential which circumstances have held down. Look with interest on these people of whom more might have been made!

Such a sight as this sometimes sets us thinking how many germs of excellence are in this world turned to no account. You see the polished diamond and the rough one side by side. It is too late now; but the dull colorless pebble might have been the bright glancing gem. And you may polish the material diamond at any time; but if you miss your season in the case of the human one, the loss can never be repaired. The bumpkin who is a bumpkin at thirty, must remain a bumpkin to threescore and ten. But another thing that makes us think how many fair possibilities are lost, is to remark the fortuitous way in which great things have often been done; and done by people who never dreamt that they had in them the power to do anything particular. These cases, one cannot but think, are samples of millions more. There have been very popular writers who were brought out by mere accident. They did not know what precious vein of thought they had at command, till they stumbled upon it as if by chance, like the Indian at the mines of Potosi. It is not much that we know of Shakespeare, but it seems certain that it was in patching up old plays for acting that he discovered within himself a capacity for producing that which men will not easily let die. When a young military man, disheartened with the service, sought for an appointment as an Irish Commissioner of Excise, and was sadly disappointed because he did not get it, it is probable that he had as little idea as any one else had that he possessed that aptitude for the conduct of war which was to make him the Duke of Wellington. And when a young mathematician, entirely devoid of ambition, desired to settle quietly down, and devote all his life to that unexciting study, he was not aware that he was a person of whom more was to be made; — who was to grow into the great Emperor Napoleon. I had other instances in my mind, but after these last it is needless to mention them. But such cases suggest to us that there may have been many Folletts who never held a brief, many Keans who never acted but in barns, many Vandyks who never earned more than sixpence a day, many Goldsmiths who never were better than penny-a-liners, many Michaels who never built their St. Peters; and perhaps a Shakespeare who held horses at the theatre door for pence, as the Shakespeare we know of did, and who stopped there.

Let it here be suggested, that it is highly illogical to conclude that you are yourself a person of whom a great deal more might have been made, merely because you are a person of whom it is the fact that very little has actually been made. This suggestion may appear a truism; but it is one of those simple truths of which we al need to be occasionally reminded. After all, the great test of what a man can do, must be what a man does. But there are folk who live on the reputation of being pebbles capable of receiving a very high polish, though from circumstances they did not choose to be polished. There are people who stand high in general estimation on the ground of what they might have done if they had liked. You will find students who took no honors at the university, but who endeavor to impress their friends with the notion that if they had chosen, they could have attained to unexampled eminence. And sometimes, no doubt, there are great powers that run to waste. There have been men whose doings, splendid as they were, were no more than a hint of how much more they could have done. In such a case as that of Coleridge, you see how the lack of steady industry, and of all sense of responsibility, abated the tangible result of the noble intellect God gave him. But as a general rule, and in the case of ordinary people, you need not give a man credit for the possession of any powers beyond those which he has actually exhibited. If a boy is at the bottom of his class, it is probably because he could not attain its top. My friend Mr. Snarling thinks he can write much better articles than those which appear in any of the magazines;

but as he has not done so, I am not inclined to give him credit for the achievement. But you can see that this principle of estimating people's abilities not by what they have done, but by what they think they could do, will be much approved by persons who are stupid, and at the same time conceited. It is a pleasing arrangement that every man should fix his own mental mark, and hold by his estimate of himself. And then, never measuring his strength with others, he can suppose that he could have beat them if he had tried.

Yes, we are all mainly fashioned by circumstances; and had the circumstances been more propitious, they might have made a great deal more of us. You sometimes think, middle-aged man, who never have passed the limits of Britain, what an effect might have been produced upon your views and character by foreign travel. You think what an indefinite expansion of mind it might have caused; how many narrow prejudices it might have rubbed away; how much wiser and better a man it might have made you. Or more society and wider reading in your early youth might have improved you; might have taken away the shyness and the intrusive individuality which you sometimes feel painfully; might have called out one cannot say what of greater confidence and larger sympathy. How very little, you think to yourself, you have seen and known! While others skim great libraries, you read the same few books over and over; while others come to know many lands and cities, and the faces and ways of many men, you look, year after year, on the same few square miles of this world, and you have to form your notion of human nature from the study of but few human beings, and these very commonplace. Perhaps it is as well. It is not so certain that more would have been made of you if you had enjoyed what might seem greater advantages. Perhaps you learned more by studying the little field before you earnestly and long, than you would have learned if you had bestowed a cursory glance upon fields more extensive by far. Perhaps there was compensation for the fewness of the cases you had to observe, in the keenness with which you were able to observe them. Perhaps the Great Disposer saw that in your case the pebble got nearly all the polishing it would stand; the man nearly all the chances he could improve.

If there be soundness and justice in this suggestion, it may afford consolation to a considerable class of men and women. I mean those people who, feeling within themselves many defects of character, and discerning in their outward lot much which they would wish other than it is, are ready to think that some one thing would have put them right; that some one thing would put them right even yet; but something which they have hopelessly missed, something which can never be. There was just one testing event, which stood between them and their being made a vast deal more of. They would have been far better and far happier, they think, had some single malign influence been kept away which has darkened all their life; or had some single blessing been given which would have made it happy. If you had got such a parish which you did not get; if you had married such a woman; if your little child had not died; if you had always the society and sympathy of such an energetic and hopeful friend; if the scenery round your dwelling were of a different character; if the neighboring town were four miles off instead of fifteen; if any one of these circumstances had been altered, what a different man you might have been! Probably many people, even of middle age, conscious that the manifold cares and worries of life forbid that it should be evenly joyous, do yet cherish, at the bottom of their heart, some vague yet rooted fancy, that if but one thing were given on which they had set their hearts, or one care removed forever, they would be perfectly happy, even here. Perhaps you overrate the effect which would have been produced on your character by such a single cause. It might not have made you much better; it might not even have made you very different. And assuredly you are wrong in fancying that any such single thing could have made you happy; that is, entirely happy. Nothing in this world could ever make you *that.* It is not God's purpose that we should be entirely happy here. "This is not our rest." The day will never come which will not bring its worry. And the possibility of terrible misfortune and sorrow hangs over all. There is but one place where we shall be right; and *that* is far away.

Yes, more might have been made of all of us; probably, in the case of most, not much more *will* be made in this world. We are now, if we have reached middle life, very much what we shall be to the end of the chapter. We shall not, in this world, be much better; let us humbly trust that we shall not be worse. Yet, if there be an undefinable sadness in looking at the marred material of which so much more might have been made, there is a sublime hopefulness in the contemplation of material, bodily and mental, of which a great deal more and better will certainly yet be made. Not much more may be made of any of us in life; but who shall estimate what may be made of us in immortality? Think of a "spiritual body;" think of a perfectly pure and happy soul! I thought of this on a beautiful evening of this summer, walking with a much valued friend through a certain grand ducal domain. In front of a noble sepulchre, where is laid up much aristocratic dust, there are sculptured by some great artist, three colossal faces, which are meant to represent Life, Death, and Immortality. It was easy to represent death: the face was one of solemn rest, with closed eyes; and the sculptor's skill was mainly shown in distinguishing Life from Immortality. And he had done it well. *There* was Life, a careworn, anxious, weary face, that seemed to look at you earnestly, and with a vague inquiry for something — the something that is lacking in all things here. And *there* was Immortality: life-like, but oh! how different from mortal Life! *There* was the beautiful face; calm, satisfied, self-possessed, sublime; and with eyes looking far away. I see it yet, the crimson sunset warming the gray stone; and a great hawthorn tree, covered with blossoms, standing by. Yes, *there* was Immortality; and you felt, as you looked at it, that it was MORE MADE OF LIFE!

CHAPTER VI.

CONCERNING PEOPLE WHO CARRIED WEIGHT IN LIFE.

WITH SOME THOUGHTS ON THOSE WHO NEVER HAD A CHANCE.

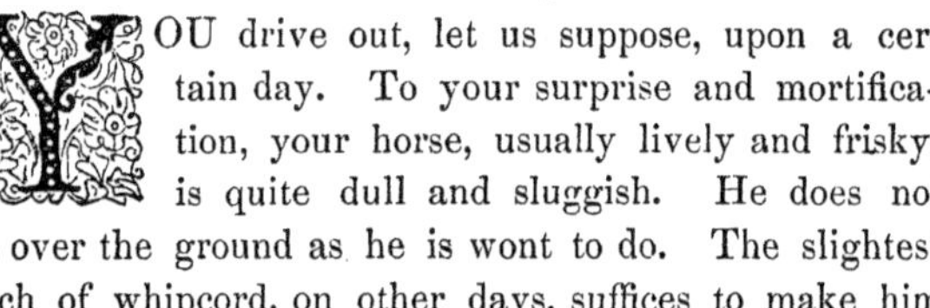

YOU drive out, let us suppose, upon a certain day. To your surprise and mortification, your horse, usually lively and frisky, is quite dull and sluggish. He does not get over the ground as he is wont to do. The slightest touch of whipcord, on other days, suffices to make him dart forward with redoubled speed; but upon this day, after two or three miles, he needs positive whipping, and he runs very sulkily with it all. By and bye his coat, usually smooth and glossy and dry through all reasonable work, begins to stream like a water-cart. This will not do. There is something wrong. You investigate; and you discover that your horse's work, though seemingly the same as usual, is in fact immensely greater. The blockheads who oiled your wheels yesterday have screwed up your patent axles too tightly; the friction is enormous; the hotter the metal gets, the greater grows the friction; your horse's work is quadrupled. You drive slowly home; and severely upbraid the blockheads.

There are many people who have to go through life at an analogous disadvantage. There is something in their constitution of body or mind; there is something in their circumstances; which adds incalculably to the exertion they must go through to attain their ends; and which holds them back from doing what they might otherwise have done. Very probably, that malign something exerted its influence unperceived by those around them. They did not get credit for the struggle they were making. No one knew what a brave fight they were making with a broken right arm; no one remarked that they were running the race, and keeping a fair place in it too, with their legs tied together. All they do, they do at a disadvantage. It is as when a noble race-horse is beaten by a sorry hack; because the race-horse, as you might see if you look at the list, is carrying twelve pounds additional. But such men, by a desperate effort, often made silently and sorrowfully, may (so to speak) run in the race; and do well in it; though you little think with how heavy a foot and how heavy a heart. There are others, who have no chance at all. *They* are like a horse set to run a race, tied by a strong rope to a tree; or weighted with ten tons of extra burden. *That* horse cannot run, even poorly. The difference between their case and that of the men who are placed at a disadvantage, is like the difference between setting a very near-sighted man to keep a sharp look-out, and setting a man who is quite blind to keep that sharp look-out. Many can do the work of life with difficulty; some cannot do it at all. In short, there are PEOPLE WHO CARRY WEIGHT IN LIFE; and there are some WHO NEVER HAVE A CHANCE.

And you, my friend, who are doing the work of life well and creditably: you who are running in the front rank, and likely to do so to the end; think kindly and charitably of those who have broken down in the race. Think kindly of him who, sadly over-weighted, is struggling onwards away half-a-mile behind you; think more kindly yet, if that be possible, of him who, tethered to a ton of granite, is struggling hard and making no way at all; or who has even sat down and given up the struggle in dumb despair. You feel, I know, the weakness in yourself which would have made you break down if sorely tried like others. You know there is in your armor the unprotected place, at which a well-aimed or a random blow would have gone home and brought you down. Yes, you are nearing the winning-post, and you are among the first; but six pounds more on your back, and you might have been nowhere. You feel, by your weak heart and weary frame, that if you had been sent to the Crimea in that dreadful first winter, you would certainly have died. And you feel, too, by your lack of moral stamina, by your feebleness of resolution, that it has been your preservation from you know not what depths of shame and misery, that you never were pressed very hard by temptation. Do not range yourself with those who found fault with a certain great and good Teacher of former days, because he went to be guest with a man that was a sinner. As if He could have gone to be guest with any man who was not!

There is no reckoning up the manifold *impedimenta* by which human beings are weighted for the race of life; but all may be classified under the two heads of unfavorable influences arising out of the mental or physical nature of the human beings themselves, and unfavorable influences arising out of the circumstances in which the human beings are placed. You have known men who, setting out from a very humble position, have attained to a respectable standing: but who would have reached a very much higher place but for their being weighted with a vulgar, violent, wrong-headed, and rude-spoken wife You have known men of lowly origin, who had in them the makings of gentlemen; but whom this single malign influence has condemned to coarse manners and a frowsy repulsive home for life. You have known many men whose powers are crippled and their nature soured by poverty; by the heavy necessity for calculating how far each shilling will go; by a certain sense of degradation that comes of sordid shifts. How can a poor parson write an eloquent or spirited sermon, when his mind all the while is running upon the thought how he is to pay the baker, or how he is to get shoes for his children? It will be but a dull discourse which, under that weight, will be produced even by a man who, favorably placed, could have done very considerable things. It is only a great genius here and there who can do great things, who can do his best, no matter at what disadvantage he may be placed; the great mass of ordinary men can make little headway with wind and tide dead against them. Not many trees would grow well if watered daily (let us say) with vitriol. Yet a tree which would speedily die under that nurture, might do very fairly, might even do magnificently, if it had fair play; if it got its chance of common sunshine and shower. Some men, indeed, though always hampered by circumstances, have accomplished much; but then you cannot help thinking how much more they might have accomplished had they been placed more happily. Pugin, the great Gothic architect, designed various noble buildings; but I believe he complained that he never had fair play with his finest; that he was always weighted by considerations of expense, or by the nature of the ground he had to build on, or by the number of people it was essential the building should accommodate. And so he regarded his noblest edifices as no more than hints of what he could have done. He made grand running in the race; but oh what running he could have made if you had taken off those twelve additional pounds! I dare say you have known men who labored to make a pretty country-house on a site which had some one great drawback. They were always battling with that drawback, and trying to conquer it; but they never could quite succeed. And it remained a real worry and vexation. Their house was on the north side of a high hill, and never could have its due share of sunshine. Or you could not reach it but by climbing a very steep ascent; or you could not in any way get water into the landscape. When Sir Walter was at length able to call his own a little estate on the banks of the Tweed he loved so well, it was the ugliest, bleakest, and least interesting spot upon the course of that beautiful river; and the public road ran within a few yards of his door. The noble-hearted man made a charming dwelling at last; but he was fighting against nature in the matter of the landscape round it; and you can see yet, many a year after he left it, the poor little trees of his beloved plantations, contrasting with the magnificent timber of various grand old places above and below Abbotsford. There is something sadder in the sight of men who carried weight within themselves; and who, in aiming at usefulness or at happiness, were hampered and held back by their own nature. There are many men who are weighted with a hasty temper; weighted with a nervous, anxious constitution; weighted with an envious, jealous disposition; weighted with a strong tendency to evil speaking, lying, and slandering; weighted with a grumbling, sour, discontented spirit; weighted with a disposition to vaporing and boasting; weighted with a great want of common sense; weighted with an undue regard to what other people may be thinking or saying of them; weighted with many like things of which more will be said by and bye. When that good missionary, Henry Martyn, was in India, he was weighted with an irresistible drowsiness. He could hardly keep himself awake. And it must have been a burning earnestness that impelled him to ceaseless labor, in the presence of such a drag-weight as that. I am not thinking or saying, my friend, that it is wholly bad for us to carry weight; that great good may not come of the abatement of our power and spirit which may be made by that weight. I remember a greater missionary than even the sainted Martyn, to whom the Wisest and Kindest appointed that he should carry weight, and that he should fight at a sad disadvantage. And the greater missionary tells us that he knew why that weight was appointed him to carry; and that he felt he needed it all to save him from a strong tendency to undue self-conceit. No one knows, now, what the burden was which he bore; but it was heavy and painful; it was "a thorn in the flesh;" three times he earnestly asked that it might be taken away; but the answer he got implied that he needed it yet; and that his Master thought it a better plan to strengthen the back than to lighten the burden. Yes, the blessed Redeemer appointed that St. Paul should carry weight in life; and I think, friendly reader, that we shall believe that it is wisely and kindly meant, if the like should come to you and me.

We all understand what is meant when we hear it

is said that a man is doing very well, or has done very well, *considering*. I do not know whether it is a Scotticism to stop short at that point of the sentence. We do it, constantly, in this country: the sentence would be completed by saying, *considering the weight he has to carry*, or *the disadvantage at which he works*. And things which are *very good, considering*, may range very far up and down the scale of actual merit. A thing which is *very good, considering*, may be very bad, or may be tolerably good. It never can be absolutely very good; for, if it were, you would cease to use the word *considering*. A thing which is absolutely very good, if it have been done under extremely unfavorable circumstances, would not be described as *very good, considering;* it would be described as *quite wonderful, considering*, or as *miraculous considering*. And it is curious how people take a pride in accumulating unfavorable circumstances, that they may overcome them, and gain the glory of having overcome them. Thus, if a man wishes to sign his name, he might write the letters with his right hand; and though he write them very clearly and well and rapidly, nobody would think of giving him any credit. But if he write his name rather badly with his left hand, people would say it was a remarkable signature, considering. And if he wrote his name, very ill indeed, with his foot, people would say the writing was quite wonderful, considering. If a man desire to walk from one end of a long building, to the other, he might do so by walking along the floor; and though he did so steadily, swiftly, and gracefully, no one would remark that he had done anything worth notice. But if he choose for his path a thick rope, extended from one end of the building to the other, at a height of a hundred feet; and if he walk rather slowly and awkwardly along it, he will be esteemed as having done something very extraordinary; while if, in addition to this, he is blindfolded, and has his feet placed in large baskets instead of shoes, he will, if in any way he can get over the distance between the ends of the building, be held as one of the most remarkable men of the age. Yes, load yourself with weight which no one asks you to carry: accumulate disadvantages which you need not face unless you choose; then carry the weight in any fashion, and overcome the disadvantages in any fashion; and you are a great man, considering; that is, considering the disadvantages and the weight. Let this be remembered: if a man is so placed that he cannot do his work, except in the face of special difficulties, then let him be praised if he vanquish these in some decent measure, and if he do his work tolerably well. But a man deserves no praise at all for work which he has done tolerably or done rather badly, because he chose to do it under disadvantageous circumstances, under which there was no earthly call upon him to do it. In this case he probably is a self-conceited man, or a man of wrong-headed independence of disposition; and in this case, if his work be bad absolutely, don't tell him that it is good, considering. Refuse to consider. He has no right to expect that you should. There was a man who built a house entirely with his own hands. He had never learned either mason work or carpentry: he could quite well have afforded to pay skilled workmen to do the work he wanted; but he did not choose to do so. He did the whole work himself. The house was finished: its aspect was peculiar. The walls were off the perpendicular considerably, and the windows were singular in shape, the doors fitted badly, and the floors were far from level. In short, it was a very bad and awkward-looking house; but it was a wonderful house, considering. And people said that it was so, who saw nothing wonderful in the beautiful house next it, perfect in symmetry and finish and comfort, but built by men whose business it was to build. Now, I should have declined to admire that odd house, or to express the least sympathy with its builder. He chose to run with a needless hundredweight on his back: he chose to walk in baskets instead of in shoes. And if, in consequence of his own perversity, he did his work badly, I should have refused to recognize it as anything but bad work. It was quite different with Robinson Crusoe, who made his dwelling and his furniture for himself, because there was no one else to make them for him. I dare say his cave was anything but exactly square, and his chairs and tables were cumbrous enough; but they were wonderful, considering certain facts which he was quite entitled to expect us to consider. Southey's *Cottonian Library* was all quite right; and you would have said that the books were very nicely bound, considering; for Southey could not afford to pay the regular binder's charges; and it was better that his books should be done up in cotton of various hues by the members of his own family, than that they should remain not bound at all. You will think, too, of the poor old parson who wrote a book which he thought of great value, but which no pubisher would bring out. He was determined that all his labor should not be lost to posterity. So he bought types and a printing-press, and printed his precious work, poor man; he and his man-servant did it all. It made a great many volumes; and the task took up many years. Then he bound the volumes with his own hands; and carrying them to London, he placed a copy of his work in each of the public libraries. I dare say he might have saved himself his labor. How many of my readers could tell what was the title of the work, or what was the name of its author? Still, *there* was a man who accomplished his design, in the face of every disadvantage.

There is a great point of difference between our feeling towards the human being who runs his race much overweighted, and our feeling towards the inferior animal that does the like. If you saw a poor horse gamely struggling in a race, with a weight of a ton extra, you would pity it. Your sympathies would all be with the creature that was making the best of unfavorable circumstances. But it is a sorrowful fact, that the drag weight of human beings not unfrequently consists of things which make us angry rather than sympathetic. You have seen a man carrying heavy weight in life, perhaps in the form of inveterate wrongheadedness and suspiciousness; but instead of pitying him, our impulse would rather be to beat him upon that perverted head. We pity physical malformation or unhealthiness; but our bent is to be angry with intellectual and moral malformation or unhealthiness. We feel for the deformed man, who must struggle on at that sad disadvantage; feeling it, too, much more acutely than you would readily believe. But we have only indignation for the man weighted with far worse things; and things which, in some cases at least, he can just as little help. You have known men whose extra pounds, or even extra ton, was a hasty temper, flying out of a sudden into ungovernable bursts: or a moral cowardice leading to trickery and falsehood: or a special disposition to envy and evil speaking: or a very strong tendency to morbid complaining about his misfortunes and troubles: or an invincible bent to be always talking of his sufferings through the derangement of his digestive organs. Now, you grow angry at these things. You cannot stand them. And there is a substratum of truth to that angry feeling. A man *can* form his mind more than he can form his body. If a man be well-made, physically, he will, in ordinary cases, remain so: but he may, in a moral sense, raise a great hunchback where nature made none. He may foster a malignant temper, a grumbling, fretful spirit, which by manful resistance might be much abated, if not quite put down. But still, there should often be pity, where we are prone only to blame. We find a person in whom a truly disgusting character has been formed: well, if you knew all, you would know that the person had hardly a chance of being otherwise: the man could not help it. You have known people who were awfully unamiable and repulsive: you may have been told how very different they once were, — sweet-tempered and cheerful. And surely the change is a far sadder one than that which has passed upon the wrinkled old woman, who was once (as you are told) the loveliest girl of her time. Yet many a one who will look with interest upon the withered face and the dimmed eyes, and try to trace in them the vestiges of radiant beauty gone, will never think of puzzling out in violent spurts of petulance the perversion of a quick and kind heart; or in curious oddities and pettinesses the result of long and lonely years of toil in which no one sympathized; or in cynical bitterness and misanthropy, an old disappointment never got over. There is a hard knot in the wood, where a green young branch was lopped away. I have a great pity for old bachelors. Those I have known have for the most part been old fools. But the more foolish and absurd they are, the more pity is due to them. I believe there is something to be said for even the most unamiable creatures. The shark is an unamiable creature. It is voracious. It will snap a man in two. Yet it is not unworthy of sympathy. Its organization is such that it is always suffering the most ravenous hunger. You can hardly imagine the state of intolerable famine in which that unhappy animal roams the ocean. People talk of its awful teeth and its vindictive eye. I suppose it is well ascertained that the extremity of physical want, as reached on rafts at sea, has driven human beings to deeds as barbarous as ever shark was accused of. The worse a human being is, the more he deserves our pity. Hang him, if *that* be needful for the welfare of society; but pity him even as you hang. Many a poor creature has gradually become hardened and inveterate in guilt, who would have shuddered at first had the excess of it ultimately reached been at first presented to view. But the precipice was sloped off: the descent was made step by step. And there is many a human being who never had a chance of being good: many who have been trained, and even compelled, to evil from very infancy. Who that knows anything of our great cities, but knows how the poor little child, the toddling innocent, is sometimes sent out day by day to steal; and received in his wretched home with blows and curses if he fail to bring back enough: who has not heard of such poor little things, unsuccessful in their sorry work, sleeping all night in some wintry stair, because they durst not venture back to their drunken, miserable, desperate parents? I could tell things at which angels might shed tears, with much better reason for doing so than seems to me to exist in some of those more imposing occasions on which bombastic writers are wont to describe them as weeping. Ah, there is One who knows where the responsibility for all this rests! Not wholly with the wretched parents: far from *that*. *They*, too, have gone through the like: they had as little chance as their children. *They* deserve our deepest pity too. Perhaps the deeper pity is not due to the shivering, starving child, with the bitter wind cutting through its thin rags, and its blue feet on the frozen pavement, holding out a hand that is like the claw of some beast, but rather to the brutalized mother who could thus send out the infant she bore. Surely the mother's condition, if we look at the case aright, is the more deplorable. Would not you, my reader, rather endure any degree of cold and hunger than come to this! Doubtless, there is blame somewhere that such things should be: but we all know that the blame of the most miserable practical evils and failures can hardly be traced to particular individuals. It is through the incapacity of scores of public servants that an army is starved. It is through the fault of millions of people that our great towns are what they are: and it must be confessed that the actual responsibility is spread so thinly over so great a surface, that it is hard to say it rests very blackly upon any one spot. Oh, that we could but know whom to hang, when we find some flagrant, crying evil! Unluckily, hasty people are ready to be content if they can but hang anybody, without minding much whether that individual be more to blame than many beside. Laws and kings have something to do here: but management and foresight on the part of the poorer classes have a great deal more to do. And no laws can make many persons managing or provident. I do not hesitate to say, from what I have myself seen of the poor, that the same short-sighted extravagance, the same recklessness of consequences, which are frequently found in them, would cause quite as much misery if they prevailed in a like degree among people with a thousand a-year. But it seems as if only tolerably well-to-do people have the heart to be provident and self-denying. A man with a few hundreds annually does not marry unless he thinks he can afford it: but the workman with fifteen shillings a-week is profoundly indifferent to any such calculation. I firmly believe that the sternest of all self-denial is that practised by those who, when we divide mankind into rich and poor, must be classed (I suppose) with the rich. But I turn away from a miserable subject, through which I cannot see my way clearly, and on which I cannot think but with unutterable pain. It is an easy way of cutting the knot to declare that the rich are the cause of all the sufferings of the poor; but when we look at the case in all its bearings, we shall see that *that* is rank nonsense. And on the other hand, it is unquestionable that the rich are bound to do something. But what? I should feel deeply indebted to any one who would write out, in a few short and intelligible sentences, the practical results that are aimed at in the *Song of the Shirt.* The misery and evil are manifest: but tell us whom to hang; tell us what to do!

One heavy burden with which many men are weighted for the race of life, is depression of spirits. I wonder whether this used to be as common in former days as it is now. There was, indeed, the man in Homer, who walked by the sea-shore in a very gloomy mood; but his case seems to have been thought remarkable. What is it in our modern mode of life, and our infinity of cares; what little thing is it about the matter of the brain, or the flow of the blood, that makes the difference between buoyant cheerfulness and deep depression? I begin to think that almost all educated people, and especially all whose work is mental rather than physical, suffer more or less from this indescribable gloom. And although a certain amount of sentimental sadness may possibly help the poet, or the imaginative writer, to produce material which may be very attractive to the young and inexperienced, I suppose it will be admitted by all that cheerfulness and hopefulness are noble and healthful stimulants to worthy effort, and that depression of spirits does (so to speak) cut the sinews with which the average man must do the work of life. You know how lightly the buoyant heart carries people through entanglements and labors under which the desponding would break down, or which they never would face. Yet, in thinking of the commonness of depressed spirits, even where the mind is otherwise very free from anything morbid, we should remember that there is a strong temptation to believe that this depression is more common and more prevalent than it truly is. Sometimes there is a gloom which overcasts all life, like that in which James Watt lived and worked, and served his race so nobly; like that from which the gentle, amiable poet, James Montgomery, suffered through his whole career. But in ordinary cases the gloom is temporary and transient. Even the most depressed are not always so. Like, we know, suggests like powerfully. If you are placed in some peculiar conjuncture of circumstances, or if you pass through some remarkable scene, the present scene or conjuncture will call up before you in a way that startles you, something like itself which you had long forgotten, and which you would never have remembered but for this touch of some mysterious spring. And accordingly, a man depressed in spirits thinks that he is always so, or at least fancies that such depression has given the color to his life in a very much greater degree than it actually has done so. For this dark season wakens up the remembrance of many similar dark seasons which in more cheerful days are quite forgot, and these cheerful days drop out of memory for the time. Hearing such a man speak, if he speak out his heart to you, you think him inconsistent, perhaps you think him insincere. You think he is saying more than he truly feels. It is not so; he feels and believes it all at the time. But he is taking a one-sided view of things: he is undergoing the misery of it acutely for the time: by and bye he will see things from quite a different point. A very eminent man (there can be no harm in referring to a case which he himself made so public) wrote and published something about his *miserable home.* He was quite sincere, I do not doubt. He thought so at the time. He *was* miserable just then; and so, looking back on past years, he could see nothing but misery. But the case was not really so, one could feel sure. There had been a vast deal of enjoyment about his home and his lot; it was forgotten, then. A man in very low spirits, reading over his diary, somehow lights upon and dwells upon all the sad and wounding things; he involuntarily skips the rest, or reads them with but faint perception of their meaning. In reading the very Bible, he does the like thing. He chances upon that which is in unison with his present mood. I think there is no respect in which this great law of the association of ideas holds more strictly true, than in the power of a present state of mind, or a present state of outward circumstances, to bring up vividly before us all such states in our past history. We are depressed, we are worried; and when we look back, all our departed days of worry and depression appear to start up and press themselves upon our view to the exclusion of anything else: so that we are ready to think that we have never been otherwise than depressed and worried all our life. But when more cheerful times come, they suggest only such times of cheerfulness, and no effort will bring back the depression vividly as when we felt it. It is not selfishness or heartlessness, it is the result of an inevitable law of mind, that people in happy circumstances should resolutely believe that it is a happy world after all; for looking back, and looking around, the mind refuses to take distinct note of anything that is not somewhat akin to its present state. And so, if any ordinary man, who is not a distempered genius or a great fool, tells you that he is always miserable, don't believe him. He feels so now, but he does not always feel so. There are periods of brightening in the darkest lot. Very, very few live in unvarying gloom. Not but what there is something very pitiful (by which I mean deserving of pity) in what may be termed the Micawber style of mind; in the stage of hysteric oscillations between joy and misery. Thoughtless readers of *David Copperfield* laugh at Mr. Micawber, and his rapid passages from the depth of despair to the summit of happiness, and back again. But if you have seen or experienced that morbid condition, you would know that there is more reason to mourn over it than to laugh at it. There is acute misery felt now and then; and there is a pervading, never-departing sense of the hollowness of the morbid mirth. It is but a very few degrees better than "moody madness, laughing wild, amid severest woe." By depression of spirits, I understand a dejection without any cause that could be stated, or from causes which in a healthy mind would produce no such degree of dejection. No doubt many men can remember seasons of dejection which was not imaginary, and of anxiety and misery whose causes were only too real. You can remember, perhaps, the dark time in which you knew quite well what it was that made it so dark. Well, better days have come. That sorrowful, wearing time, which exhausted the springs of life faster than ordinary living would have done, which aged you in heart and frame before your day, dragged over, and it is gone. You carried heavy weight, indeed, while it lasted. It was but poor running you made, poor work you did, with that feeble, anxious, disappointed, miserable heart. And you would many a time have been thankful to creep into a quiet grave. Perhaps that season did you good. Perhaps it was the discipline you needed. Perhaps it took out your self-conceit, and made you humble. Perhaps it disposed you to feel for the grief and cares of others, and made you sympathetic. Perhaps, looking back now, you can discern the end it served. And now that it has done its work, and that it only stings you when you look back, let that time be quite forgotten!

There are men, and very clever men, who do the work of life at a disadvantage, through *this*, that their mind is a machine fitted for doing well only one kind of work; or that their mind is a machine which, though doing many things well, does some one thing, perhaps a conspicuous thing, very poorly. You find it hard to give a man credit for being possessed of sense and talent, if you hear him make a speech at a public dinner, which speech approaches the idiotic for its silliness and confusion. And the vulgar mind readily concludes that he who does one thing extremely ill, can do nothing well; and that he who is ignorant on one point, is ignorant on all. A friend of mine, a country parson, on first going to his parish, resolved to farm his glebe for himself. A neighboring farmer kindly offered the parson to plough one of his fields. The farmer said that he would send his man John with a plough and a pair of horses on a certain day. "If ye 're goin' aboot," said the farmer to the clergyman, "John will be unco' weel pleased if you speak to him, and say it's a fine day, or the like o' that; but dinna," said the farmer, with much solemnity, "dinna say onything to him aboot ploughin' and sawin'; for John," he added, "is a stupid body, but he has been ploughin' and sawin' all his life, and he'll see in a minute that *ye* ken naething aboot ploughin' and sawin'. And then," said the sagacious old farmer, with extreme earnestness, "if he comes to think that ye ken naething aboot ploughin' and sawin', he'll think that ye ken naething aboot onything!" Yes, it is natural to us all to think that if the machine breaks down at that work in which we are competent to test it, then the machine cannot do any work at all.

If you have a strong current of water, you may turn it into any channel you please, and make it do any work you please. With equal energy and success it will flow north or south; it will turn a corn-mill, or a threshing-machine, or a grindstone. Many people live under a vague impression that the human mind is like that. They think — Here is so much ability, so much energy, which may be turned in any direction, and made to do any work; and they are surprised to find that the power, available and great for one kind of work, is worth nothing for another. A man very clever at one thing, is positively weak and stupid at another thing. A very good judge may be a wretchedly bad joker; and he must go through his career at this disadvantage, that people, finding him silly at the thing they are able to estimate, find it hard to believe that he is not silly at everything. I know for myself that it would not be right that the Premier should request me to look out for a suitable Chancellor. I am not competent to appreciate the depth of a man's knowledge of equity; by which I do not mean justice, but chancery law. But though quite unable to understand how great a Chancellor Lord Eldon was, I am quite able to estimate how great a poet he was; also how great a wit. Here is a poem by that eminent person. Doubtless he regarded it as a wonder of happy versification, as well as instinct with the most convulsing fun. It is intended to set out in a metrical form, the career of a certain judge, who went up as a poor lad from Scotland to England, but did well at the bar, and ultimately found his place upon the bench. Here is Lord Chancellor Eldon's humorous poem:

James Allan Parke
Came naked stark,
From Scotland:
But he got clothes,
Like other beaux,
In England!

Now the fact that Lord Eldon wrote that poem, and valued it highly, would lead some folk to suppose that Lord Eldon was next door to an idiot. And a good many other things which that Chancellor did, such as his quotations from Scripture in the House of Commons, and his attempts to convince that assemblage (when Attorney-General) that Napoleon I. was the Apocalyptic

Beast or the Little Horn, certainly point towards the same conclusion. But the conclusion, as a general one, would be wrong. No doubt Lord Eldon was a wise and sagacious man as judge and statesman, though as wit and poet he was almost an idiot. So with other great men. It is easy to remember occasions on which great men have done very foolish things. There never was a truer hero nor a greater commander than Lord Nelson; but in some things he was merely an awkward, overgrown midshipman. But, then, let us remember, that a locomotive engine, though excellent at running, would be a poor hand at flying. *That* is not its vocation. The engine will draw fifteen heavy carriages fifty miles in an hour; and *that* remains as a noble feat, even though it be ascertained that the engine could not jump over a brook which would be cleared easily by the veriest screw. We all see this. But many of us have a confused idea that a great and clever man is (so to speak) a locomotive that can fly; and when it is proved that he cannot fly, then we begin to doubt whether he can even run. We think he should be good at everything, whether in his own line or not. And he is set at a disadvantage, particularly in the judgment of vulgar and stupid people, when it is clearly ascertained that at some things he is very inferior. I have heard of a very eminent preacher who sunk considerably (even as regards his preaching) in the estimation of a certain family, because it appeared that he played very badly at bowls. And we all know that occasionally the Premier already mentioned reverses the vulgar error, and in appointing men to great places, is guided by an axiom which amounts to just this: this locomotive can run well, therefore it will fly well. This man has filled a certain position well, therefore let us appoint him to a position entirely different; no doubt he will do well there too. Here is a clergyman who has edited certain Greek plays admirably: let us make him a bishop.

It may be remarked here, that the men who have attained the greatest success in the race of life, have generally carried weight. *Nitor in adversum* might be the motto of many a man, besides Burke. It seems to be almost a general rule, that the raw material out of which the finest fabrics are made, should look very little like these, to start with. It was a stammerer, of uncommanding mien, who became the greatest orator of graceful Greece. I believe it is admitted that Chalmers was the most effective preacher, perhaps the most telling speaker, that Britain has seen for at least a century; yet his aspect was not dignified, his gestures were awkward, his voice was bad, and his accent frightful. He talked of an *oppning* when he meant an *opening;* and he read out the text of one of his noblest sermons, "He that is fulthy, let him be fulthy stull." Yet who ever thought of these things, after hearing the good man for ten minutes! Aye, load Eclipse with what extra pounds you might, Eclipse would always be first! And, to descend to the race-horse, *he* had four white legs, white to the knees; and he ran more awkwardly than racer ever did, with his head between his forelegs, close to the ground, like a pig. Alexander, Napoleon, and Wellington, were all little men; in places where a commanding presence would have been of no small value. A most disagreeably affected manner has not prevented a barrister, with no special advantages, from rising with general approval to the highest places which a barrister can fill. A hideous little wretch has appeared for trial in a Criminal

Court, having succeeded in marrying seven wives at once. A painful hesitation has not hindered a certain eminent person from being one of the principal speakers in the British Parliament, for many years. Yes, even disadvantages never overcome have not sufficed to hold in obscurity men who were at once able and fortunate. But sometimes the disadvantage was thoroughly overcome. Sometimes it served no other end than to draw to one point the attention and the efforts of a determined will; and that matter, in regard to which nature seemed to have said that a man should fall short, became the thing in which he attained unrivalled perfection.

A heavy drag-weight upon the powers of some men, is the uncertainty of their powers. The man has not his powers at command. His mind is a capricious thing, that works when it pleases, and will not work except when it pleases. I am not thinking now of what to many is a sad disadvantage; that nervous trepidation which cannot be reasoned away, and which often deprives them of the full use of their mental abilities just when they are most needed. It is a vast thing in a man's favor that, whatever he can do, he should be able to do at any time, and to do at once. For want of coolness of mind, and that readiness which generally goes with it, many a man cannot do himself justice; and in a deliberative assembly he may be entirely beaten by some flippant person who has all his money (so to speak) in his pocket, while the other must send to the bank for his. How many people can think next day, or even a few minutes after, of the precise thing they ought to have said, but which would not come at the time! But very frequently the thing is of no value, unless it come at the time when it is wanted. Coming next day, it is like the offer of a thick fur great-coat on a sweltering day in July. You look at the wrap, and say, Oh if I could but have had you on the December night when I went to London by the limited mail, and was nearly starved to death! But it seems as if the mind must be, to a certain extent, capricious in its action. Caprice, or what looks like it, appears of necessity to go with complicated machinery, even material. The more complicated a machine is, the liker it grows to mind, in the matter of uncertainty and apparent caprice of action. The simplest machine — say a pipe for conveying water — will always act in precisely the same way. And two such pipes, if of the same dimensions, and subjected to the same pressure, will always convey the self-same quantities. But go to more advanced machines. Take two clocks, or two locomotive engines; and though these are made in all respects exactly alike, they will act (I can answer at least for the locomotive engines) quite differently. One locomotive will swallow a vast quantity of water at once; another must be fed by driblets; no one can say why. One engine is a *fac-simile* of the other; yet each has its character and its peculiarities, as truly as a man has. You need to know your engine's temper before driving it, just as much as you need to know that of your horse, or that of your friend. I know, of course, there is a mechanical reason for this seeming caprice, if you could trace the reason. But not one man in a thousand could trace out the reason. And the phenomenon, as it presses itself upon us, really amounts to this: that very complicated machinery appears to have a will of its own; appears to exercise something of the nature of choice. But there is no machine so capricious as the human mind.

The great poet who wrote those beautiful verses, could not do *that* every day. A good deal more of what he writes is poor enough; and many days he could not write at all. By long habit the mind may be made capable of being put in harness daily for the humbler task of producing prose; but you cannot say, when you harness it in the morning, how far or at what rate it will run that day.

Go and see a great organ, of which you have been told. Touch it, and you hear the noble tones at once. The organ can produce them at any time. But go and see a great man; touch *him;* that is, get him to begin to talk. You will be much disappointed if you expect, certainly, to hear anything like his book or his poem. A great man is not a man who is always saying great things; or who is always able to say great things. He is a man who on a few occasions has said great things; who on the coming of a sufficient occasion may possibly say great things again; but the staple of his talk is commonplace enough. Here is a point of difference from machinery, with all machinery's apparent caprice. You could not say, as you pointed to a steam-engine, The usual power of that engine is two hundred horses; but once or twice it has surprised us all by working up to two thousand. No; the engine is always of nearly the power of two thousand horses, if it ever is. But what we have been supposing as to the engine, is just what many men have done. Poe wrote *The Raven;* he was working then up to two thousand horse power. But he wrote abundance of poor stuff, working at about twenty-five. Read straight through the volumes of Wordsworth: and I think you will find traces of the engine having worked at many different powers, varying from twenty-five horses or less, up to two thousand or more. Go and hear a really great preacher when he is preaching in his own church upon a common Sunday; and possibly you may hear a very ordinary sermon. I have heard Mr. Melvill preach very poorly. You must not expect to find people always at their best. It is a very unusual thing that even the ablest men should be like Burke, who could not talk with an intelligent stranger for five minutes, without convincing the stranger that he had talked for five minutes with a great man. And it is an awful thing when some clever youth is introduced to some local poet who has been told how greatly the clever youth admires him; and what vast expectations the clever youth has formed of his conversation; and when the local celebrity makes a desperate effort to talk up to the expectations formed of him. I have witnessed such a scene; and I can sincerely say that I could not previously have believed that the local celebrity could have made such a fool of himself. He was resolved to show that he deserved his fame; and to show that the mind which had produced those lovely verses in the country newspaper, could not stoop to commonplace things.

Undue sensitiveness, and a too lowly estimate of their own powers, hang heavily upon some men; probably upon more men than one would imagine. I believe that many a man whom you would take to be ambitious, pushing, and self-complacent, is ever pressed with a sad conviction of inferiority, and wishes nothing more than quietly to slip through life. It would please and satisfy him if he could but be assured that he is just like other people. You may remember a touch of nature (that is, of some people's nature) in Burns; you remember the simple exultation of the peasant mother when her daughter gets a sweetheart: she is "well pleased to see *her* bairn respeckit *like the lave*," that is, like the other girls round. And undue humility, perhaps even befitting humility, holds back sadly in the race of life. It is recorded that a weaver in a certain village in Scotland, was wont daily to offer a singular petition; he prayed daily and fervently for a better opinion of himself. Yes, a firm conviction of one's own importance is a great help in life. It gives dignity of bearing; it does (so to speak) lift the horse over many a fence at which one with a less confident heart would have broken down. But the man who estimates himself and his place humbly and justly, will be ready to shrink aside, and let men of greater impudence and not greater desert step before him. I have often seen, with a sad heart, in the case of working people, that manner, difficult to describe, which comes of being what we in Scotland sometimes call *sair hadden down*. I have seen the like in educated people too. And not very many will take the trouble to seek out and to draw out the modest merit that keeps itself in the shade. The energetic, successful poople of this world are too busy in pushing each for himself, to have time to do *that*. You will find that people with abundant confidence, people who assume a good deal, are not unfrequently taken at their own estimate of themselves. I have seen a Queen's Counsel walk into court, after the case in which he was engaged had been conducted so far by his junior, and conducted as well as mortal could conduct it. But it was easy to see that the complacent air of superior strength with which the Queen's Counsel took the management out of his junior's hands, conveyed to the jury (a common jury) the belief that things were now to be managed in quite different and vastly better style. And have you not known such a thing as that a family, not a whit better, wealthier, or more respectable than all the rest in the little country town or the country parish, do yet, by carrying their heads higher (no mortal could say why), gradually elbow themselves into a place of admitted social superiority? Everybody knows exactly what they are, and from what they have sprung; but somehow, by resolute assumption, by a quiet air of being better than their neighbors, they draw ahead of them, and attain the glorious advantage of one step higher on the delicately graduated social ladder of the district. Now it is manifest that if such people had sense to see their true position, and the absurdity of their pretensions, they would assuredly not have gained that advantage, whatever it may be worth.

But sense and feeling are sometimes burdens in the race of life; that is, they sometimes hold a man back from grasping material advantages which he might have grasped had he not been prevented by the possession of a certain measure of common sense and right feeling. I doubt not, my friend, that you have acquaintances who can do things which you could not do for your life, and who by doing these things, push their way in life. They ask for what they want, and never let a chance go by them. And though they may meet many rebuffs, they sometimes make a successful venture. Impudence sometimes attains to a pitch of sublimity; and at that point it has produced a very great impression upon many men. The incapable person who started for a professorship, has sometimes got it. The man who, amid the derision of the county, published his address to the electors, has occasionally got into the House of Commons. The vulgar, half-educated preacher, who without any introduction asked a patron for a vacant living in the Church, has now and then got the living. And however unfit you may be for a place, and however discreditable may have been the means by which you got it, once you have actually held it for two or three years, people come to acquiesce in your holding it. They accept the fact that you are there, just as we accept the fact that any other evil exists in this world, without asking why, except on very special occasions. I believe too, that in the matter of worldly preferment, there is too much fatalism in many good men. They have a vague trust that Providence will do more than it has promised. They are ready to think that if it is God's will that they are to gain such a prize, it will be sure to come their way without their pushing. That is a mistake. Suppose you apply the same reasoning to your dinner. Suppose you sit still in your study and say, "If I am to have dinner to-day, it will come without effort of mine; and if I am not to have dinner to-day, it will not come by any effort of mine; so here I sit still and do nothing." Is not *that* absurd? Yet that is what many a wise and good man practically says about the place in life which would suit him, and which would make him happy. Not Turks and Hindoos alone have a tendency to believe in their *Kismet*. It is human to believe in that. And we grasp at every event that seems to favor the belief. The other evening, in the twilight, I passed two respectable-looking women, who seemed like domestic servants; and I caught one sentence which one said to the other with great apparent faith. "You see," she said, "if a thing 's to come your way, it'll no gang by ye!" It was in a crowded street but if it had been in my country parish where every one knew me, I should certainly have stopped the women, and told them that though what they said was quite true, I feared they were understanding it wrongly; and that the firm belief we all hold in God's Providence which reaches to all events, and in His sovereignty which orders all things, should be used to help us to be resigned, after we have done our best and failed; but should never be used as an excuse for not doing our best. When we have set our mind on any honest end, let us seek to compass it by every honest means; and if we fail after having used every honest means, *then* let us fall back on the comfortable belief that things are ordered by the Wisest and Kindest; *then* is the time for the *Fiat Voluntas Tua.*

You would not wish, my friend, to be deprived of common sense and of delicate feeling, even though you could be quite sure that once *that* drag-weight was taken off, you would spring forward to the van, and make such running in the race of life as you never made before. Still you cannot help looking with a certain interest upon those people who, by the want of these hindering influences, are enabled to do things and say things which you never could. I have sometimes looked with no small curiosity upon the kind of man who will come uninvited, and without warning of his approach, to stay at another man's house: who will stay on, quite comfortable and unmoved, though seeing plainly he is not wanted: who will announce, on arriving, that his visit is to be for three days, and who will then, without further remark, and without invitation of any kind, remain for a month or six weeks: and all the while sit down to dinner every day with a perfectly easy and unembarrassed manner. You and I, my reader, would rather live on much less than sixpence a day than do all this. We *could not* do it. But some people not merely can do it, but can do it without any appearance of effort. Oh, if the people who are victimized by these horse-leeches of society could but gain a little of the thickness of skin which characterizes the horse-leeches, and bid them be off, and not return again till they are invited! To the same pachydermatous class belong those individuals who will put all sorts of questions as to the private affairs of other people, but carefully shy off from any similar confidence as to their own affairs: also those individuals who borrow small sums of money and never repay them, but go on borrowing till the small sums amount to a good deal. To the same class may be referred the persons who lay themselves out for saying disagreeable things: the "candid friends" of Canning: the "people who speak their mind," who form such pests of society. To find fault is to right-feeling men a very painful thing; but some take to the work with avidity and delight. And while people of cultivation shrink, with a delicate intuition, from saying anything which may give pain or cause uneasiness to others, there are others who are ever painfully treading upon the moral corns of all around them. Sometimes this is done designedly: as by Mr. Snarling, who by long practice has attained the power of hinting and insinuating, in the course of a forenoon call, as many unpleasant things as may germinate into a crop of ill-tempers and worries which shall make the house at which he called uncomfortable all that day. Sometimes it is done unawares, as by Mr. Boor, who, through pure ignorance and coarseness, is always bellowing out things which it is disagreeable to some one, or to several, to hear. Which was it,

I wonder, Boor or Snarling, who once reached the dignity of the mitre; and who, at prayers in his house, uttered this supplication on behalf of a lady visitor who was kneeling beside him: "Bless our friend, Mrs. ——: give her a little more common sense; and teach her to dress a little less like a tragedy queen than she does at present?"

But who shall reckon up the countless circumstances which lie like a depressing burden on the energies of men, and make them work at that disadvantage which we have thought of under the figure of *carrying weight in life?* There are men who carry weight in a damp, marshy neighborhood, who, amid bracing mountain air, might have done things which now they will never do. There are men who carry weight in an uncomfortable house: in smoky chimneys: in a study with a dismal look-out: in distance from a railway-station: in ten miles between them and a bookseller's shop. Give another hundred a year of income, and the poor, struggling parson who preaches dull sermons will astonish you by the talent he will exhibit when his mind is freed from the dismal depressing influence of ceaseless scheming to keep the wolf from the door. Let the poor little sick child grow strong and well, and with how much better heart will its father face the work of life! Let the clergyman who preached in a spiritless enough way, to a handful of uneducated rustics, be placed in a charge where weekly he has to address a large cultivated congregation; and with the new stimulus, latent powers may manifest themselves which no one fancied he possessed, and he may prove quite an eloquent and attractive preacher. A dull, quiet man, whom you esteemed as a blockhead, may suddenly be valued very differently when circumstances unexpectedly call out the solid qualities he possesses, unsuspected before. A man, devoid of brilliancy, may on occasion show that he possesses great good sense; or that he has the power of sticking to his task, in spite of discouragement. Let a man be placed where dogged perseverance will stand him in stead, and you may see what he can do when he has but a chance. The especial weight which has held some men back — the thing which kept them from doing great things and attaining great fame — has been just this: that they were not able to say or to write what they have thought and felt. And indeed a great poet is nothing more than the one man in a million who has the gift to express that which has been in the mind and heart of multitudes. If even the most commonplace of human beings could write all the poetry he has felt, he would produce something that would go straight to the hearts of many.

It is touching to witness the indications and vestiges of sweet and admirable things which have been subjected to a weight which has entirely crushed them down: things which would have come out into beauty and excellence if they had been allowed a chance. You may witness one of the saddest of all the losses of nature in various old maids. What kind hearts are there running to waste! What pure and gentle affections blossom to be blighted! I dare say you have heard a young lady of more than forty sing; and you have seen her eyes fill with tears at the pathos of a very commonplace verse. Have you not thought that there was the indication of a tender heart which might have made some good man happy; and, in doing so, made herself happy too? But it was not to be. Still, it is sad to think that sometimes upon cats and dogs there should be wasted the affection of a kindly human being! And you know, too, how often the fairest promise of human excellence is never suffered to come to fruit. You must look upon gravestones to find the names of those who promised to be the best and noblest specimens of the race. They died in early youth; perhaps in early childhood. Their pleasant faces, their singular words and ways, remain, not often talked of, in the memories of subdued parents, or of brothers and sisters now grown old, but never forgetting how *that* one of the family that was as the flower of the flock was the first to fade. It has been a proverbial saying, you know, even from heathen ages, that those whom the gods love die young. It is but an inferior order of human beings that makes the living succession to carry on the human race.

CHAPTER VII.

COLLEGE LIFE AT GLASGOW.

N the last days of October, just when winter is fairly settling down upon smoky and noisy Glasgow; when every leaf has gone (for the leaves go early) from the trees near it, and when fogs shorten the day at its beginning and its end; there begins to appear, intermingled with the crowd in the Trongate, and staring in at the shop-windows of Buchanan-street with a curiosity fresh from the country, a host of lads, varying in age from decided boyhood to decided manhood, conspicuous by the scarlet mantle they wear. Those glaring robes have not been seen before since May-day — for the vacation at Glasgow College lasts from the first of May to about the twenty-sixth of October: — and now their appearance announces to the citizens that winter has decidedly set in; the season, in Glasgow, of ceaseless rain, fog, and smoke; of eager business, splendid hospitality, and laborious study. Through the close stifling *wynds* or alleys of the High-street the word runs, that "The Colley dougs have come back again;" and by the time that November is a few days old, the college courts, which through the summer months lay still and deserted, are thronged with a motley crowd of many hundreds of young men, students of arts, theology, medicine, and law.

The stranger in Glasgow who has paid a visit to the noble cathedral, has probably, in returning from it, walked down the High-street, a steep and filthy way of tall houses, now abandoned to the poorest classes of the community, where dirty women in *mutches*, each followed by two or three squalid children, hold loud conversations all day long; and the alleys leading from which pour forth a flood of poverty, disease, and crime. On the left hand of the High-street, where it becomes a shade more respectable, a dark, low-browed building, of three stories in height, fronts the street for two or three hundred yards. *That* is Glasgow College, or the University of Glasgow; for here, as also at Edinburgh, the University consists of a single College. The first gate-way at which we arrive opens into a dull-looking court, inhabited by the professors, eight or ten of whom have houses here. Further down, a low archway, which is the main entrance to the building, admits to two or three quadrangles, occupied by the various class-rooms. There is something impressive in the sudden transition from one of the most crowded and noisy streets of the city, to the calm and stillness of the College courts. The first court we enter is a small one, surrounded by buildings of a dark and venerable aspect. An antique staircase of massive stone leads to the Faculty Hall, or Senate-house; and a spire of considerable height surmounts a vaulted archway leading to the second court. This court is much larger than the one next the street, and with its turrets and winding staircases, narrow windows and high-pitched roofs, would quite come up to our ideas of academic architecture; but unhappily, some years since one side of this venerable quadrangle was pulled down, and a large building in the Grecian style erected in its place, which, like a pert interloper, contrasts most disagreeably with the remainder of the old monastic pile. Passing out of this court by another vaulted passage, we enter an open square, to the right of which is the University library, and at some little distance an elegant Doric temple, which is greatly admired by those who prefer Grecian to Gothic architecture. This is the Hunterian Museum, and contains a valuable collection of subjects in natural history and anatomy, bequeathed by the eminent surgeon whose name it bears. Beyond this building, the College gardens stretch away to a considerable distance. The ground is undulating — there are many trees, and what was once a pleasant country stream flows through the gardens; but Glasgow factories and Glasgow smoke have quite spoiled what must once have been a delightful retreat from the dust and glare of the city. The trees are now quite blackened, the stream (named the Molendinar Burn) became so offensive that it was found necessary to arch it over, and drifts of stifling and noisome smoke trail slowly all day over the College gardens. There are no evergreens nor flowers; and the students generally prefer to take their "constitutional" in the purer air of the western outskirts of Glasgow.

Let us suppose that the young student, brought from the country by parent or guardian, has come to town to enter upon his university career. The order in which the classes are taken is as follows: first year, Latin and Greek; second, Logic and Greek; third, Moral Philosophy and Mathematics; fourth, Natural Philosophy. The classes must be attended in this order by those students who intend taking their degree, or going into the church; but any person may attend any class upon signing a decaration to the effect that he is not studying for the church. Practically, the classes are almost invariably attended in the order which has been mentioned, which is called the College *curriculum*. For several days before the classes open, the professors remain in their houses, that students may call upon them to enter their class. Our young friend and his governor call upon the professor whose class is to be entered. They find him seated in his study, a low-roofed chamber of small dimensions, but abundantly provided with the comforts which beseem a sedentary and studious life. There is the writing-table at which to sit; by the window, the desk at which to write or read while standing; there is the cool seat of polished birch, without a trace of cushion; and the vast easy-chair, where horse-hair and morocco have done their utmost, to receive the weary man of learning in the day's last luxurious hour of leisure. The professor is seated at his table, fresh and hearty from his six months' holiday, brown from his shooting-box in the Highlands, or his ramble over the Continent, or his pretty villa on the beautiful Frith of Clyde. Three or four lads who have come to enter the class, fidget uneasily on their chairs, with awe-struck faces. The professor may perhaps, for his own guidance, make some inquiry as to the previous acquirements of the student, but there is no preliminary test applied to ascertain the student's fitness for entering college. The ceremony of entering the class is completed by paying the professor his fee, which in almost every class is three guineas. In return, the professor gives the student a ticket of admission to the class-room; on which, at the end of the session, he writes a certificate of the student's having attended his class. The more civilized students take care to have the exact amount of the fee prepared beforehand, which they place on the professor's table, and which he receives without remark, thus softening the mercantile transaction as much as may be. Others hand their money to the professor, and demand the change in regular shop fashion. It is amusing to remark the demeanor of the different professors in taking their three guineas. Some are dignifiedly unconscious of the sum received, and although a sharp glance may ascertain that the amount is there, no remark is made. Others take up the money, count it over, and pocket it with a bow, saying, "Thank you, Sir; much obliged to you, Sir."

And what a strange mixed company the thirteen or fourteen hundred students of Glasgow College make up! Boys of eleven or twelve years old (Thomas Campbell entered at the latter age); men with gray hair, up to the age of fifty or sixty; great stout fellows from the plough; men in considerable number from the north of Ireland; lads from counting-houses in town, who wish to improve their minds by a session at the logic class; English dissenters, long excluded from the Universities of England, who have come down to the enlightened country where a Turk or a Buddhist may graduate if he will; young men with high scholarship from the best public schools; and others not knowing a letter of Greek and hardly a word of Latin. Mr. Lockhart (formerly editor of the *Quarterly Review*), says with truth that "the greater part of the students attending the Scotch colleges, consists of persons whose situation in life, had they been born in England, must have left them no chance of being able to share the advantages of an academical education." "Any young man who can afford to wear a decent coat, and live in a garret upon porridge or herrings, may, if he pleases, come to Edinburgh, and pass through his aca demical career just as creditably as is required or expected." And, in consequence of all this, "the Universities of Scotland educate, in proportion to the size and wealth of the two countries, twenty times a larger number than those of England educate."[1]

Let us imagine our student now fairly entered upon his work. In company with three or four hundred of the newest and brightest gowns, he has, no doubt, attended the ceremony of opening the session in the Common Hall, and listened to many good advices from the Principal, who used regularly to beg his youthful auditors to remember they were "no longer schoolboys;" a request invariably received with loud applause. The bustle of the first start over, the student has fallen into the regular order of his work. The Latin and Greek classes he finds are very much like classes at school, the main difference being that they are attended by larger numbers, and accordingly that each student is but rarely called on for examination. When a student is "called," he construes five or six lines; the professor then puts a number of questions upon what has been read. Should he fail to answer any question, the professor asks if any one in the same bench can answer it. If no one can, he next names the numbers of the various benches one after another, and the students in each have then an opportunity of making their knowledge and application apparent to their fellow-students; by whom, at the end of the session, the class prizes are voted. Lockhart says with justice of the Scotch professors of Latin and Greek, that

"The nature of the duties they perform of course reduces them to something quite different from what we (in England) should under-

[1] *Peter's Letters to his Kinsfolk.* Vol. i. pp. 187, 192, 198.

stand by the name they bear. They are not employed in assisting young men to study, with greater facility or advantage, the poets, the historians, or the philosophers of antiquity; nay, it can scarcely be said, in any proper meaning of the term, that they are employed in teaching the principles of language. They are schoolmasters in the strictest sense of the word; for their time is spent in laying the very lowest part of the foundation on which a superstructure of learning must be reared. A profound and accomplished scholar may at times be found discharging these duties; but most assuredly there is no need either of depth or elegance to enable him to discharge them as well as the occasion requires."

The reiterated complaints of Professor Blackie, of the Greek Chair at Edinburgh, prove what indeed needs no proof to any one acquainted with the Universities of Scotland, that no improvement has taken place in the years since Lockhart thus wrote. Greek professors are still expected to begin with the alphabet. The truth is, that while things remain as at present, a good, energetic teacher from a public school would make a better Latin or Greek professor than a man of fine scholarship. Fancy Mr. Blackie patiently listening to a dunce blundering through ὁ ἡ το! Or think of assigning the task of grounding a ploughman in the inflections of τυπτω, to the gentle and refined Mr. Lushington of Glasgow! We do not think that Mr. Tennyson was sketching the characteristics of the right man for such work when he wrote of Lushington thus:—

And thou art worthy; full of power;
As gentle; liberal-minded, great,
Consistent; wearing all that weight
Of learning lightly like a flower.

It is the old story of "cutting blocks with a razor;" it is like setting the winner of the Derby to pull a dray. And so long as the work remains what it is, we believe it would be better and more cheerfully done by machinery a good deal more rough and ready.

The students attending the Latin class may number about 250; but the class is taught in two separate divisions. The Greek class (which meets in three divisions) has about 300 students; when Sir Daniel Sandford was professor, it sometimes numbered 500. The Logic class has from 150 to 180 students, the Moral Philosophy, 100 to 120; the Natural Philosophy, 70 to 90.

It is a curious thing to witness the beginning of a working day at Glasgow College. We must, to do so, rise at six A. M. in a dark winter morning; for if we live in the better part of the town, we have a walk of half-an-hour to get over before the classes meet. Through darkness and sleet we make our way to the College, which we reach, say at twenty minutes past seven A. M. A crowd of students, old and young, wrapped in the red mantles, shivering and sleepy, is pouring in at the low archway already mentioned. The lights shining through the little windows point out the class-rooms which are now to be occupied. At the door of each stands an unshaven servant, in whose vicinity a fragrance as of whisky pervades the air. The servants in former days were always shabby and generally dirty; not unfrequently drunk. They wear no livery of any kind. By long intercourse with many generations of students, they have acquired the power of receiving and returning any amount of "chaff." At length a miserable tinkling is heard from the steeple; the students pour into the class-rooms, and arrange themselves in benches, like the pews of a church. A low pulpit is occupied by the professor. The business of the day is commenced by a short prayer. After prayer, a student, placed in a subsidiary pulpit, calls over the names of the students, who severally signify their presence by saying *Adsum*. The work of the class then goes on till the hour is finished. An hour is the invariable period for which the class remains. The Latin and Greek classes meet at the early hour we have mentioned; and, strange to say, it is at this unseasonable time that the eloquent Professor of Moral Philosophy lectures. It is a remarkable proof of his power, that he is able to touch and excite such a wretchedly cold and sleepy auditory. The applause which generally attends his lectures, makes the houses nearest his class-room the least desirable in the professor's court. At half-past eight many of the classes are in operation — as the Latin, Greek, Logic, Natural Philosophy, and Theology. Though it is always an effort to be at College at hours so early, still the arrangement soon comes to be liked by both professors and students. By half-past nine the hardest of the day's work is over; and thus these early morning hours, which otherwise would probably be turned to little account, save the more valuable hours of the morning and afternoon.

Each of the Philosophy Classes meets two hours a day. The morning hour is occupied by a lecture; and an hour later in the day is given to the examination of the students on the lectures they have heard, and to hearing them read essays on the subjects under consideration. Thus Scotch students have the pen in their hand from the very commencement of their course; and the same system is kept up to the close of even the long course of eight years for the church. A very large proportion of young men thus acquire no inconsiderable command of that noble instrument, the English language; which is very seldom written with ease and accuracy, except as the result of long-continued practice. The lectures read are *verbatim* the same, session after session, so that a Scotch Professor of Philosophy, with his two hours a day of work, and his six months' holiday in the pleasantest part of the year, has (once his course of lectures is written) a very comfortable place of it.

The present Professor of Latin (or *Humanity*, as it is called) is Mr. Ramsay, a graduate of Cambridge, and the author of the work on "Roman Antiquities" in the *Encyclopædia Metropolitana.* Mr. Lushington is the Professor of Greek, having succeeded Sir Daniel Sandford in 1838. He was the first Grecian of his time at Cambridge. The Chair of Logic has been filled by Mr. Buchanan for many years. There is no more admirable teacher in the University. Many a young man has dated his intellectual birth to the period of his attendance on the Logic class at Glasgow. Mr. Buchanan is a clergyman of the Scotch church, but resigned his parish on his appointment to the chair. Dr. Fleming is the Professor of Moral Philosophy: he, too, was a parish clergyman before his appointment. He is a man of vast information in every department of metaphysical philosophy, and is, perhaps, not surpassed in a somewhat tawdry eloquence by any man in Scotland. He is a heavy-looking man when in repose, but when animated, brightens up wonderfully. The intensity with which he himself feels, gives him a great power in moving the feelings of his hearers. Mr. Thomson, a few years since second Wrangler and first Smith's Prizeman, is the Professor of Natural Philosophy. He took a leading part in the laying of the Atlantic Telegraph Cable.

At the end of three years, students may take the degree of Bachelor of Arts, on passing an examination in

Classics, Logic, and Moral Philosophy. At the end of four years, on passing a further examination in Mathematics and Natural Philosophy, they may take their Master's degree. Few students comparatively graduate. It is not necessary in order to enter the church; and not many young men are willing to undertake no inconsiderable amount of study to attain an honor which, in Scotland, brings with it no advantage whatever. And even the small fee, of from three to five guineas, which is paid at graduation, is a serious consideration to most Scotch students. A university education in Scotland, comes far down in the social scale; and while at the universities of England the great majority of the young men are the sons of gentlemen, in Scotland the vast preponderance consists of sons of farmers, tradesmen, and working men; and of poor lads, without relations or friends, struggling on amid unheard-of difficulties and privations. No one can look round the benches of any class-room in Scotland, without being struck by the harsh features and coarse attire of most of the young men; no one can converse with nine out of ten of them, without being struck by their vulgar accent and manner. A writer in the *Quarterly Review* perhaps speaks somewhat severely when he alludes to "those tag-rag and bob-tail concerns, the Scotch Universities:" but there is truth in Lockhart's remark, that —

A person whose eyes had been accustomed only to such places as the schools of Oxford, would certainly be very much struck with the *prima facie* mean condition of the majority of the students assembled at the prælections of these Edinburgh [and Glasgow] professors. Here and there one sees some small scattered remnant of the great flock of dandies, trying to keep each other in countenance, in a corner of the class-room; but these only heighten, by the contrast of their presence, the general effect of the slovenly and dirty mass which on every side surrounds them with its contaminating atmosphere.[1]

[1] *Peter's Letters.* Vol. i. p. 187.

Yet ability is given by nature with little regard to social position: many of those rough specimens of humanity possess no ordinary talent; many will take on polish wonderfully, before they pass from college to life: and there is really a deep pathos in the story of toil, privation, and resolution, which is the story of many a Glasgow student's college days.

There are, of course, young men of good families at Glasgow College. There are students who wear all-round collars of extreme stiffness, who walk down to their classes from the aristocratic districts of Blythswood-square and Woodside-terrace; who are in much request at evening parties, and who strut in the afternoon in the Sauchyhall-road, the fashionable promenade of Glasgow. But most of the students live in very plain lodgings, in various parts of the town, and know no more of Glasgow society than if they were living in the Sandwich Islands. There are some streets near the College, consisting of tall houses divided into *flats*, in which great numbers of students dwell. The life of almost all is one of struggle and self-denial. It touches us, and that deeply, to think of poor lads of eighteen or nineteen, toiling on with their studies, with many a thought as to how they are to get food and raiment; with all those cares upon their heads which are heavy enough, God knows, when they press upon maturer years, yet supported by the hope that at some time in the distant future they may get into the church at last, or even into a parish school. What a princely dwelling must a country manse seem to such; what an inexhaustible revenue a living of three or four hundred a year! We have been told that many students have managed to live upon fifteen or twenty pounds a year. After writing this, we were almost startled on recurring to it; but Mr. Lockhart, a Glasgow student himself, and the son of a Glasgow minister, confirms us: "I am assured," he says, "that the great majority of students here have seldom more than thirty or forty pounds per annum, and that *very many most respectable students contrive to do with little more than half so much money*."[1] Our readers may perhaps remember the touching fact recorded in the life of Dr. Adam, the very eminent Rector of the High School of Edinburgh, — that when at College, his dinner consisted of a penny roll; and that to save the expense of a fire, he was accustomed to eat it as he climbed some long and lonely stair in the Old Town, where there are houses of fourteen stories in height.[2] We have heard of students from Ireland who brought with them a bag of *scones*, or cakes of oatmeal, on which *alone* they lived in some poor garret. And many a poor family is pinching itself at home, to keep the clever son at College. A clergyman of the Church of Scotland who published a work on *Clerical Economics* dedicated it "To a father who, on a hundred pounds a year, brought up six sons to learned professions, and who has often sent his last shilling to each of them in their turn, when they were at College." The motto which Sydney Smith proposed for the *Edinburgh Review*, "*Tenui musam meditamur avena*," — "We cultivate literature on a little oatmeal," might be the motto of many a Glasgow student. A few years since, a poor fellow, whose education was so deficient that he could not earn anything by teaching others, supported himself by becoming a night-watchman, and studied his Greek Testament by the light of the

1 *Peter's Letters.* Vol. i. p. 193.

2 "Life of Dr. Adam," in Chambers' *Scottish Biographical Dictionary.*

street lamps. The Census of 1851 in Glasgow was in a great degree taken up by students, thankful thus to make a few shillings. We cannot refrain from making a quotation which tells a story which, to our personal knowledge is true in scores of cases, — aye, in hundreds : —

> My father was a poor man — a common working wright, in a little village not far from Glasgow. My mother and he pinched themselves blue to give me my education. I went to college when I was about fifteen years old, and they sent me in cheese and vegetables, even oatmeal to make my porridge, every week by the carrier. I did not taste butcher's meat three times, I believe, in the first three years I was a student. But then I began to do something for myself. I got a little private teaching, and by degrees ceased to be a burden on the old people. Step by step I wrought on, till I became tutor in a gentleman's family. Then I was licensed, and I remained a preacher for twenty years, — sometimes living in a family, sometimes teaching from house to house, and latterly I had a school of my own in Glasgow. I was forty years old and upwards ere I got the kirk, Mr. Wald; and my dear parents never lived to see me in it.[1]

Not less true and not less touching is another passage from the same masterly pen : —

> If I was poor, I had no objections to living poorly. After attending classes and hospitals from daybreak to sunset, I contented myself with a dinner and supper in one, of bread and milk, — or perhaps a mess of potatoes, with salt for their only sauce. A deal table, a half-broken chair, and a straw pallet, were all the furniture I had about me; and very rarely did I indulge myself with a fire. But I could wrap a blanket over my legs, trim my lamp, and plunge into the world of books, and forget everything.[2]

There is not a whit of exaggeration in Sir Walter Scott's description of the early struggles of Dominie Sampson. And we confess we cannot read without emotion the description in *Matthew Wald*, of the poor tutor going for his evening's work with his pupils, to the house

[1] *History of Matthew Wald*, pp. 148-9.
[2] *Matthew Wald*, 203-5.

of some wealthy burgess, and being saluted in his lobby "with the amiable fragrance of soup, roast meat, rum-punch, and the like dainties," himself just from his spare mess of potatoes and salt. Ah, there is much pathos about the daily life of the poor students of Glasgow! Let no one indulge in the heartless sneer at the poor fellow's threadbare coat, his whity-brown paper, his linen so coarse that it looks like sail-cloth, his patched boots and his worn anxious face. God bless him, and help him, say we! Speak kindly to him, dandified young student; deal gently with him, grave professor; his heart is very likely so full already that it will almost break with one drop more. He is the hope and pride, and the anxious care, too, of some poor family far away, whose members are grinding themselves down to life's last necessaries to give him advantages which (sad that in the nature of things it must be) will, when obtained, draw a line of separation between him and themselves. They will make him, perhaps, the scholar and the gentleman, but all this will only serve to introduce him into a world of which they know nothing. They may be proud of him still, when he gets a kirk at last; but he will perhaps marry a lady, and then they will hardly ever see him, and it will be with a vague, blank feeling of disappointment when they do. And the old parents — it may be, left alone in the last days of life, with the single return for years of struggle, that they can say that the son whom they hardly ever see, is a parish minister a hundred miles off — may think that, after all, it might have been better had he saved his home-bred virtues in his parents' lowly lot, and by his daily presence smoothed his parents' passage to their lowly grave.

It is sad to think that not unfrequently all this effort

and self-denial on the part of the family at home, and the student at college, are found in the case of poor fellows who are so completely deficient in ability, that it is impossible that they should ever get on in life. The Divinity Hall of each University is never without a sprinkling of lads who would have made excellent ploughmen, or schoolmasters, or mechanics, but whose whole future life must be blasted by the unfortunate fact that nothing would serve themselves or their relations but that they must try to get into the church. We have known of poor deformed creatures who toiled and starved on year after year, hoping, with a despairing earnestness that in some cases settled down into monomania, that they might yet pass the Presbytery, and be presented to a living. It is a very painful duty which the Presbyteries have sometimes to perform, in rejecting applicants for orders who are manifestly unfit, yet whose rejection crushes the cherished hopes and foils the utmost endeavors of a poor family for many years. We believe that such a case has been as that such a person has come up for examination five or six successive times at intervals of a year or two, before abandoning the hope of passing. We have heard of a case in which a grown-up man, on being told by the Moderator or President of the Presbytery that he "was recommended still further to prosecute his studies," the mild formula by which rejection is conveyed, dropped senseless on the floor of the court, and lay for long as dead. We know of a case in which a person, in like manner rejected, had to be conveyed to a place of restraint, a wild raving maniac. The dogged energy and determination of the Scottish character can bear a man through almost anything so long as hope remains; but when the last hope breaks down, we believe that the firm

Scottish heart may be roused to a frenzy of despair as keen as ever stirred in the hot blood of the tropics.

Those students who are poor and who possess fair scholarship, very generally maintain themselves by private teaching. They instruct lads in the junior classes, hastening from house to house in the evenings, and usually remaining one hour with each pupil. The fee for such attendance is a guinea a month. We find it mentioned in the *Life of James Halley*, one of the most distinguished of Glasgow students in recent years, that during the period in which he made his reputation, "his principal source of maintenance was the product of his own exertion as a private tutor. A very considerable portion of his time — always four, and sometime five, hours a day — was taken up in this way. This very materially enhances his merit in maintaining so high a position in all the classes." [1] Campbell the poet, writing of a period when he was just eighteen years old, records that "after my return from Mull, I supported myself during the winter by private tuition." [2] We have known of students who made a respectable figure in their classes, who were engaged in teaching for six, eight, or ten hours a day. There are a great many exhibitions, or *Bursaries*, as they are called, which are intended to aid deserving students. These vary in amount from three or four pounds a year up to forty. But, unhappily, hardly any of them are open to competition, and they are very frequently given to those students who least need them and least deserve them.

On the whole, looking at the way in which Glasgow

1 *Memoir of James Halley, B.A., Student of Theology*, p. 17. Edinburgh. 1842.

2 Life, prefixed to *Poems*. Edition of 1851; p. 28.

students generally *do* live, and the way in which they *may* live, we must admit that it was not without reason that the old Glasgow merchant in *Cyril Thornton* boasted of the accessibility of a Scotch University education :—

So ye've come down here to be a colleaginer. It's a lang gait to gang for learning. But after a', I am no sure that you could ha'e done better. Our colleges here are no bund down like yours in the south, by a wheen auld and fizzionless rules, and we dinna say to ilka student, either bring three hundred pounds in your pouch, or gang about your business. We dinna lock the door o' learning, as they do at Oxford and Cambridge, and shut out a' that canna bring a gouden key in their hand, but keep it on the sneck, that onybody that likes may open it.[1]

At the end of the four years' course in Arts, students for the church begin their theological studies, which extend over four years more. On "entering the Divinity Hall," as it is termed, the student lays aside the red gown, and for the remainder of his college course wears no distinguishing dress. During each of these four sessions he attends the lectures of the Professor of Theology, and the lectures of the Professors of Hebrew and Church History for two sessions each. The Professor of Theology is necessarily a clergyman, and is, *ex officio*, a member of the Presbytery of Glasgow. Laymen are eligible for the Chairs of Hebrew and Church History; but in practice they are always filled by clergymen. Dr. Hill is the Professor of Theology; Mr. Weir, a young clergyman, has lately succeeded to the Chair of Hebrew; and that of Church History is filled by Dr. Jackson, an able man, whose besetting sin is a tendency to become most abstrusely metaphysical in his lectures. The Hebrew class is taught very much as the Latin and Greek classes

1 *Youth and Manhood of Cyril Thornton.* Vol. i. p. 60.

are ; the Theology and Church History, like the Philosophy classes. The number of students attending the Divinity Hall is, we believe, above a hundred. The vacancies in the Church caused by death average about thirty-five annually, and Glasgow College alone could supply nearly that number of candidates for orders. The University of Edinburgh turns out yearly almost as many; the Universities of St. Andrew's and Aberdeen as many more. Our readers may suppose that there is a pretty sharp competition for every living that becomes vacant, while the supply is thus nearly threefold in excess of the demand.

After the student for the Church has completed his college course, he applies for orders to the Presbytery within whose bounds he resides. He is "taken on trials" by that Church-court. He is examined in all the branches he has studied at college, and is required to compose and read to the Presbytery five or six discourses. These "trials" occupy perhaps six months, at the end of which time he is licensed to preach. He is not permitted to administer the sacraments until he has been ordained; and in practice no one is ever ordained till he has been appointed to a church as minister. It will thus be seen that nearly nine years pass from the time a student enters college, down to the period at which he is licensed to preach. If licensed at the age of twenty-two, as is not unfrequently the case, having left off his classical studies six or seven years before, it may be left to our readers to imagine how much claim he can have to be regarded as a *scholar*, in the English sense. We think that reform in the Scotch University system is imperatively needed, and in no respect more imperatively than in the abbreviation of the enormous course for the

Church. To finish that course in anything like reasonable time, the student must enter college at an absurdly early age.

The competition for academic honors is as keen at Glasgow as it can be anywhere. The prizes for general eminence in each class are voted by the students in it, at the end of the session. The prizes are almost always given with perfect fairness; so the system is better in practice than it looks in theory. When ten or twelve prizes are given in a class, it may be supposed that the degrees of merit are less strongly marked among the lowest on the list of prizemen, and private feeling may weigh in the adjudication of the inferior prizes. But there is hardly an instance on record of the first, second, or third prize going otherwise than as the professor would have awarded it. The first prize in each class is of course a matter of special ambition; it has often been contested with an eagerness prejudicial to health and even life. We have known of Glasgow students who for five months of the session, have allowed themselves not more than three or four hours of sleep nightly, the entire waking day being devoted to study. In such cases the feverish anxiety of the competition has sometimes kept up the student in working trim to the end of the session, while at its close, the stimulus removed, he has utterly broken down. The higher Latin and Greek prizes are keenly contested, as success in obtaining any of them marks out a student for appointment to one of the *Snell Exhibitions.* Under the Snell endowment, the University of Glasgow sends ten students to Balliol College, Oxford, giving to four of them a stipend of £135 a year each, and to the remaining six £120 a year each. These exhibitions are tenable for ten years. And for the credit of the University, the professors generally send to Oxford the best classical students who are willing to go. Classical learning, however, is undervalued in Scotland, and the principal honors of the University go for proficiency in Mental Philosophy, in its various departments. For students who purpose completing their course in Scotland, the testing classes are those of Logic and Moral Philosophy — Moral Philosophy implying at Glasgow a complete course of Metaphysics. Whoever obtains the first prize in that class, is pretty safe to carry the honors of the Divinity classes. The work of these classes demands the same kind of ability; and, with the exception of importations from other universities, which are rarely of first-class students, the competition in these classes will be with the same men.

Among the most coveted distinctions of the University, are the prizes for the "University Essays." These prizes are eight or nine in number annually, and the competition for them is extensive. Two gold medals, given on alternate years, are open to the competition of all students attending any class in the University; one of these is given for an essay in history, the other for an essay in political economy. Then there are one or two prizes open to the competition of all students of theology; two or three to all students of philosophy; one to all students of medicine. The following, from the published prize-list, will give an idea of the kind of subjects prescribed.

In 1842, the Gartmore gold medal was given for the best essay on "The Expediency or Inexpediency of Capital Punishments." In 1844, for the best essay on "Secondary Punishments." In 1848, for the best essay on "Under what Circumstances, and in what Mode, should a Constitutional State encourage Emigration?"

In 1843, the Ewing gold medal was given for the best account of "The Circumstances which led to the Peace of Westphalia in 1648, with the Results of that Treaty." In 1845, the subject was, "An Account of the First Partition of Poland in 1772." In 1847, "An Account of the Establishment and Progress of the British Empire in India, to the termination of the Government of Warren Hastings." Among the subjects to be written on in different years by students of Philosophy, we find "An Analysis of the Faculty of Judging;" "Poetic Diction, its Use and Abuse by the Orators;" "The Nature and Influence of Motives in Moral Action;" "The Historical Episode and its Conditions, Critically Considered, Illustrated by Examples;" "A Classification and Analysis of the Passions." Among the subjects for students of Theology, we have, "The Analogy of the Mosaic and Christian Dispensations;" "The Extent of the Atonement of Christ;" "Baptismal Regeneration;" "Apostolical Succession;" "Auricular Confession." And in Physics, "The Principles and Practicability of Atmospheric Railways;" "The Form and Construction of Arches;" "The Methods of Supplying Large Towns with Water."

These essays are very laboriously written. They are often complete works on the subjects proposed, extending to some hundreds of pages, and the result of original research and protracted thought. We have reason to know that the prize essays written by one very successful student in one year extended to nearly two thousand pages. There are generally two or three of the University essay prizes open to the competition of each student each year; and besides the prizes for general eminence voted by the students, there is usually, in each class, a prize for an essay, which is adjudicated by the professor. A student of extraordinary energy may thus compete for five or six essay prizes in one session. Sometimes a man who has carried all the honors which belong to his own department, makes an excursion into another field, to find a fresh subject and new competitors. An amusing instance of this is recorded in the *Life of Halley*: —

In the summer of 1834 he enrolled as a student in the botanical class. This was done chiefly with a view to benefit his health. The garden in which the lecture-room was situated lay at a distance of about two miles from his place of residence, and the hour of lecture was from eight to nine in the morning. This secured for three months a system of early and regular exercise. It happened that during that session a gentleman, whose name was not given, empowered Dr. (now Sir William) Hooker to offer a gold medal for the best essay on "The Natural History and Uses of the Potato." Halley had not paid much attention to the study of botany, and the prescribed subject of the essay did not at all lie in his way, yet he determined to write by way of amusement, and, as he said, "to beat the medicals." The result was a treatise of 172 closely-written quarto pages It was pronounced the best; and the interloper carried off the medal, fairly won, from the medical students on their own proper field. Whether this achievement had found its way into the *Farmer's Magazine*, we cannot tell, but it had nearly procured for him a reputation of which he was not desirous. One day a stranger was ushered into his room, announcing himself as an Irish agriculturist, who had devoted considerable attention to the failure of the potato crop. Having heard that Mr. Halley had been studying the same subject, he had waited upon him to hear the result of his researches. Mr. Halley received his visitor with due politeness and gravity; laid aside his folios, and entered, with all becoming solemnity, into the comparative merits of late and early planting — of whole sets and single eyes, and after a long consultation dismissed his visitor, highly delighted with the interview.[1]

The subjects of the University prize essays are announced on the first of May in each year; the essays are taken into the Principal's house in December following. Each essay bears two mottoes, and is accompanied by a

[1] *Halley's Life*, pp. 23, 24.

sealed letter bearing the same mottoes, and containing the name of the author, with a declaration that the essay is of his unaided composition. The successful essay is announced at the distribution of prizes in the Common Hall on the first of May, and the letter containing the author's name is opened in the presence of the assembled *Comitia.* The other letters are destroyed unopened. The prize essay is placed in the library, where, however, it is accessible only to the professors. A proof how fairly the students vote the highest prizes, is furnished by the fact that these prizes for essays, adjudicated by the professors in utter ignorance of their authorship, are given in nineteen cases out of twenty to students who have "taken" (such is the college phrase) the first prize in their respective classes by the students' votes. We have examined the prize-list for a number of years, and we find that the honors awarded by students and professors almost invariably fall to the same men.

The distribution of prizes on May-day is a gay scene. Students and professors alike are in high spirits in the anticipation of their holiday time. Tickets of admission to the ceremony are in great request. Our readers may perhaps remember that the first poetical composition of the author of the *Pleasures of Hope*, was *A Description of the Distribution of Prizes in the Common Hall of the University of Glasgow, on the first of May*, 1793. All old Glasgow students have many pleasant associations with this day of the year.

The first of May is the day fixed by immemorial usage in the University for the distribution of the prizes, a day looked forward to with "hopes, and fears that kindle hope," by many youthful and ardent spirits. The Great Hall of the college on that day certainly presents a very pleasing and animated spectacle. The academical distinctions are bestowed with much of ceremonial pomp, in the presence of a vast concourse of spectators, and it is not uninteresting to mark the flush of bashful triumph on the cheek of the victor; the sparkling of his downcast eye as the hall is rent with loud applause, when he advances to receive the badge of honor assigned him by the voice of his fellow-students. It is altogether a sight to stir the spirit in the youthful bosom, and stimulate into healthy action faculties which, but for such excitement, might have continued in unbroken slumber.[1]

The Common Hall is a plain square apartment, with a gallery at each end. It is capable of containing about a thousand persons. Along one side runs a raised bench, occupied by the professors. The Principal presides at the distribution, unless when the Lord Rector is present. Long before the appointed hour, which is always ten A. M., the body of the hall is thronged with students, and the galleries with ladies. The students beguile the time by throwing volleys of peas at one another; after a distribution, several bushels are gathered up from the floor. There is a prescriptive toleration for peas, but no other missile is permitted; and a strong-minded man who introduced eggs, narrowly escaped expulsion. The bald heads of some of the servants present tempting marks, and are furiously assailed. At length the professors (all of whom wear gowns) enter in procession, preceded by the *bedellus*, bearing a huge mace of silver. A prayer in Latin is offered by the Principal. Then the University prize essays are announced; the letters containing the authors' names are opened, and the prizes are delivered to the successful students by the Lord Rector or Principal. The divinity prizes are given next; then the medical, then the philosophy and classical. The proceedings are over about one o'clock; and ere the sun has set, the last red gown, now sadly faded from its November brightness, has disappeared from the streets of Glasgow. The

[1] *Cyril Thornton.* Vol. i. pp. 215, 216.

students are scattered over the country; tutors in gentlemen's families, teaching parish schools, acting as missionaries or catechists under the clergy of large towns, watching sheep, busy at farm-work, and some of the more distinguished, by the time a week has passed, busy collecting materials for next year's University essays.

The names of the students stand in the class catalogue *in Latin;* and the professor, in addressing a student, uses his Latinized Christian name in the vocative. There is no such thing known in Scotland as that entire sinking of the Christian name which is usual in the public schools of England. At one period the professors at Glasgow always addressed their students in the Latin language. The impression produced on a stranger was decidedly that of the ridiculous. Mr. Lockhart tells us that when he went to the class-room of Mr. Young, the very eminent Greek Professor at Glasgow, forty years since, the first thing done was calling over the roll of the class, which was done by one of the students: —

> The professor was quite silent during this space, unless where some tall, awkward Irishman, or young indigenous blunderer happened to make his *entrée* in a manner more noisy than suited the place, on which occasion a sharp cutting voice from the chair was sure to thrill in their ears some brief but decisive query, or command, or rebuke: — "*Quid agas tu, in isto angulo, pedibus strepitans et garriens!*" "*Cave tu tibi, Dugalde M'Quhirter, et tuas res agas!*" "*Notetur, Phelimius O'Shaughnessy, sero ingrediens, ut solvat duas asses sterlinenses!*" "*Iterumne admonendus es, Nicolaei Jarvie?*" "*Quid hoc rei, Francisce Warper?*" &c. &c. &c.

The custom of the Professor addressing the class in Latin has now almost entirely disappeared. The last vestiges of it linger in the Philosophy class-rooms, in such beautifully classical sentences as "Silentium, gentlemen, silentium!" "Nigellius M'Lamroch is breaking silentium!" The fact is, the custom was found to be a very inconvenient one at once to professors and students. It is not too much to say that most of the latter understood English very much better than Latin, and few of the professors had such a command of Latin as to be able to express themselves in it correctly when they got angry. It is a tradition in Glasgow College that a professor, who died some years since, once commanded a noisy student to be still. The lad replied that he had been perfectly so. The professor's indignation at this misstatement was too much for his Latinity. He burst out, "*Nonne video te jumpantem over the table!*"

The University library is a very good one. We believe that in Scotland it ranks second only to the Advocates' library in Edinburgh. It was founded in the fifteenth century. We understand that the Senate can afford to expend on the purchase of new books about £1,000 a year. Of this sum the Treasury pays £700 annually as compensation for the loss of the Stationers' Hall privilege. Each student has likewise to pay seven shillings annually to the library, and in return has the privilege of having two volumes at a time during the session at his own home, and of consulting as many as he pleases in the reading-room. "No novels, romances, tales, nor plays" are lent to the students. These, however, pour into the library in great profusion for the use of the wives and daughters of the professors.

At one time, degrees in Arts were granted after a merely formal examination. The examination is now a real one, so far as it extends. It may interest some of our readers to know its extent. For the ordinary degree of Bachelor of Arts, the subjects of examination are as follows: —

In Latin: Livy, Three Books; Virgil, Æneid, Three Books; Horace, Odes, Three Books.

In Greek: The Four Gospels; Homer, Three Books.

In Logic: The Intellectual Powers; the Ancient or Aristotelian Logic; the Modern or Inductive Logic.

In Moral Philosophy: The Intellectural, Active, and Moral Powers; the Will; Practical Ethics; Natural Theology.

To obtain the degree of M. A., the student must further be examined

In Natural Philosophy: The subjects lectured on in the class.

In Mathematics; Euclid, first Six Books; Plane Trigonometry; Simple and Quadratic Equations.

For the degrees with honors, the examinations are much more severe.

The examinations for degrees are held on the Thursdays in March and April. With very little exception, they are conducted *vivâ voce*. The statute requires that they should take place in the presence of at least two professors, but in practice the candidate for a degree is examined in each branch by the professor under whom he has studied it, the other professor present not interfering in the examination, nor even attending to it. A strong effort has been made of late years to raise the standard of attainment required in graduates; and sometimes as many as one third of the students who go up for examination are plucked. In the good old times no one was ever rejected; to ask for a degree, and to get it, were convertible terms. We have already stated that very many students take no degree; no advantage is derived in after-life from having taken one. It is not required of men entering the Church, that they should have one. And in the case of the ordinary run of young men, whose desire is to get through their "*curriculum*" with as little trouble as possible, it is hardly to be expected that some toil and some anxiety will be endured, with no inducement of countervailing advantage. Still (counting both Bachelors and Masters), some sixty or seventy students take their degree in each year; and among the graduates, we may say, are all students of any eminence who have advanced so far in their course as to have it in their power to go up. The degree in honors is very seldom sought, even by the most distinguished, except under the stimulus of an occasional prize. In order to go up for such a degree with the least hope of success, a man must spend on his preparations an amount of labor which would yield a better return if given to class-work or the composition of prize essays. College distinction in Scotland, though so eagerly sought, does not aid a man in after-life as it does in England. Even in the Church it goes for very little. It may lead to a good deal being expected of a young preacher at his first outset: but it is his popularity with ordinary congregations that determines his success, unless where patronage is administered with a higher hand than it has been of late years in Scotland; and very great dunces indeed are often endowed by nature with very loud voices, and are quite competent to practise a howling and sudorific oratory, which goes down amazingly with the least intelligent of the Scottish peasantry.

A marked feature of Glasgow college life is what is termed the *Blackstone Examination*. The name is derived from an antique chair of oak, with a seat of black marble, which is occupied by the student under examination. This examination is compulsory. Before entering the Logic class, the students are examined on the Blackstone in Greek. Before entering the Moral Philosophy, in Logic; and before entering the Natural Philosophy, in Moral Philosophy. This examination is a mere form: no one is ever turned at it. It is amusing to witness the odd mixture of Latin and English in which, on this occasion, communication is held between the student and the professor. The latter is seated in a large chair at one side of the table; on the other side stands the formidable Blackstone. A great crowd of students fills the examination-room; "Carole Dickie," says the professor. Carolus, pale and trembling, walks up to the table. "Well, Carole," says the professor, "what do you profess?" Answer: "Doctissime Professor, Evangelium secundum Joannem profiteor." Carolus then takes his seat on the Blackstone, and construes a verse or two.

A prize is given yearly to the student who passes the best examination on the Blackstone, in Latin; also for the best in Greek. This prize is a matter of very keen competition, as success in obtaining it, coming at the commencement of the session, almost insures a student of the first prize in the class. A very great number of books is often "professed" by competitors for these prizes. There are traditions in the college of students who arrived at the examination-room with a wheelbarrow, containing the works on which they were willing to be examined. The examination is *vivâ voce*, and lasts for several hours. A number of years since, three competitors went in for the Greek Blackstone prize: Tait, Smith, and Halley. Halley made a most brilliant appearance, and carried off the prize. He studied for the Scotch Church, but died before obtaining license. Of his competitors, Smith went to Cambridge, where he became Senior Wrangler; Tait succeeded Dr. Arnold as head-master of Rugby, and is now Bishop of London. It cannot be said that any special brilliancy of talent recommended him to that eminent place; but it is generally admitted that he has filled it with great judgment.

The character and conduct of the students of Glasgow are generally unexceptionable. There may be a black sheep now and then, but such cases are very rare. Indeed, no one without considerable moral stamina would ever think of living the life of nine tenths of the Glasgow students. And "their lot circumscribes" the errors and follies of which they could by possibility be guilty. They have not the money to indulge the tastes, whether good or bad, of most English University men. Wine-parties, riding-horses, escapades to London, coursing and hunting, even rowing matches, are beyond the tether of a man to whom every penny is a serious consideration; and who cannot but think of his poor sisters wearing out their eyes at needlework, and his old father denying himself the long-prized solace of a little tobacco, to keep the brother and the son at college. He would be a black-hearted villain who could be vicious or even extravagant, when either extravagance or vice would be sure to frustrate *their* hopes and break *their* hearts. The grosser vices are, we believe, unknown. An occasional *gaudeamus*, at which whisky-toddy is the chief luxury; a visit to the theatre, made with fear and trembling; a row with the police once in eight or ten years; constitute the utmost dissipation of the mass of Glasgow students. Mr. Lockhart's description of the *morale* at the University of St. Andrew's holds true of Glasgow as well:

I lived a life almost solitary, and in general certainly very simple and innocent. The lads there were mostly poor, and had few means of signalizing themselves by any folly. Our greatest diversion in the way of sport was a game at golf; and we had little notion of any debauch beyond a pan of toasted cheese, and a bottle or two of the College ale, now and then on a Saturday night.[1]

The service of the Scotch Church used to be performed on Sundays during the session in the Common Hall, but hardly any one went to it, and a few years since the arrangement was allowed to drop. The students are now permitted to dispose of themselves on Sunday as they please.

We have mentioned that a number of professors have houses in the College. One court is filled entirely with these houses, and a few others are jammed in, in unexpected corners of the class-room courts. They are all quaint, old-fashioned dwellings, with a strong smack of academic repose about them. The apartments are small, and the ceilings very low. The very filthiest lane in Glasgow runs parallel to one side of the quadrangle, at a distance of some twenty yards. During the railway mania, a company obtained an act to remove the College buildings to a pretty situation in the western outskirts of the town, converting the present College and gardens into a terminus. Although the New College was to have been a magnificent piece of Gothic architecture, the general feeling was against the abandonment and desecration of the old walls. But the resident professors and their wives and daughters, long poisoned by the vile odors of the "Havannah Vennel," were delighted at the idea of a transference to the pleasant slopes of Kelvin Grove. The railway company, however, went to ruin, and the New College scheme fell to the ground.

[1] *Matthew Wald*, p. 57.

Glasgow has by far the best endowed University in Scotland. The professors form a close corporation, and keep their affairs very much to themselves; so it is only from common report we can speak of the value of the several chairs. But upon that authority, we believe that the Chair of Greek is worth above £1,000 a year; those of Philosophy from £800 to £900. That of Theology, though the premier chair of the University, does not stand first in point of emolument. It is said to be worth about £600 a year. The sums mentioned do not include the value of the residences. Many of the more recently-founded chairs have exceedingly small endowments, and their income is derived mainly from the fees paid by the students. In all the classes, the professors retain the fees paid them: so that a professor's income may be materially increased should his fame attract a greater number of disciples. When Sir D. Sandford was Greek professor, he crowded his class-room not merely with regular students, but with Glasgow clergymen, lawyers, and merchants, who attended his eloquent and enthusiastic prelections. And we have heard it said that in those days the revenue of the Greek chair was above £1,500 a year.

Among other little advantages, the professors are free from payment of the local taxes; they are also supplied with coals and gas. An abundant supply of newspapers and periodicals is provided for themselves and their families. And the fine old "Fore Hall," a large apartment, wainscoted with black oak, and by far the most picturesque chamber in the University, is occupied by the professors as a club-room. On the whole, a Glasgow professor on the old foundation leads a very comfortable life.

One or two of the professors are unable to induce

any one to attend their lectures. It may therefore be regarded as difficult to explain what purpose these professors serve. Dr. Nichol, the late eloquent Professor of Astronomy, gave occasionally short courses of popular lectures, which were open to all students, and which were well attended. But no class demanding labor and sustained attention will find students, unless attendance upon it is made compulsory. We think it would be utterly useless to found new chairs in the Scotch Universities, as has lately been proposed. We believe that to do so would be the very reverse of a reform or improvement. Unless attendance upon them is made an essential part of the *curriculum*, no one would attend them. And we believe that to make attendance upon them compulsory would, in the case of many a student who has more than enough to do already, be the last pound that breaks the camel's back. It is in the Latin and Greek classes that reform is needed. Raise the standard of scholarship by an examination at entering College; give the professors of Latin and Greek *professor's* work to do, not that of hedge schoolmasters; shorten to half, the preposterously extended course for the Church; let students enter the University at eighteen or nineteen instead of at twelve or thirteen: they will thus not be hurried through the Philosophy classes while mere children, — and the Scotch Universities will have all the reform they need. But on this subject we have not time to enter.

The first fortnight of the session, every alternate year is taken up with a series of violent disturbances connected with the election of the Lord Rector. We believe that at one time this officer had various duties to perform; but for many years past his sole function has been to give an address to the students in the Common

Hall upon his inauguration. The Lord Rector is elected by the professors and students. The election goes almost invariably upon political grounds, and is conducted with unparalleled bitterness of party feeling. Although the professors always vote at the election, they profess to leave the management of it in the hands of the students; the leaders of whom, however, are virtually directed in their movements by the professors of their own party. All the arts usual at other contested elections are brought into play, aggravated by the hot-headedness incidental to the youth of the parties engaged. Public meetings are held, and addresses and squibs of all kinds are printed and circulated in immense profusion. The most violent attacks are made by either party upon the leaders of the other, and upon the opposing candidate. Sometimes these attacks end in physical violence. At a meeting in one of the class-rooms, a few years ago, the platform was charged by a large force of antagonistic students. It was gallantly defended with cudgel and fist, and more than one of the attacking party was felled like an ox. The air is darkened in the Hall on the election-day by clouds of peas, of which missiles the professors get even more than their share. These dignitaries always behave with great good-humor upon the occasion; and the *saturnalia* once over, discipline is restored, and all parties return quietly to work.

Among the Lord Rectors of the last thirty years, are, Lord Jeffrey, Sir James Mackintosh, Lord Brougham, Thomas Campbell (who was elected in opposition to Sir Walter Scott), the Marquis of Lansdowne, the Earl of Derby, Sir Robert Peel, Sir James Graham, Earl Russell, Lord Macaulay, the Duke of Argyle, and Sir E. Bulwer Lytton. The inaugural addresses since Jeffrey's time have been published in a large volume. Edmund Burke was rector in 1783; he fairly broke down in his address, and stopped in the middle of it. Brougham's address is regarded as the most eloquent; Macaulay's was a very fine one. We remember that great man, in a large yellow waistcoat, getting on in a slow sing-song through his address, and drinking a little water at the close of each short paragraph. The Rector wears at his inauguration a very ancient and shabby gown, decorated with faded gold lace. It is never forgot in Glasgow College, that Sir Robert Peel said, on assuming it, that he felt greater pride in putting on that gown, than in putting on the robes of Prime Minister.

This chapter has run to such a length that we must forego our intention of saying something about the conflicts with the police, few and far between, yet very desperate when they occur; of the occasional breaches of discipline; of traditions of the odd professors of the last generation; of publications written by the students, most of which are remarkably poor; of the extraordinary scenes which are sometimes presented at the breakfast-parties given by the professors in the course of the session. Every Saturday morning in the months of March and April, each professor has fifteen or twenty of his class at breakfast, till he has got through his roll. It would require another pen than ours to depict the sheepishness and timidity of some poor fellows on entering The Presence, their gradually growing confidence, and the jaunty and jocular free-and-easiness which they occasionally attain before the close of the entertainment.

We have thus endeavored to afford our readers some

idea of how things go on in the University of Glasgow: an institution which sends forth from its plain and even tumble-down class-rooms, "a mighty population of men, who have a kind and measure of education which fits them for taking a keen and active management in the affairs of ordinary life;" and whose long course of study many a one has entered on a raw boy, and emerged from comparatively a thoughtful man. We can but very rarely trace the after career of Glasgow students, as we often may trace that of Oxford and Cambridge men, in the history of the senate and the country. A seat on the Scotch Bench is about the highest thing that a Glasgow man can look to, and by far the most eminent among the students of Glasgow pass into the simple life of a Scotch parish minister. It is quite remarkable to what a degree the Church absorbs the highest talent of the University. And it is a significant fact, that only two Glasgow students — Campbell and Jeffrey — have ever risen to the dignity of Lord Rector.

Yet there are few Glasgow students who do not cherish a fond recollection of their College life, even though it may have been a hard one at the time. For ourselves, as we look back, not so many years, that time rises again before us. We call to mind the dark mornings on which we hurried to College, only half awake; the midnight hours of solitary study, when we heard the clock strike two, three, four, five, through the silent house; the time when we wearily rose to our day's work, and saw the moon hardly moved from that place in the sky which it held when we lay down to our poor hour of rest. We call to mind the half-dozen chairs littered with old books, fished out from the dustiest corners of the college library; the pages of paper daily covered, with a pleasant sense, unknown to other work, that here was something tangible accomplished; the indescribable feeling of weariness growing day by day; the pen which, towards the end of the session, we could sometimes scarcely hold in the trembling hand, till we had got warmed with half an hour's work; the "constitutional walk" for an hour before dinner; the delightful Saturday evening allowed to relaxation; the carrying in the prize essays; the list made out of all the prizes we were competing for, how many we shall not say; the thankfulness rather than pride with which, during the last fortnight of the session, we marked off each in succession as won; the throbbing anxiety of the first of May, which was to decide the University essay prizes; and how musical the Principal's voice as he read out the mottoes we knew so well; then the delightful relief of total leisure in those bright days of May; the summer-time spent in research and labor against another session; the intense veneration for *work* which a man comes to have when he knows what it means. Nothing to others, all these things are deeply interesting to one's own self; and perhaps they may touch some chords of recollection in some of our old college companions, now scattered over every quarter of the earth. We believe that for real hard work, for real mental discipline, for training to habits of industry and self-denial, for fitting average men to fill respectably an average place in society, there are very few things better than *College Life at Glasgow.*

CHAPTER VIII.

CONCERNING THE WORLD'S OPINION:

WITH SOME THOUGHTS ON COWED PEOPLE.

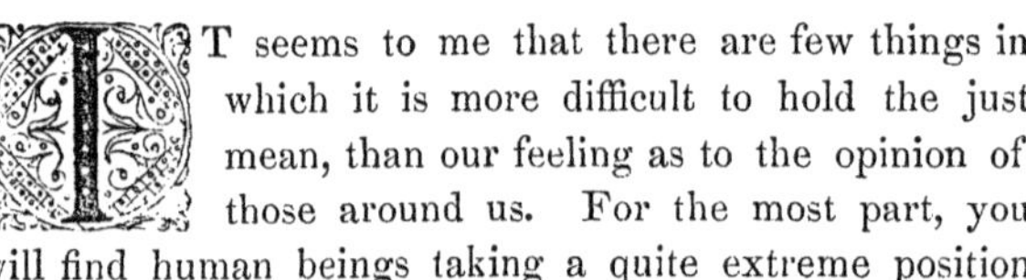

IT seems to me that there are few things in which it is more difficult to hold the just mean, than our feeling as to the opinion of those around us. For the most part, you will find human beings taking a quite extreme position as to what may be called the World's Opinion. They pay either too much regard to it, or too little. Either they are thoroughly cowed by it, or they stand towards it in an attitude of defiance. The cowed people, unquestionably, are in the majority. Most people live in a vague atmosphere of dread of the world, and of what the world is saying of them. You may discern the belief which prevails with the steady-going mass of humankind, in the typical though not historical fact which was taught most of us in childhood, — that DON'T CARE came to a bad end. The actual idea which is present to very many minds is difficult to define. Even to attempt to define it takes away that vagueness which is of the essence of its nature, and which is a great reason of the fear it excites. And the actual idea varies much in different minds, and in the same mind at different times. Sometimes, if put into shape, it would amount to this: — that some great and uncounted number of human beings is watching the person, is thinking of him, is forming an estimate of him, and an opinion as to what he ought to do. Sometimes the world's opinion becomes a more tangible thing: it means the opinion of the little circle of the person's acquaintance; or the opinion of the family in which he or she lives; or the opinion of even some single individual of a somewhat strong, and probably somewhat coarse and meddlesome nature. In such a case the world becomes personified in the typical Mrs. Grundy; and the fear of the world's opinion is expressed in the well-known question — What will Mrs. Grundy say?

Most people, then, live in a vague fear of that which may be styled Mrs. Grundy: and are cowed into abject submission not merely to her ascertained opinions, but also to what they fancy that possibly her opinions may be. Others, again — a smaller number, and a number lessening as the individuals who constitute it grow older — confront Mrs. Grundy, and defy her. DON'T CARE was a leader of this little band. But even though Don't Care had not come to trouble, it is highly probable that as he advanced in years he would have found that he must care, and that he did care. For a good many years I have enjoyed the acquaintance and the conversation of a man who, even after he became Solicitor-General, held bravely yet temperately by the forlorn hope of which a large part has always consisted of the young and the wrongheaded; and from which, with advancing years and increasing experience, men are so apt to drop away. I know that it was not vaporing in him to say, "The hissing of collected Europe, provided I knew the hissers could not touch me, would be a grateful sound rather than the reverse — that is, if heard at a reasonable distance."[1] But though I believe the words were sincere when he said them, yet I am convinced it was only by the stiffening of a moral nature, implying effort too great to last, that he was able to keep the feeling which these words express. I see in these words the expression of a desperate reaction against a strong natural bias; and I believe that time would gradually crumble that resolute purpose down. By a determined effort you may hold out a heavy weight at arm's length for a few minutes; you may defy and vanquish the law of gravitation for that short space; but the law of gravitation, quietly and unvaryingly acting, will beat you at last. And even if Ellesmere could peacefully go about his duty, and tranquilly enjoy his home, with that universal hiss in his ears, I know of those into whose hearts that hiss would sink down,—whose hearts that hiss would break. How about his wife and children? And how would the strong man himself feel, when day by day he saw by the pale cheek, the lined brow, the anxious eye, the unnatural submissiveness, that *they* were living in a moral atmosphere that was poisoning them? Think of the little children coming in and saying that the other children would not play with them or speak to them. Think of the poor wife going to some meeting of charitable ladies, and left in a corner without one to notice her or take pity on her. Ah, my friend Ellesmere, once you have given hostages to fortune, we know where the world can make you feel!

Let us give a little time to clearing up our minds on this great practical question, as to the influence which of right belongs to the world's opinion; as to the deference which a wise man will accord to it. Let us try to define that great shadowy phantom which holds numbers

[1] Ellesmere, in *Companions of my Solitude.*

through all their life in a slavery which extends to all they say and do; to the food they eat, and the raiment they put on, and the home they dwell in; and in many cases even to what they think, and to what they will admit to themselves that they think. The tyranny of the world's opinion is a tyranny infinitely more subtle and farther-reaching than that of the Inquisition in its worst days; one which passes its sentences, though no one knows who are the judges that pronounce them; and one which inflicts its punishments by the hands of numbers who utterly disapprove them. And yet, one has not the comfort of feeling able to condemn this strange tribunal out and out; you are obliged to confess that in the main its judgments are just, and its supervision is a wholesome one. Now and then it does things that are flagrantly unjust and absurd; but if I could venture, with my experience of life, to lay down any general principle, it would be the principle, abhorent to warm young hearts and to hasty young heads, that in the main the world's opinion is right in those matters to which the world's opinion has a right to extend. I dare say you will think that this is a general principle promulgated with considerable reservation. So it is; and I hardly know to which thing, the principle or the reservation, it seems to me that the greater consideration is due.

It is wrong, doubtless, to be always thinking what people will say. It is a low and wretched state of mind to come to. There is no more contemptible or miserable mortal than one of whom *this* can be said: —

While you, you think
What others think, or what you think they'll say;
Shaping your course by something scarce more tangible
Than dreams, at best the shadows on the stream
Of aspen trees by flickering breezes swayed —

Load me with irons, drive me from morn till night,
I am not the utter slave which that man is
Whose sole thought, word, and deed are built on what
The world may say of him!

The condition of mind described in these indignant lines is doubtless wrong and wretched. But still one feels that these lines must be understood with much qualification and restriction. Neither in moral principle, nor in common sense or taste, can one go with those who run to the other extreme. It is as well for most people to be cowed by a rule which in the main will keep them right, as to be suffered to run wild with no rule at all. The road to insanity is even more short and direct to the man who resolves that he shall do nothing like anybody else, than to the poor subdued creature in whom the fear of the world's judgment has run to that morbid excess that she fancies that as she goes along the street every one is pointing at her. There was nothing fine in Shelley's wearing a round blue jacket after he was a married man, just because men in general do not wear boys' jackets. And his writing *Atheist* after his name in the tourists' book, to shock people, does not strike me for its profanity half so much as for its idiotic silliness and its contemptible littleness. I do not admire the woman who walks about, a limp and conspicuous figure, in the days when crinoline is universally accepted. The extreme of crinoline is silly; the utter absence of it is silly; the wise and safe course is the middle one. I do not think it wise or admirable for a lady to walk a quarter of a mile bareheaded along a crowded street to a friend's house, even though thus she may save the trouble of going up-stairs for her bonnet. I do not approve the young fellow who tells you, when you speak to him about some petty flying in the face of the conventional notion of propriety, that he will do exactly what he likes, and that he does not care a straw what any one may think or say. That young fellow is in a very unsafe, and a very unstable position. It is not likely that he will long remain at his present moral stand-point. It is extremely probable that after a few signal instances of mischief brought upon himself by that defiant spirit, he will be cowed into abject submission to what people may think, and become afraid almost to move or breathe for fear of what may be said by folk whose opinion he secretly despises. He will gain a reputation for want of common sense, which it will be very difficult to get rid of. And even the humblest return to his allegiance to Mrs. Grundy may fail to conciliate that individual's favor, lost by many former insults.

There are some persons who are bound, not merely in prudence, but in principle, to consider the world's opinion a good deal. They are bound, not merely to avoid evil, but to avoid even the appearance of evil. And this because their usefulness in this world may be very prejudicially affected by the unfavorable opinion of those around them. It is especially so with the clergy. A clergyman's usefulness depends very much on the estimation in which he is held by his parishioners. It is desirable that his parishioners should like him: it is quite essential that they should respect him. It is not wise in the parson to shock the prejudices of those around him. It will be his duty sometimes to yield to opinions which he thinks groundless. However fond a clergyman of the Anglican Church may be of a choral service, it will be extremely foolish and wrongheaded in him to endeavor to thrust such a service upon a congregation of people who in their ignorance think it Popish. And it will not be prudent in a clergyman of the Scotch Church, placed in a remote country parish where the population retains a good deal of the old covenanting leaven, to fill his church windows with stained glass, or even to put a cross above the eastern gable. And such a man will also discern that it is his duty to practise a certain economy and reticence in the explaining of his views as to instrumental music in church, and liturgical services. If it be the fact that many rustics in the parish regard these things as marks of the Beast, he need not obtrude the fact that he holds a different opinion. For he would then, in some quarters, bring all his teaching into suspicion. Let Mr. Snarling take notice, that I am counselling no reserve in the grave matters of doctrine: no reserve, that is, in the sense of making your people fancy that you believe what you do not believe, or that you do not believe what you do. The only economy in doctrine which I should approve would be that of bringing out and applying the truth which seems most needful at the time, and best fitted for its exigencies. But as to other things, both in statement and in conduct, I hold by a high authority which states that many things may be lawful for the parson which are not expedient. And I believe that in little things the world's judgment is right in the main. There is a gravitation of society towards common sense: at least to approving it, if not to acting upon it. I am not going to defend hats and the like; or to stand up for our angular Western dress against the flowing garments of the East, though I believe our dress is more convenient if it be less graceful. And I do not believe there is any perverse bent of society to what is ugly and inconvenient at least in male attire: if any hatter or tailor produced a better covering, which would be as cheap, it would doubtless find acceptance. But I hold that it is not wise for any ordinary man to take issue with his race on any point of dress. He will not be the wisest of judges who shall first lay aside the venerable wig of gray horsehair. It is not expedient that a young clergyman should fly in the face of his parishioners on such a question as the wearing of a shooting-coat or a black neck-tie, or as going out with the hounds. It was not wise in John Foster, the great Baptist preacher, to horrify his simple flock by appearing in his pulpit in a gray coat and a red waistcoat. No doubt, in logic, his position was unassailable. For people who reject all clerical robes as Popish, it is manifestly absurd to make a stand for a black coat and a white neckcloth. By making a stand for these, you cut the ground from under your feet: you admit the principle which justifies satin and lawn. Let me say, a sound and reasonable principle too. It is not fitting that in every-day attire a man should conduct the worship of God's house. But even with folk who thought differently, John Foster acted unwisely. As lawyers would say, it was a bad issue to take. I know how a certain eminent essayist, whom I much revere, stands up for eccentricity. He holds it to be a useful protest against our tendency to a dead conformity. I venture to say that, generally, it is not wise to be eccentric. You find that eccentric people are usually eccentric in little things, not worth fighting about. We all know that there are great and important things in which the world thinks wrongly: take issue *there* with the world, if you like: but it is not worth while to do so in small matters of dress and behavior.

It is not worth while to take a beard into the pulpit where it will interfere with the congregation's attention to the sermon; nor to appear in the same place in lavender gloves in a country where lavender gloves, in such a locality, are unknown. It is wise to give in to the little requirements on which the world's opinion has been plainly expressed. If you are resolved to take a part of opposition to all the world, do so in the behalf of things which are worth the trouble of the strife. Let it not be engraven on your tombstone, Here lies the man who confronted the human race on the question of the wide-awake hat. Stand up for truth and right, if you are fond of fighting: you will have many opportunities in this life. Smite the flunkey, pierce the humbug, violently kick the aristocratic liar and seducer, and probably you will find abundant occupation. But though you know it is a pleasant and enjoyable thing for yourself and your children to sit on the steps of your country-house in the sunshine after breakfast, you will not gain the approval of wise men by doing the like on the steps of your town-house in a much-frequented street: say, for example, in Princes-street in Edinburgh. And though you often roll on the grass with your little boy in the country, do not attempt the like on the pavement of such a public way. For in that case it is conceivable that you may be jeered at by the passers-by, and apprehended by the police. And while you are being conveyed to the station-house, instead of being esteemed as a philosopher and revered as a martyr, it is not impossible that you may be laughed at as a fool. "We sat on the bridge, and swung our legs over the water:" with these words an eloquent writer lately began an essay. Of course, the bridge was in a quiet rural spot. If the writer and his friend had done the like on London bridge, the small boys would have hallooed at them, and the constable would have moved them on. Yet the merits of the deed are the same in either case. Only in the one case the world says You may; in the other case it says You must not. And the human being who resists the world's judgment in these little matters, shows, not strength, but weakness. Where principle is involved, it is noble to swing your legs; but not otherwise. But doubtless you have remarked that it is a common thing to find great obstinacy in petty concerns in a man who has no real firmness. You will find people who are squeezable and facile in the great affairs of life, and in their larger opinions have not a mind of their own, but adopt the opinion of the last person they heard express one; yet who persistently stick to some little absurd or bad habit which they have often been entreated to leave off, which annoys their friends, and makes them ridiculous. You will find a man whom you might turn round with a straw in his belief on any question political, moral, or literary, but who, having taken up the ground that once one is three, would go to the stake rather than give in to the world's way of thinking on that point.

I beg the reader to observe, that I do not counsel a general conformity to the appointments of his particular world, merely on the ground that non-conformity may cause him to be derided, or disliked, or suspected. I wish him to think of the injury which his non-conformity may occasion to others. If your shooting-coat, my clerical brother, however light and easy to walk in on a hot summer day, is to stand between a poor dying girl and the comfort and profit she might get from your counsels and prayers, why, I think, if you are the man

I mean, that you will determine never to go beyond your own gate but in the discomfort (often very great in country parishes) of severely clerical attire. Possibly few of my readers know that in various rural districts of Scotland a sermon, however admirable, will do no good if the preacher reads it: he must either give it extempore, or appear to do so by having previously written it and committed it to memory. "I canna thole the paper," I have heard an intelligent farmer say. He meant, he could not bear the sight of the manuscript discourse. It is fair to add that this prejudice is fast dying out, even in rural parishes; while in large towns in Scotland, it has entirely disappeared. But however unreasonable and stupid may have been the prejudice which condemned overwrought ministers to several hours weekly of the irksome school-boy labor of getting their sermons by heart, and however painful the anxiety which a man with an uncertain memory must often have felt on a Sunday morning, in the fear that he might forget what he had painfully prepared, and be reduced to a state of utter blankness, and ignominiously stick in his sermon; still, you will think that a conscientious man, earnest to do good, would make this painful sacrifice, not to his popularity, but to his usefulness. Let me confess, for myself, that I cannot imagine how the elder clergy of the Scotch Church were able to accomplish this awful toil. The father of the present writer, for thirty years, wrote and committed to memory two sermons of forty minutes each, every week; and hundreds of his brethren did the same. I could not do it, to save my life. Surely the intellectual fibre of the new generation is less muscular than that of their fathers. I have made mention of a judicious economy in giving instruction. You may discern the result of the want of it in what we are told about a poor dying laborer, in one of the midland counties of England. It is quite unquestionable that the world goes round the sun; but it is not in the weakness of the parting hours of life that a poor uneducated man should be called to reconstruct the theory of the universe under which he had lived all his days. And though it was certainly needful to explain to the dying man the meaning of Christian faith, it might have been done without going into anything like metaphysics; and in a way in which a child of six years old might understand it, possibly as well as the parson himself. But a young parson could not see this. He would correct all the intellectual errors of his humble parishioner. He would pour upon him a flood of knowledge. Possibly you may smile at the odd expressions; but I remember few sentences which have so touched me with their hopeless pathos, as that with which the dying man feebly turned to the wall, and spoke no more. "Wut wi' faeth," he said, "and wut wi' the earth goin' round the sun, and wut wi' the railways all a-whuzzin' and a-buzzin', I'm clean muddled, confoozled, and bet!" Well, let us hope that light came at the evening-time upon that blind, benighted way.

It should be borne in mind, that as to any particular subject, there is sometimes great difficulty in ascertaining what the world (by which I mean our own particular world) is actually saying. It seems to me especially difficult to know, in a small community, what is the general opinion upon almost any matter. For you may fall in with people holding quite exceptional opinions. And exceptional opinions are often very strongly held; and held by very clever men. I remember hearing a really able man (one whom the great world has recognized as such) declare that in his judgment a certain clergyman, not remarkable for talent, earnestness, oddity, or anything but self-conceit, was the greatest preacher he had ever listened to; incomparably greater than A, B, C, or D, each of whom is well known to fame. The man who expressed this opinion was one you would have been obliged to admit as most competent to form an opinion; yet somehow, for some inexplicable reason, some sympathy or antipathy beyond the reach of reasoning, he had come firmly to hold an opinion which was entirely exceptional, which was shared by no other human being. And thus the world may be saying one thing at one tea-table, and just the opposite at another tea-table, in some little country town. At one tea-table, the sermon of last Sunday may be very good; at the other it may be very bad. The like difference of opinion may exist as to the efficiency of the member of parliament. At one table, he may be a worthy, hard-working man; at the other, a poor silly creature. So with the singing of Miss X. If you are enjoying the cup that does not particularly cheer with Mrs. Smith and her set of friends, you may be informed, as a stranger to the town, that a great treat awaits you in listening to Miss X's songs. Her voice is splendid, and admirably cultivated; her taste exquisite. She is generally regarded as singing better than Jenny Lind. You naturally go away with the belief that in the opinion of the world at Drumsleekie, Miss X is a very great singer. But all this is due to the accident of your taking tea with Mrs. Smith. Had it been Mrs. Jones, you would have been told that Miss X overstrained her voice; that she sang untruly; that she sang flat; that she sang harshly;

that her affectation in singing was such that it was hard to refrain from throwing something at her head; and finally, that she could not sing at all. All this is perplexing. It would be a comfort to get over the preliminary difficulty, and to find out what it is that the world actually does say. Its voice, however, conveys an uncertain sound. And it would cost more time and trouble than the result would be worth, to add up the tea-tables on one side, and the tea-tables on the other side, and then discover on which side is the preponderant weight. And in case it should be found that the tea-tables on either side exactly balanced each other, the difficulty would arise, that it would appear that in Drumsleekie, on the subject of Miss X's singing, the world had no opinion at all. The favorable and unfavorable would just neutralize one another. And as with the singing of Miss X, so will you find it with the beauty of Miss Y, and the manners of Miss Z. Likewise with the horses of Mr. Q, and the poems of Mr. R. In short, to sum the matter up, it depends entirely on the set into which you get in a small community, what impression you are to carry away as to the general opinion upon any question. For though one slice taken from a leg of mutton will give you a fair idea of the general flavor of all the joint; yet you may (so to speak) cut a slice out of the talk of the town which shall be entirely different from all the rest. You may have chanced on the faction which cries up the new town-hall, or on the faction which cries it down. You may have chanced on the party which thinks the parson the greatest of men, or on the party which esteems him as one of the least.

Then it is certain that Mrs. Grundy may be made to appear to say almost anything, by the skilful management and the energy of two or three pushing individuals. It is possible for a very small number of persons to *get up a sough* (to use the Scotch phrase) either for or against a man. A few clacking busybodies, running about from house to house, may disseminate a vague unfavorable impression. A few hearty, active, energetic friends may cause the world's opinion, in a little place, to seem to be setting very strongly in a man's favor. You have probably heard the legend, which very likely is fabulous, of the fashion in which the blacking of a certain eminent man rose into universal fame. The eminent man hired four footmen, of loud and fluent power of expression, and of brazen countenance. He arrayed them in gorgeous liveries; the livery of each being quite different from that of the other three. Then, each alone, from morning to evening they pervaded London; and this was what they did. When each footman saw a shop in which blacking appeared likely to be sold, he rushed into it with great appearance of excitement, and exclaimed in a hurried manner, "Give me some of Snooks's blacking instantly." Snooks, it should be mentioned, was the name of his eminent employer. "Snooks's blacking," said the man in the shop; "we never heard of it!" "Not heard of Snooks's blacking!" exclaimed the footman; "why, my master won't let me brush his boots with any other; and just now he is roaring at me for brushing his boots this morning with that of Stiggins; I must be off elsewhere and get Snooks's blacking forthwith." This interview naturally startled the man in the shop; he began to think, "I must get some of Snooks's blacking; everybody must be using Snooks's blacking!" And when, in the course of the day, the other three footmen severally visited his shop as the first had done; one exclaiming, "the Chancellor wont use anything but Snooks's blacking;"

another "his Grace wont use anything but Snooks's blacking;" the last (in crimson livery), "his Majesty wont use anything but Snooks's blacking;" the man in the shop took his resolution. He found out the factory of Snooks, and ordered a large quantity of his blacking.

That which has pushed blacking into fame, has done the like for other things. Two or three individuals, vigorously puffing a book, may cause it to seem that the world's judgment in the locality where they live is in that book's favor. And most people will bow to that judgment. Not very many people have so much firmness, or confidence in themselves, as to hold their own opinion in the presence of the strongly expressed opinion of the world on the other side. And a loud and confident declaration that something is very bad, will silence and put down many people, who in their secret soul think it very good.

The *sough*, or general opinion and belief in a country district, may occasionally be got up by persons who are little better than idiots. Let me relate a story which I heard, long ago. A very distinguished preacher once went to preach in the parish church of a certain big and ugly village in Scotland. The village lies among the hills, in a pastoral district. It had no railway communication; no near neighbors; no large town within many miles. The people, many of them, were very ignorant, very pragmatical and self-conceited. The big and ugly village thought it was the centre of the world; possibly, that it was the whole world. Its population formed an unfavorable estimate of the preaching of the great orator. It was generally said in the village that "his sermons were no' very weel conneckit." It happens that the discourses of that clergyman are remarkable for their logical linkedness of thought; for the symmetry and beauty of their skeleton, no less than for the brilliance and range of their illustrations. But some blockhead said (not having anything particular to say) that they were " no' very weel conneckit." Other blockheads grasped at this. It was something to say; and to say it seemed to imply the possession of some critical acumen. So the voice of Mrs. Grundy, in that village, reëchoed that statement on every side. The statement was, indeed, absurd. You might as well have said that the sermons were distinguished by their ignorant impatience of the relaxation of taxation, or by their want of mezzotinto. But people seized it, and repeated it. I remember going as a boy to that locality; and hearing several persons, all densely stupid, and most of them very conceited, speak of the great preacher. They all criticized him in the selfsame terms: " His sermons were no' very weel conneckit!" But there is no opinion expressed with so great confidence as the opinion of the man who is incapable of forming any opinion. I remember an old gentleman telling me how he went to hear Dr. Chalmers. " I could not understand the man," said he; " I could not see what he was driving at." I am entirely satisfied that the old gentleman told the truth. Like the Squire in the *Vicar of Wakefield*, Dr. Chalmers could supply argument, but he could not supply intellect to comprehend it.

An unfavorable *sough* may be got up in a rural district, by a man who combines caution with malignity; and all in such a way that you cannot lay hold of the malicious but cautious man. Let us suppose a new doctor is coming to the village. You, the old doctor, may go about the village and beg the people to try and receive him civilly; he may not be such a bad man after all. The truth probably is, that nobody supposes him a bad man, or intends to receive him otherwise than civilly; but a few days judiciously spent may excite a prejudice which it will take some time to allay. Some one speaks to you in praise of an acquaintance. You may reply, in a hesitating way, "Yes; he is rather a nice fellow; but —— well, I don't want to say anything bad of any one." In this way you have not committed yourself; but you have conveyed a worse impression than you could probably have conveyed by any definite charge you could have made against the man. Honest and manly folk, indeed, may possibly call you a sneak. What do you care? Some muscular Christian may kick you. In that case you will have the comfort of knowing that it unquestionably serves you right.

There is something worrying and vexatious, in thinking that the *sough of the country-side*, which in Scotland signifies the general opinion of the neighborhood, is running against yourself and your possessions; even though you heartily despise the individuals whose separate judgments go to make up that *sough*. For you gradually come to attach considerable importance to the opinion of the people among whom you live, even though that opinion be in itself worth nothing. There is compensation, however, in the fact, that if the unfavorable opinions of stupid and incompetent people are able to depress a man, the favorable opinions of stupid and incompetent people are able to elate and encourage even a very clever and wise man. Many such men are kept up to the mark at which they do good and even great things, by rumors of the high estimation in which they are held by Mrs. Grundy. There is probably as much happiness communicated to a human being by the favorable estimate of those around him — though they are people of no great standing, and not very wise — as if they were the wisest and noblest of the land. For, by degrees, even the wise man begins to fancy that these people who think so highly of him are not quite ordinary folk; they are more capable judges of human excellence than people in their station in life usually are. I can quite understand that the author who finds his book praised in the *Little Peddlington Gazette*, or the *Whistlebinkie Banner of Freedom*, will conclude that these are important newspapers, conducted with intelligence much surpassing that of country papers in general. He will be quite cheerful for a whole forenoon after reading in either of those journals, that he is one of the most original thinkers of the age. So a clergyman, who is popular in his own parish, will quite honestly come to think that its population is remarkable for its intelligence and its power of appreciating a good sermon. Of course, as has been said, the converse case holds good. The ill opinion of those around you, if quite universal, is depressing, however much you may despise that opinion. Not only is that unfavorable estimate always around you, like an unhealthy atmosphere, but you gradually come to think that the people who hold it are rather wise and important people. A parson, going from a large and intelligent parish to one where the people are few and uncultivated, knows at first very nearly what is the mark of his present position and his present congregation. He knows that, seriously, the opinion which his parishioners form of him is neither here nor there. But he learns very soon that comfort and discomfort may be caused by judgments which are absolutely valueless. You may remember what Philip Van Artevelde says of that which may be regarded as the most favorable of all individual estimates of man : —

> How little flattering is a woman's love! —
> Worth to the heart, come how it may, a world;
> Worth to men's measures of their own deserts,
> If weighed in wisdom's balance, merely nothing!

And gradually you go farther than Van Artevelde. Probably even that philosophic man, as he found day by day new indications of the warm affection and the hearty admiration of the woman he had in his mind when he said such words, began to think that, after all, there must be something unusual about him to elicit all that devotion ; began to think that her opinion was sound and just ; and that she must be a person of no ordinary sagacity who arrived at a judgment so true. You will do all that. You will not only be pleased by the favorable estimate of incompetent judges: you will come to think that they are very competent judges. A clergyman who at one time used to preach to a great crowd of cultivated folk in London, told me that after he had been a few months in a little country-parish, he felt quite pleased when he found the mill-girls of a manufacturing town four miles off, walking over on Sundays to hear him preach ; and also that he began to think these mill-girls very intelligent people, whose appreciation was worth having. Your "nature is subdued to what it works in." You stand in considerable awe of things amid which you always live. And the truth is, that almost everything, when you come to know it well, is bigger than the stranger fancies it. It is because things, when you come to know them, are really so good, that the *lues Boswelliana* prevails to such a degree in biographers; that each parson thinks his own church in some one respect superior to the general run;

and that the rustics of each parish think their own the finest in the country. The things are really very good; and it is difficult to estimate how good, relatively to others. When a wise man finds himself second, or ninth, or nineteenth, in competition with others, whether the competition be in the size of his turnips, the speed of his horses, the beauty of his pictures, the bitterness of his reviews, the amiability of his children, or the badness of his headaches (all matters of which people are given to boast), the wise man will not necessarily conclude that he himself or his belongings are less good or great than he had previously bestowed. The right conclusion is this: that other men and their belongings are better or bigger than he had fancied them. And though the favorable appreciation of judges, barristers, cabinet ministers, and the like, is undoubtedly worth more than that of factory-girls, still the favorable appreciation of the factory-girls may be regarded as worth a good deal, by one who lives exclusively among factory-girls.

Besides this, there is a further consideration that comes in to give weight to the unfavorable judgment of Mrs. Grundy. A wise man, knowing how human vanity leads people to over-estimate their own merits, would, if he found that everybody thought he was a fool, begin to fear that he was one; and also to fear that the fact that he could not see he was a fool showed the hopelessness of his condition; as we know that a maniac occasionally believes that he is the only sane person in the world. I believe that there is nothing that can hold a man up against the depressing effect of being held in little esteem by those around him, as his family, or his neighbors; but the fact of his being held in good estimation by some person or persons elsewhere, whom he can regard as wiser and worthier judges of him than those around him are. I have known a great preacher, whose church was nearly empty on Sundays. It was in a remote rural district. But whenever he went to preach in any large town, the church in which he preached was crowded to excess. So he could set the opinion of the remote Mrs. Grundy against that of the near Mrs. Grundy, and, though surrounded by the unfavorable estimation of the near Mrs. Grundy, he could retain composure and confidence in himself, by backing up his estimate of himself with that of the distant world. And there are people with no distant friends to lean on, who yet, in a remote situation, find the support and sympathy they want, in the better part of our periodical literature. The *Times*, coming daily to an educated man in a very rustic place, is a great blessing. So is the *Saturday Review* to the country parson. So are the Quarterly Reviews generally. He will find much in them with which he cannot agree; a good deal which is extremely distasteful to him. But in reading them, he breathes a different atmosphere from that in which he is placed by many of his daily concerns and acquaintances. He finds in them something to prevent him from being cowed into conformity. He finds the thoughts of cultivated men, holding the same canons of taste with himself; and, in the main, holding nearly the same great points of belief on more important things. I felt it as a comfort, after lately hearing a man say that a certain noble cathedral was "a great ugly jail of a place," to read a brilliant article in praise of Gothic architecture. And when you are building a pretty Elizabethan house, with all its graceful characteristics, you do not mind a bit that Mrs. Grundy, Mr. Snarling, and Miss Limejuice go about saying that it is gimcrack, barbarous, Popish, inconvenient, dark, and fit only for monks and nuns, when you are able to turn to many pages on which competent men have set out the beauties and comforts of that delightful style, and shown up the nonsense of the stupid and tasteless folk who abuse it. But if you stood alone in the world in your love for the well-shown gable and the pointed arch, it may be feared that, unless you had the determination of the martyr, you would be badgered into keeping your opinions to yourself, and into conforming your practice to that of other people. There are few more delightful things to any one who has long lived among those with whom he feels no sympathy, than to find himself among people who think and feel as he does. And there is more than pleasure in the case; there is something in this that will strengthen and vivify his tastes and beliefs into redoubled energy.

You will not unfrequently find people who loudly profess their contempt for the world's opinion, who are really living in abject terror of it. A coward, you know, often assumes a bullying manner. And there is no weaker or sillier way of considering Mrs. Grundy, than to be ever on the watch for opportunities of shocking her. It is for the most part nervous people, very much afraid of her, who do this. We all know persons who take great delight in trying to astonish mankind by the awful opinions they express, and by conduct flatly opposed to the rules of civilized society. You will find parsons who in their sermons like to frighten people, by sailing as near unsound doctrine as possible; or by a manner very devoid of that gravity which becomes the time and place. So with young ladies who smoke cigars, or talk in a fast manner to gentlemen on subjects and about people of which they ought to know nothing. So with the greater part of all eccentricity. One can bear eccentricity, however great, when it is genuine. One can bear the man, however oddly he may act, who acts in Mrs. Grundy's presence as though he saw her not; and who *bonâ fide* does not see her. But it is a very wretched and contemptible thing, to witness a man doing very bold things, going through all kinds of eccentric gyrations, with a side-glance all the while at Mrs. Grundy, and with an ear upon the stretch to remark what she is going to say.

There are men who are right in carefully observing the world's opinion of them and their doings: whose duty it is to observe these things carefully. There are men who know for certain that the world has an opinion of them: an opinion varying from day to day; and an opinion upon whose variations very tangible results depend. Such a man is the Prime Minister in Britain. His possession of actual power and of profitable place depends just upon the world's opinion of him; an opinion which ebbs and flows from week to week: which is indicated unmistakably by his parliamentary majority as it rises and sinks; and which is affected by a host of circumstances quite away from the Premier's merits. If the Premier is desirous to retain his place, I should fancy that, till he gets indurated to it, it must be a most disagreeable one. From what a variety of quarters the voice of Mrs. Grundy must be borne to his ears; and how difficult it must be to know precisely what importance to attach to this or that specific bellow! Judging from the easy way in which the present head of the government bears his functions, one would suppose that to be Prime Minister must be like being stoker of an American high-pressure steamer. At first, you will be in momently expectation of being blown up; but by and by you will come to take it quite coolly; indeed, with a hardihood rather appalling to most people to see. There is no one who has it in his power to know so certainly and immediately what his own world thinks of him, as a great actor. It is an index of his popularity, as certain as the mercury in the thermometer is of the temperature, how the theatre fills at which he performs. And to him, popularity is more than empty praise. It is substantial pudding. The bread and butter of his wife and children depend upon it. There are cases in which it is a miserable spectacle to see a man eagerly anxious about the world's opinion. There is no more contemptible and degrading sight, than a clergyman who sets his heart upon popularity as a preacher; who is always fishing for compliments, and using claptrap arts to draw a crowd and amaze people. You come to hear of preachers who, it is plain, are prepared to go any length: men who would preach standing on their head rather than fail of creating a sensation. I thank God I never listened to such; but I have read in print addresses described as having been given in buildings professedly used for the worship of the Almighty, which addresses, in their title, subject, and entire tone, were perfectly analogous to the advertisements and exhibitions of a juggler. Their vulgar buffoonery and disgusting profanity were intended as a bait to the lowest and worst classes in the community. You may have known persons, in various walks of life, who were in the possession of the world's good opinion, but who could not be said to be in the enjoyment of it. It did not make them happy to have it, but it would have made them miserable to lose it. To go down a peg or two in the scale of fame would have been unendurable. And you would find them occasionally putting out feelers, to try whether the popular gale was slackening. Should it show signs of slackening, you have various acquaintances who will be careful to inform you. I knew a young divine who preached for almost the first time at a certain country church. A few days after, a man from the parish, a vulgar person, and almost a stranger, came and assured him that his sermon did not by any means guv sahtisfawkshun. I have known a person, a stupid and ignorant blockhead, who devoted himself to going about and retailing to every one he knew, any wretched little piece of tattle which might be disagreeable to hear. I don't believe the man was malignant. I suppose he yielded to an impulse analogous to that which makes a hen cackle when it has laid an egg. Unhappily, some men are so weak that though they find it unpleasant to be informed that the world is pronouncing opinion against them, they yet find a certain fascination impelling them to learn all particulars as to this unfriendly opinion. And so the ignorant blockhead found many attentive auditors. Doubtless this gratified him. My readers, cut such a man short at once. Snub him. Shut him up. As you would close the window through which a bitter north-east wind is blowing into your chamber on a winter day, so shut up this wretched gutter that conveys to you the dregs of Mrs. Grundy!

As you go on through life, my friend, you will discover a good many *Cowed People.* These people have been fairly beaten by their fear of what the world will say. They are always in a vague alarm. They are afraid of doing or saying the most innocent thing, lest in some way, they cannot say how, it may turn to their prejudice.

They are in mortal dread of committing themselves. They live in some general confused apprehension of what may come next. They are always thinking that Mr. A bowed rather stiffly to them, and wondering what it can mean; that Mrs. B looked the other way as they passed, and no doubt intends to finally cut their acquaintance; and the like. All this shades off into developments which pass the limit of sanity; as believing that the entire population of the place have combined against them, and that the human race at large is resolved to thwart their plans and crush their hopes. I do not mention these things to be laughed at. The sincerest sympathy is due to such as suffer in this way. No doubt all this founds upon a nervous, anxious nature; but it has been greatly fostered by lending a ready ear to such stupid, if not malicious, tatlers as have just been mentioned. There is, indeed, much of natural temperament here; much of physical constitution. There are boys who go to school each morning, trembling with vague apprehension, they cannot say of what. Possibly there is some idea that all their companions may league against them. There is not much of the magnanimous about boys; and such a poor little fellow probably leads a sad enough school life. And years afterwards, when he is a man in business, you may find him going away from his cottage on the outskirts into town each morning, to get his letters and attend to the day's transactions, as Daniel might have gone into the den. To many human beings the world is as a great, fierce machine, whirring and grinding inexorably on; and their great desire is to keep away from it. And possibly the man who is most thoroughly cowed by the world is not the man who lives in an even and equable awe of it; but rather he who now and then rebels, makes a frantic, foolish fight for freedom, gets terribly mauled in a quarrel with the world on some stupid issue, and then gives up, and sinks down beaten into a state of utter prostration. Probably such a man, for a while after each desperate rally, is the most cowed of cowed men.

There are human beings of this temperament who seem to feel as though any street in which an acquaintance lives were barricaded against their passage. They will tell you they don't like to pass Mr. Smith's house, lest he should see them. You listen with wonder, and possibly you reply: "Suppose he does, what then?" Of course they cannot answer your question; they cannot fix on any specific evil result which would follow if Mr. Smith did happen to see them; they have simply a vague fear of the consequences of that event. You will find such people, if they are walking along the street, and see any one they know coming in their direction, instantly get out of the way by turning down some side lane. I believe that in the hunting-field the cry of "*Ware wheat!*" warns the horseman to keep off the ground sown with that precious grain, lest the crop suffer damage. I think I have seen human beings, the voice of whose whole nature, as they advanced through creation, appeared to be "*Ware Friends!*" Their wish was just to keep out of anybody's way. It was vain to ask what harm would follow even if they met Mr. Green or the Miss Browns. They did not know exactly why they were afraid: they were vaguely cowed. Is it because the present writer feels within himself something which might ultimately land him in that wretched condition of moral prostration, that he is anxious to describe it accurately and protest against it bitterly? You find people so thoroughly cowed, that they appear to be always apologizing for venturing to be in this world. They seem virtually to say to every one they meet, but especially to all baronets, lords, and the like, "I beg your pardon for being here." You will find them saying this even to wealthy mercantile men. Not only is this a painful and degrading point to arrive at; I do not hesitate to say that it is a morally wrong one. It implies a forgetfulness of Who put you in this world, my friend, that you should wish to skulk through it in that fashion. Is not *this* the right thing for a human being to feel. The Creator put me here, in my lowly place indeed; but I have as good a right in this world, in my own place in it, as the Queen or the President. My title to be here is exactly the same as that of the greatest and noblest: it is the will of my Maker. And I shall follow the advice of a good and resolute man in an early century, who was always ready to give honor to whom it was due, but who would not abnegate his rights as man, for mortal. I intend to do what he said should be done by "every man," — I intend, "wherein I am called, therein to abide with God."

There are few more contemptible exhibitions of human slavery than you may find in cowed people who, in every little thing they do, are guided not by their notion of what is right, but by their belief as to what Mrs. Grundy may say, more especially the Grundy whose income and social standing somewhat surpass their own. I once heard a parson, who had a large income, say that he could not venture to put his man-servant into livery, because the gentry in his parish would not like it! I suggested that it was no concern of the gentry how he might attire his servant; that the questions to be considered concerned only himself, and appeared to me to be these: —

1. Whether he could afford it;
2. Whether he would like it.

And that for myself, if I could answer these questions in the affirmative, I should like to see the man in my parish who would venture to interfere with what I thought fit to do in the matter. Not but what I believe that vulgar and impertinent individuals might be found who would not like to see my friend approximating too closely to their own magnificence; but if there be a thing in this world to be decisively and instantly snubbed, it assuredly would be the insolence of venturing to express, in my friend's presence, either liking or dislike in the case. I have known a talking busybody, a relation of Miss Limejuice, who called at the house of a family lately come to settle in a remote country region, to inform them that their dining so late as they did was regarded as presumptuous; and that various neighboring families felt aggrieved that their own dinner-hour, hitherto esteemed the most advanced in fashion, had been transcended by the new-comers. It may suffice to say, that though the relation of Miss Limejuice was treated with entire civility, she never ventured in that house to recur to that topic again. It is curious how rapidly it comes to be understood, whether any individual possesses that cowed and abject nature which permits impertinent interference in his private concerns, or not. The most meddlesome of tattling old women knows when she may venture to repeat Mrs. Grundy's opinion, and when she had better not. And all this without the least noisy demonstration; all this with very little reference to the absolute social position of the person to be interfered with. It is a question of the nature of the animal. An eagle, you know, is a smaller animal than a goose; but it is inexpedient to interfere with the former bird. If you have any unpleasant advice to offer, stick to the goose, my friend!

It is worthy of notice, that in the respect of the attitude which men assume towards the world's opinion, the most remarkable change sometimes passes over them. We all know that human beings, in the course of their lives, go through many phases of opinion and feeling as to most matters: but I think there is no single matter in which they may exhibit extremes so far apart as in the matter of confidence and cowedness. You will find men who as school-boys were remarkable for their forwardness: who were always ready to start up and roar out an answer in their class; and who even at college were pushing and confident, and quite willing to take a lead among their fellow-students; but who ten years after leaving the university, have shrunk into very modest and retiring and timid men. I have known several cases in which this was so; always in the case of men who had carried off very high honors. Doubtless this loss of confidence is in some measure the result of growing experience, and of the lowlier estimate of one's own powers which *that* seldom fails to bring to men of sense; but I believe that it is in no small measure the result of a nervous system early overdriven, and of a mental constitution from which the elasticity has been taken by too hard work, gone through too soon. You know that if you put a horse in harness at three years old, he will, if he be a good horse, do his work splendidly; but he will not do it long. At six years old, he will be a spiritless, broken-down creature. You took it out of him too soon. He is used up. And the cleverest young men at the universities are often like the horse set to hard work at three. By the time they are two and twenty, you have sometimes taken out of them the best that will ever come. They will probably die about middle age; and till that time they will go heavily through life, with little of the cheerful spring. They will not rise to the occasion. They cannot answer the spur. They are prematurely old: weary, jaded, cowed. Oh that the vile system of midnight toil at the universities, of England and Scotland and America, were finally abolished! It directly encourages many of the most promising of the race to mortgage their best energies and their future years, to sustain the reckless expenditure of the present. It would be an invaluable blessing if it were made a law, inexorable as those of the Medes, that no honors should ever be given to any student who was not in bed by eleven o'clock at latest.

It is a sad thing when any person, old or young, goes through his work in a cowed spirit. I do not mean, goes through his work in a jaded, heartless way merely, but goes through his work in the bare hope of escaping blame. A great part of all that is done in this world is done in this way. Many children, many servants, many clerks, and even several parsons, go through their daily round thus. I need not say how poorly that work will usually be done which the man wishes just to get through without any great reprobation; but think how unhappily it will be done, and what a miserable training of mind and heart it is! It seems to me that few people do their work heartily, and really as well as they can. And people whose desire is merely to get through somehow, seem to stand to their work as at a level below it. The man who honestly does his best, works from above; his task is below him; he is master of it, however hard it may be. The man who hopes no more than to escape censure, and who accordingly aims at nothing more, seems to work from below; his task is above him; he is cowed by it. Let us resolve that we shall always give praise when we can. You will find many people who are always willing to find fault with their servants, if their servants do anything wrong, but who never say an approving word when their servants do right. You will find many people who do the like as to their children. And only too often that wretched management breaks the spring of the youthful spirit. Yes, many little children are cowed; and the result is either a permanent dull quiescence, never to be got over, or a fierce reaction against the accursed tyranny that embittered early years — a reaction which may sometimes cast off entirely the bonds of natural affection, and even of moral restraint. How it encourages and cheers the cowed little fellow, growing up in the firm belief that he is hopelessly wicked, and never can do anything to please any one, to try reward as a change from constant punishment and bullying! I have seen the good effect upon such a one of the kind approving word. How much more cheerfully the work will be done; how much better it will be done; and how much happier a man he will be that does it! A poor fellow who never expects that he can please, and who barely hopes that he may pass without censure and abuse, will do his task very heartlessly. Let us praise warmly and heartily wherever praise is deserved. And if we weigh the matter, we shall find that a great deal of hearty praise is deserved in this world on every day that shines upon it.

May I conclude by saying, that many worthy people

go through their religious duties in a thoroughly cowed spirit? They want just to escape God's wrath — not to gain His kind favor. The great spring of conduct within them is not love, but abject terror. Truly a mistaken service! You have heard of the devil-worshippers in India; do you know why they worship the devil? Because they think him a very powerful being, who can do them a mischief if they don't. Does not the worship of the Almighty, rendered in that cowed spirit, partake of the essential nature of devil-worship? Let us not love and serve our Maker, my reader, because we are in fear that He will torment us if we do not. Let us humbly love and serve Him because He is so good, so kind to you and me, because He loved us first, and because we can see Him and His glory in the kindest face this world ever saw! I do not think we should have been afraid of Jesus of Nazareth. I do not think we need have gone in a cowed spirit to Him. And in Him we have the only manifestation that is level to our understanding, of the Invisible God. I think we could have gone to Him confidingly as a little child to a kind mother. I think we should have feared no repulse, no impatience, as we told to Him the story of all our sins and wants and cares. We can picture to ourselves, even yet, the kindly, sorrowful features which little children loved, and which drew those unsophisticated beings to gather round Him without a fear. Let there be deep humility, but nothing of that unworthy terror. You remember what we know on the best of all authority is the first and great thing we are to do. It is not to cultivate a cowed spirit. It is to LOVE our Maker with heart and soul and mind.

CHAPTER IX.

CONCERNING THE SORROWS OF CHILDHOOD.

NCE upon a time, Mr. Smith, who was seven feet in height, went out for a walk with Mr. Brown, whose stature was three feet and a half. It was in a distant age, in which people were different from what they are now, and in which events occurred such as do not usually occur in these days. Smith and Brown, having traversed various paths, and having passed several griffins, serpents, and mail-clad knights, came at length to a certain river. It was needful that they should cross it; and the idea was suggested that they should cross it by wading. They proceeded, accordingly, to wade across; and both arrived safely at the farther side. The water was exactly four feet deep, — not an inch more or less. On reaching the other bank of the river, Mr. Brown said, —

"This is awful work; it is no joke crossing a river like *that*. I was nearly drowned."

"Nonsense!" replied Mr. Smith; "why make a fuss about crossing a shallow stream like this? Why, the water is only four feet deep: *that* is nothing at all!"

"Nothing to you, perhaps," was the response of Mr. Brown, "but a serious matter for me. You observe," he went on, "that water four feet deep is just six inches over my head. The river may be shallow to you, but it is deep to me."

Mr. Smith, like many other individuals of great physical bulk and strength, had an intellect not much adapted for comprehending subtile and difficult thoughts. He took up the ground that things are what they are in themselves, and was incapable of grasping the idea that greatness and littleness, depth and shallowness, are relative things. An altercation ensued, which resulted in threats on the part of Smith that he would throw Brown into the river; and a coolness was occasioned between the friends which subsisted for several days.

The acute mind of the reader of this page will perceive that Mr. Smith was in error; and that the principle asserted by Mr. Brown was a sound and true one. It is unquestionable that a thing which is little to one man may be great to another man. And it is just as really and certainly great in this latter case as anything ever can be. And yet, many people do a thing exactly analogous to what was done by Smith. They insist that the water which is shallow to them shall be held to be absolutely shallow; and that, if smaller men declare that it is deep to themselves, these smaller men shall be regarded as weak, fanciful, and mistaken. Many people, as they look back upon the sorrows of their own childhood, or as they look round upon the sorrows of existing childhood, think that these sorrows are or were very light and insignificant, and their causes very small. These people do this, because to them, as they are now, *big people*, (to use the expressive phrase of childhood,) these sorrows would be light, if they should befall. But though these sorrows may seem light to us now, and their causes small, it is only as water four feet in depth was shallow to the tall

Mr. Smith. The same water was very deep to the man whose stature was three feet and a half; and the peril was as great to him as could have been caused by eight feet depth of water to the man seven feet high. The little cause of trouble was great to the little child. The little heart was as full of grief and fear and bewilderment as it could hold.

Yes, I stand up against the common belief that childhood is our happiest time. And whenever I hear grown-up people say that it is so, I think of Mr. Smith and the water four feet deep. I have always, in my heart, rebelled against that common delusion. I recall, as if it were yesterday, a day which I have left behind me more than twenty years. I see a large hall, the hall of a certain educational institution, which helped to make the present writer what he is. It is the day of the distribution of the prizes. The hall is crowded with little boys, and with the relations and friends of the little boys. And the chief magistrate of that ancient town, in all the pomp of civic majesty, has distributed the prizes. It is neither here nor there what honors were borne off by me; though I remember well that *that* day was the proudest that ever had come in my short life. But I see the face and hear the voice of the kind-hearted old dignitary, who has now been for many years in his grave. And I recall especially one sentence he said, as he made a few eloquent remarks at the close of the day's proceedings.

"Ah, boys," said he, "I can tell you this is the happiest time of all your life!"

"Little you know about the matter," was my inward reply.

I knew that our worries, fears, and sorrows were just as great as those of any one else.

The sorrows of childhood and boyhood are not sorrows of that complicated and perplexing nature which sit heavy on the heart in after-years; but in relation to the little hearts that have to bear them, they are very overwhelming for the time. As has been said, great and little are quite relative terms. A weight which is not absolutely heavy is heavy to a weak person. We think an industrious flea draws a vast weight, if it draws the eighth part of an ounce. And I believe that the sorrows of childhood task the endurance of childhood as severely as those of manhood do the endurance of the man. Yes, we look back now, and we smile at them, and at the anguish they occasioned, because they would be no great matter to us now. Yet in all this we err just as Mr. Smith the tall man erred, in that discussion with the little man, Mr. Brown. Those early sorrows were great things then. Very bitter grief may be in a very little heart. "The sports of childhood," we know from Goldsmith, "satisfy the child." The sorrows of childhood overwhelm the poor little thing. I think a sympathetic reader would hardly read without a tear, as well as a smile, an incident in the early life of Patrick Fraser Tytler, recorded in his biography. When five years old, he got hold of the gun of an elder brother and broke the spring of its lock. What anguish the little boy must have endured, what a crushing sense of having caused an irremediable evil, before he sat down and printed in great letters the following epistle to his brother, the owner of the gun: — "Oh, Jamie, think no more of guns, for the mainspring of that is broken, and *my heart is broken!*" Doubtless the poor little fellow fancied that for all the remainder of his life he never could feel as he had felt before he had touched the unlucky weapon. And looking back over many years, most of us can remember a child crushed and overwhelmed by some trouble which it thought could never be got over; and we can feel for our early self as though sympathizing with another being.

What I wish in this essay is, that we should look away along the path we have come in life; and that we should see, that, though many cares and troubles may now press upon us, still we may well be content. I speak to ordinary people, whose lot has been an ordinary lot. I know there are exceptional cases; but I firmly believe, that, as for most of us, we never have seen better days than these. No doubt, in the retrospect of early youth, we seem to see a time when the summer was brighter, the flowers sweeter, the snowy days of winter more cheerful, than we ever find them now. But, in sober sense, we know that it is all an illusion. It is only as the man travelling over the burning desert sees sparkling water and shady trees where he knows there is nothing but arid sand.

I dare say you know that one of the acutest of living men has maintained that it is foolish to grieve over past suffering. He says, truly enough in one sense, that the suffering which is past is as truly non-existent as the suffering which has never been at all; that, in fact, past suffering is now nothing, and is entitled to no more consideration than that to which nothing is entitled. No doubt, when bodily pain has ceased, it is all over: we do not feel it any more. And you have probably observed that the impression left by bodily pain passes very quickly away. The sleepless night, or the night of torment from toothache, which seemed such a distressing reality while it was dragging over, looks a very shadowy thing the next forenoon. But it may be doubted whether you will ever so far succeed in overcoming the fancies and weaknesses of humanity as to get people to cease to feel that past sufferings and sorrows are a great part of their present life. The remembrance of our past life is a great part of our present life. And, indeed, the greater part of human suffering consists in its anticipation and in its recollection. It is so by the inevitable law of our being. It is because we are rational creatures that it is so. We cannot help looking forward to that which is coming, and looking back on that which is past; nor can we suppress, as we do so, an emotion corresponding to the perception. There is not the least use in telling a little boy who knows that he is to have a tooth pulled out to-morrow, that it is absurd in him to make himself unhappy to-night through the anticipation of it. You may show with irrefragable force of reason, that the pain will last only for the two or three seconds during which the tooth is being wrenched from its place, and that it will be time enough to vex himself about the pain when he has actually to feel it. But the little fellow will pass but an unhappy night in the dismal prospect; and by the time the cold iron lays hold of the tooth, he will have endured by anticipation a vast deal more suffering than the suffering of the actual operation. It is so with bigger people, looking forward to greater trials. And it serves no end whatever to prove that all this ought not to be. The question as to the emotions turned off in the workings of the human mind is one of fact. It is not how the machine ought to work, but how the machine does work. And as with the anticipation of suffering, so with its retrospect. The great grief which is past, even though its consequences no longer directly press upon us, casts its shadow over after-years. There are, indeed, some hardships and trials upon which it is possible that we may look back with satisfaction. The contrast with them enhances the enjoyment of better days. But these trials, it seems to me, must be such as come through the direct intervention of Providence; and they must be clear of the elements of human cruelty or injustice. I do not believe that a man who was a weakly and timid boy can ever look back with pleasure upon the ill-usage of the brutal bully of his school-days, or upon the injustice of his teacher in cheating him out of some well-earned prize. There are kinds of great suffering which can never be thought of without present suffering, so long as human nature continues what it is. And I believe that past sorrows are a great reality in our present life, and exert a great influence over our present life, whether for good or ill. As you may see in the trembling knees of some poor horse, in its drooping head, and spiritless paces, that it was overwrought when young: so, if the human soul were a thing that could be seen, you might discern the scars where the iron entered into it long ago, — you might trace not merely the enduring remembrance, but the enduring results, of the incapacity and dishonesty of teachers, the heartlessness of companions, and the idiotic folly and cruelty of parents. No, it will not do to tell us that past sufferings have ceased to exist, while their remembrance continues so vivid, and their results so great. You are not done with the bitter frosts of last winter, though it be summer now, if your blighted evergreens remain as their result and memorial. And the man who was brought up in an unhappy home in childhood will never feel that that unhappy home has ceased to be a present reality, if he knows that its whole discipline fostered in him a spirit of distrust in his kind which is not yet entirely got over, and made him set himself to the work of life with a heart somewhat soured and prematurely old. The past is a great reality. We are here the living embodiment of all we have seen and felt through all our life, — fashioned into our present form by millions of little touches, and by none with a more real result than the hours of sorrow we have known.

One great cause of the suffering of boyhood is the bullying of bigger boys at school. I know nothing practically of the English system of *fagging* at public schools, but I am not prepared to join out and out in the cry against it. I see many evils inherent in the system ; but I see that various advantages may result from it, too. To organize a recognized subordination of lesser boys to bigger ones must unquestionably tend to cut the ground from under the feet of the unrecognized, unauthorized, private bully. But I know that at large schools, where there is no fagging, bullying on the part of youthful tyrants prevails to a great degree. Human nature is beyond doubt fallen. The systematic cruelty of a school-bully to a little boy is proof enough of *that*, and presents one of the very hatefullest phases of human character. It is worthy of notice, that, as a general rule, the higher you ascend in the social scale among boys, the less of bullying there is to be found. Something of the chivalrous and the magnanimous comes out in the case of the sons of gentlemen : it is only among such that you will ever find a boy, not personally interested in the matter, standing up against the bully in the interest of right and justice. I have watched a big boy thrashing a little one, in the presence of half a dozen other big boys, not one of whom interfered on behalf of the oppressed little fellow. You may be sure I did not watch the transaction longer than was necessary to ascertain whether there was a grain of generosity in the hulking boors; and you may be sure, too, that that thrashing of the little boy was, to the big bully, one of the most unfortunate transactions in which he had engaged in his bestial and blackguard, though brief, life. *I* took care of *that*, you may rely on it. And I favored the bully's companions with my sentiments as to their conduct, with an energy of statement that made them sneak off, looking very like whipped spaniels. My friendly reader, let us never fail to stop a bully, when we can. And we very often can. Among the writer's possessions might be found by the curious inspector several black kid gloves, no longer fit for use, though apparently not very much worn. Surveying these integuments minutely, you would find the thumb of the right hand rent away, beyond the possibility of mending. Whence the phenomenon? It comes of the writer's determined habit of stopping the bully. Walking along the street, or the country-road, I occasionally see a big blackguard fellow thrashing a boy much less than himself. I am well aware that some prudent individuals would pass by on the other side, possibly addressing an admonition to the big blackguard. But I approve Thomson's statement, that "prudence to baseness verges still;" and I follow a different course. Suddenly approaching the blackguard, by a rapid movement, generally quite unforeseen by him, I take him by the arm, and occasionally (let me confess) by the neck, and shake him till his teeth rattle. This, being done with a new glove on the right hand, will generally unfit that glove for further use. For the bully must be taken with a gripe so firm and sudden as shall serve to paralyze his nervous system for the time. And never once have I found the bully fail to prove a whimpering coward. The punishment is well deserved, of course; and it is a terribly severe one in ordinary cases. It is a serious thing, in the estimation both of the bully and his companions, that he should have so behaved as to have drawn on himself the notice of a passer-by, and especially of a parson. The bully is instantly cowed; and by a few words to any of his school-associates who may be near, you can render him unenviably conspicuous among them for a week or two. I never permit bullying to pass unchecked; and so long as my strength and life remain, I never will. I trust you never will. If you could stand coolly by, and see the cruelty you could check, or the wrong you could right, and move no finger to do it, you are not the reader I want, nor the human being I choose to know. I hold the cautious and sagacious man, who can look on at an act of bullying without stopping it and punishing it, as a worse and more despicable animal than the bully himself.

Of course, you must interfere with judgment; and you must follow up your interference with firmness. Don't intermeddle, like Don Quixote, in such a manner as to make things worse. It is only in the case of continued and systematic cruelty that it is worth while to work temporary aggravation, to the end of ultimate and entire relief. And sometimes that is unavoidable. You remenber how, when Moses made his application to Pharaoh for release to the Hebrews, the first result was the aggravation of their burdens. The supply of straw was cut off, and the tale of bricks was to remain the same as before. It could not be helped. And though things came right at last, the immediate consequence was that the Hebrews turned in bitterness on their intending deliverer, and charged their aggravated sufferings upon him. Now, my friend, if you set yourself to the discomfiture of a bully, see you do it effectually. If needful, follow up your first shaking. Find out his master, find out his parents; let the fellow see distinctly that your interference is no passing fancy. Make him understand that you are thoroughly determined that his bullying shall cease. And carry out your determination unflinchingly.

I frequently see the boys of a certain large public school, which is attended by boys of the better class; and judging from their cheerful and happy aspect, I judge that bullying among boys of that condition is becoming rare. Still, I doubt not, there yet are poor little nervous fellows whose school-life is embittered by it. I don't think any one could read the poet Cowper's account of how he was bullied at school, without feeling his blood a good deal stirred, if not entirely boiling. If I knew of such a case within a good many miles, I should stop it, though I never wore a glove again that was not split across the right palm.

But, doubtless, the greatest cause of the sorrows of childhood is the mismanagement and cruelty of parents. You will find many parents who make favorites of some of their children to the neglect of others: an error and a sin which is bitterly felt by the children who are held down, and which can never by possibility result in good to any party concerned. And there are parents who deliberately lay themselves out to torment their children. There are two classes of parents who are the most inexorably cruel and malignant: it is hard to say which class excels, but it is certain that both classes exceed all ordinary mortals. One is the utterly blackguard: the parents about whom there is no good nor pretence of good. The other is the wrongheadedly conscientious and religious: probably, after all, there is greater rancor and malice about these last than about any other. These act upon a system of unnatural repression, and systematized weeding out of all enjoyment from life. These are the people whose very crowning act of hatred and malice towards any one is to pray for him, or to threaten to pray for him. These are the people who, if their children complain of their bare and joyless life, say that such complaints indicate a wicked heart, or Satanic possession; and have recourse to further persecution to bring about a happier frame of mind. Yes: the wrong-headed and wrong-hearted religionist is probably the very worst type of man or woman on whom the sun looks down. And, oh! how sad to think of the fashion in which stupid, conceited, malicious blockheads set up their own worst passions as the fruits of the working of the Blessed Spirit, and caricature, to the lasting injury of many a young heart, the pure and kindly religion of the Blessed Redeemer! These are the folk who inflict systematic and ingenious torment on their children: and, unhappily, a very contemptible parent can inflict much suffering on a sensitive child. But of this there is more to be said hereafter; and before going on to it, let us think of another evil influence which darkens and embitters the early years of many.

It is the cruelty, injustice, and incompetence of many schoolmasters. I know a young man of twenty-eight, who told me, that, when at school in a certain large city in Peru, (let us say,) he never went into his class any day without feeling quite sick with nervous terror. The entire class of boys lived in that state of cowed submission to a vulgar, stupid, bullying, flogging barbarian. If it prevents the manners from becoming brutal diligently to study the ingenuous arts, it appears certain that diligently to teach them sometimes leads to a directly contrary result. The bullying schoolmaster has now become an almost extinct animal; but it is not very long since the spirit of Mr. Squeers was to be found, in its worst manifestations, far beyond the precincts of Dotheboys Hall. You would find fellows who showed a grim delight in walking down a class with a cane in their hand, enjoying the evident fear they occasioned as they swung it about, occasionally coming down with a savage whack on some poor fellow who was doing nothing whatsoever. These brutal teachers would flog, and that till compelled to cease by pure exhaustion, not merely for moral offences, which possibly deserve it, (though I do not believe any one was ever made better by flogging,) but for making a mistake in saying a lesson, which the poor boy had done his best to prepare, and which was driven out of his head by the fearful aspect of the truculent blackguard with his cane and his hoarse voice. And how indignant, in after-years, many a boy of the last generation must have been, to find that this tyrant of his childhood was in truth a humbug, a liar, a fool, and a sneak! Yet how that miserable piece of humanity was feared! How they watched his eye, and laughed at the old idiot's wretched jokes! I have several friends who have told me such stories of their school-days, that I used to wonder that they did not, after they became men, return to the schoolboy spot that they might heartily shake their preceptor of other years, or even kick him!

If there be a thing to be wondered at, it is that the human race is not much worse than it is. It has not a fair chance. I am not thinking now of an original defect in the material provided: I am thinking only of the kind of handling it gets. I am thinking of the amount of judgment which may be found in most parents and in most teachers, and of the degree of honesty which may be found in many. I suppose there is no doubt that the accursed system of the cheap Yorkshire schools was by no means caricatured by Mr. Dickens in "Nicholas Nickleby." I believe that starvation and brutality were the rule at these institutions. And I do not think it says much for the manliness of Yorkshire men and of Yorkshire clergymen, that these foul dens of misery and wickedness were suffered to exist so long without a voice raised to let the world know of them. I venture to think, that, if Dr. Guthrie of Edinburgh had lived anywhere near Greta Bridge, Mr. Squeers and his compeers would have attained a notoriety that would have stopped their trade. I cannot imagine how any one, with the spirit of a man in him, could sleep and wake within sight of one of these schools without lifting a hand or a voice to stop what was going on there. But without supposing these extreme cases, I can remember what I have myself seen of the incompetence and injustice of teachers. I burn with indignation yet, as I think of a malignant blockhead who once taught me for a few months. I have been at various schools; and I spent six years at one venerable university (where my instructors were wise and worthy); and I am now so old, that I may say, without any great exhibition of vanity, that I have always kept well up among my school and college companions: but that blockhead kept me steadily at the bottom of my class, and kept a frightful dunce at the top of it, by his peculiar system. I have observed (let me say) that masters and professors who are stupid themselves have a great preference for stupid fellows, and like to keep down clever ones. A professor who was himself a dunce at college, and who has been jobbed into his chair, being quite unfit for it, has a fellow-feeling for other dunces. He is at home with them, you see, and is not afraid that they see through him and despise him. The injustice of the malignant blockhead who was my early instructor, and who succeeded in making several months of my boyhood unhappy enough, was taken up and imitated by several lesser blockheads among the boys. I remember particularly one sneaking wretch who was occasionally set to mark down on a slate the names of such boys as talked in school; such boys being punished by being turned to the bottom of their class. I remember how that sneaking wretch used always to mark my name down, though I kept perfectly silent: and how he put my name last on the list, that I might have to begin the lesson the very lowest in my form. The sneaking wretch was bigger than I, so I could not thrash him; and any representation I made to the malignant blockhead of a schoolmaster was entirely disregarded. I cannot think but with considerable ferocity, that probably there are many schools to-day in Britain containing a master who has taken an unreasonable dislike to some poor boy, and who lays himself out to make that poor boy unhappy. And I know that such may be the case where the boy is neither bad nor stupid. And if the school be one attended by a good many boys of the lower grade, there are sure to be several sneaky boys among them who will devote themselves to tormenting the one whom the master hates and torments.

It cannot be denied that there is a generous and magnanimous tone about the boys of a school attended exclusively by the children of the better classes, which is unknown among the children of uncultivated boors. I have observed, that, if you offer a prize to the cleverest and most industrious boy of a certain form in a school of the upper class, and propose to let the prize be decided by the votes of the boys themselves, you will almost invariably find it fairly given: that is, given to the boy who deserves it best. If you explain, in a frank, manly way, to the little fellows, that, in asking each for whom he votes, you are asking each to say upon his honor whom he thinks the cleverest and most diligent boy in the form, nineteen boys out of twenty will answer honestly. But I have witnessed the signal failure of such an appeal to the honor of the bumpkins of a country-school. I was once present at the examination of such a school, and remarked carefully how the boys acquitted themselves. After the examination was over, the master proposed, very absurdly, to let the boys of each class vote the prize for that particular class. The voting began. A class of about twenty was called up: I explained to the boys what they were to do. I told them they were not to vote for the boy they liked best, but were to tell me faithfully who had done best in the class-lessons. I then asked the first boy in the line for whom he gave his vote. To my mortification, instead of voting for a little fellow who had done incomparably best at the examination, he gave his vote for a big sullen-looking blockhead who had done conspicuously ill. I asked the next boy, and received the same answer. So all round the class: all voted for the big sullen-looking blockhead. One or two did not give their votes quite promptly; and I could discern a threatening glance cast at them by the big sullen-looking blockhead, and an ominous clinching of the blockhead's right fist. I went round the class without remark; and the blockhead made sure of the prize. Of course this would not do. The blockhead could not be suffered to get the prize; and it was expedient that he should be made to remember the occasion on which he had sought to tamper with justice and right. Addressing the blockhead, amid the dead silence of the school, I said: "You shall not get the prize, because I can judge for myself that you don't deserve it. I can see that you are the stupidest boy in the class; and I have seen reason, during this voting, to believe that you are the worst. You have tried to bully these boys into voting for you. Their votes go for nothing; for their voting for you proves either that they are so stupid as to think you deserve the prize, or so dishonest as to say they think so when they don't think so." Then I inducted the blockhead into a seat where I could see him well, and proceeded to take the votes over again. I explained to the boys once more what they had to do; and explained that any boy would be telling a lie who voted the prize unfairly. I also told them that I knew who deserved the prize, and that they knew it too, and that they had better vote fairly. Then, instead of saying to each boy, "For whom do you vote?" I said to each, "Tell me who did best in the class during these months past." Each boy in reply named the boy who really deserved the prize: and the little fellow got it. I need not record the means I adopted to prevent the sullen-looking blockhead from carrying out his purpose of thrashing the little fellow. It may suffice to say that the means were thoroughly effectual; and that the blockhead was very meek and tractable for about six weeks after that memorable day.

But, after all, the great cause of the sorrows of childhood is unquestionably the mismanagement of parents. You hear a great deal about parents who spoil their children by excessive kindness; but I venture to think that a greater number of children are spoiled by stupidity and cruelty on the part of their parents. You may find parents who, having started from a humble origin, have attained to wealth, and who, instead of being glad to think that their children are better off than they themselves were, exhibit a diabolical jealousy of their children. You will find such wretched beings insisting that their children shall go through needless trials and mortifications, because they themselves went through the like. Why, I do not hesitate to say that one of the thoughts which would most powerfully lead a worthy man to value material prosperity would be the thought that his boys would have a fairer and happier start in life than he had, and would be saved the many difficulties on which he still looks back with pain. You will find parents, especially parents of the pharisaical and wrong-headedly religious class, who seem to hold it a sacred duty to make the little things unhappy; who systematically endeavor to render life as bare, ugly, and wretched a thing as possible; who never praise their children when they do right, but punish them with great severity when they do wrong; who seem to hate to see their children lively or cheerful in their presence; who thoroughly repel all sympathy or confidence on the part of their children, and then mention as a proof that their children are possessed by the Devil, that their children always like to get away from them; who rejoice to cut off any little enjoyment, — rigidly carrying out into practice the fundamental principle of their creed, which undoubtedly is, that "nobody should ever please himself, neither should anybody ever please anybody else, because in either case he is sure to displease God." No doubt, Mr. Buckle, in his second volume, caricatured and misrepresented the religion of Scotland as a country; but he did not in the least degree caricature or misrepresent the religion of some people in Scotland. The great doctrine underlying all other doctrines, in the creed of a few unfortunate beings, is, that God is spitefully angry to see his creatures happy; and of course the practical lesson follows, that they are following the best example, when they are spitefully angry to see their children happy.

Then a great trouble, always pressing heavily on many a little mind, is that it is overtasked with lessons. You still see here and there idiotic parents striving to make infant phenomena of their children, and recording with much pride how their children could read and write at an unnaturally early age. Such parents are fools: not necessarily malicious fools, but fools beyond question. The great use to which the first six or seven years of life should be given is the laying the foundation of a healthful constitution in body and mind; and the instilling of those first principles of duty and religion which do not need to be taught out of any books. Even if you do not permanently injure the young brain and mind by prematurely overtasking them, — even if you do not permanently blight the bodily health and break the mind's cheerful spring, you gain nothing. Your child at fourteen years old is not a bit farther advanced in his education than a child who began his years after him ; and the entire result of your stupid driving has been to evercloud some days which should have been among the happiest of his life. It is a woful sight to me to see the little forehead corrogated with mental effort, though the effort be to do no more than master the multiplication table: it was a sad story I lately heard of a little boy repeating his Latin lesson over and over again in the delirium of the fever of which he died, and saying piteously that indeed he could not do it better. I don't like to see a little face looking unnaturally anxious and earnest about a horrible task of spelling; and even when children pass that stage, and grow up into school-boys who can read Thucydides and write Greek iambics, it is not wise in parents to stimulate a clever boy's anxiety to hold the first place in his class. That anxiety is strong enough already; it needs rather to be repressed. It is bad enough even at college to work on late into the night; but at school it ought not to be suffered for one moment. If a lad takes his place in his class every day in a state of nervous tremor, he may be in the way to get his gold medal, indeed; but he is in the way to shatter his constitution for life.

We all know, of course, that children are subjected to worse things than these. I think of little things early set to hard work, to add a little to their parent's scanty store. Yet, if it be only work, they bear it cheerfully. This afternoon, I was walking through a certain quiet street, when I saw a little child standing with a basket at a door. The little man looked at various passers-by; and I am happy to say, that, when he saw me, he asked me to ring the door-bell for him: for, though he had been sent with that basket, which was not a light one, he could not reach up to the bell. I asked him how old he was. "Five years past," said the child, quite cheerfully and independently. "God help you, poor little man!" I thought; "the doom of toil has fallen early upon you!" If you visit much among the poor, few things will touch you more than the unnatural sagacity and trustworthiness of children who are little more than babies. You will find these little things left in a bare room by themselves, — the eldest six years old, — while the poor mother is out at her work. And the eldest will reply to your questions in a way that will astonish you, till you get accustomed to such things. I think that almost as heart-rending a sight as you will readily see is the misery of a little thing who has spilt in the street the milk she was sent to fetch, or broken a jug, and who is sitting in despair beside the spilt milk or the broken fragments. Good Samaritan, never pass by such a sight; bring out your twopence; set things completely right: a small matter and a kind word will cheer and comfort an overwhelmed heart. That child has a truculent step-mother, or (alas!) mother, at home, who would punish that mishap as nothing should be punished but the gravest moral delinquency. And lower down the scale than this, it is awful to see want, cold, hunger, rags, in a little child. I have seen the wee thing shuffling along the pavement in great men's shoes, holding up its sorry tatters with its hands, and casting on the passengers a look so eager, yet so hopeless, as went to one's heart. Let us thank God that there is one large city in the empire where you need never see such a sight, and where, if you do, you know how to relieve it effectually; and let us bless the name and the labors and the genius of Thomas Guthrie! It is a sad thing to see the toys of such little children as I can think of. What curious things they are able to seek amusement in! I have known a brass button at the end of a string a much prized possession. I have seen a grave little boy standing by a broken chair in a bare garret, solemnly arranging and rearranging two pins upon the broken chair. A machine much employed by poor children in country-places is a slate tied to a bit of string: this, being drawn along the road, constitutes a cart; and you may find it attended by the admiration of the entire young population of three or four cottages standing in the moorland miles from any neighbor.

You will not unfrequently find parents who, if they cannot keep back their children from some little treat, will try to infuse a sting into it, so as to prevent the children from enjoying it. They will impress on their children that they must be very wicked to care so much about going out to some children's party; or they will insist that their children should return home at some preposterously early hour, so as to lose the best part of the fun, and so as to appear ridiculous in the eyes of their young companions. You will find this amiable tendency in people intrusted with the care of older children. I have heard of a man whose nephew lived with him, and lived a very cheerless life. When the season came round at which the lad hoped to be allowed to go and visit his parents, he ventured, after much hesitation, to hint this to his uncle. Of course the uncle felt that it was quite right the lad should go, but he grudged him the chance of the little enjoyment, and the happy thought struck him that he might let the lad go, and at the same time make the poor fellow uncomfortable in going. Accordingly he conveyed his permission to the lad to go by roaring out in a savage manner, "*Begone!*" This made the poor lad feel as if it were his duty to stay, and as if it were very wicked in him to wish to go; and though he ultimately went, he enjoyed his visit with only half a heart. There are parents and guardians who take great pains to make their children think themselves very bad, — to make the little things grow up in the endurance of the pangs of a bad conscience. For conscience, in children, is a quite artificial thing: you may dictate to it what it is to say. And parents, often injudicious, sometimes malignant, not seldom apply hard names to their children, which sink down into the little heart and memory far more deeply than they think. If a child cannot eat fat, you may instil into him that it is because he is so wicked; and he will believe you for a while. A favorite weapon in the hands of some parents, who have devoted themselves diligently to making their children miserable, is to frequently predict to the children the remorse which they (the children) will feel after they (the parents) are dead. In such cases, it would be difficult to specify the precise things which the children are to feel remorseful about. It must just be, generally, because they were so wicked, and because they did not sufficiently believe the infallibility and impeccability of their ancestors. I am reminded of the woman mentioned by Sam Weller, whose husband disappeared. The woman had been a fearful termagant; the husband, a very inoffensive man. After his disappearance, the woman issued an advertisement, assuring him, that, if he returned, he would be fully forgiven; which, as Mr. Weller justly remarked, was very generous, seeing he had never done anything at all.

Yes, the conscience of children is an artificial and a sensitive thing. The other day, a friend of mine, who is one of the kindest of parents and the most amiable of men, told me what happened in his house on a certain *Fast-day*. A Scotch Fast-day, you may remember, is the institution which so completely puzzled Mr. Buckle. That historian fancied that *to fast* means in Scotland to abstain from food. Had Mr. Buckle known anything whatever about Scotland, he would have known that a Scotch Fast-day means a week-day on which people go to church, but on which (especially in the dwellings of the clergy) there is a better dinner than usual. I never knew man or woman in all my life who on a Fast-day refrained from eating. And quite right, too. The growth of common sense has gradually abolished literal fasting. In a warm Oriental climate, abstinence from food may give the mind the preëminence over the body, and so leave the mind better fitted for religious duties. In our country, literal fasting would have just the contrary effect: it would give the body the mastery over the soul; it would make a man so physically uncomfortable that he could not attend with profit to his religious duties at all. I am aware, Anglican reader, of the defects of my countrymen; but commend me to the average Scotchman for sound practical sense. But to return. These Fast-days are by many people observed as rigorously as the Scotch Sunday. On the forenoon of such a day, my friend's little child, three years old, came to him in much distress. She said, as one who had a fearful sin to confess, "I have been playing with my toys this morning;" and then began to cry as if her little heart would break. I know some stupid parents who would have strongly encouraged this needless sensitiveness; and who would thus have made their child unhappy at the time, and prepared the way for an indignant bursting of these artificial trammels when the child had grown up to maturity. But my friend was not of that stamp. He comforted the little thing, and told her, that, though it might be as well not to play with her toys on a Fast-day, what she had done was nothing to cry about. I think, my reader, that, even if you were a Scotch minister, you would appear with considerable confidence before your Judge, if you had never done worse than failed to observe a Scotch Fast-day with the Covenanting austerity.

But when one looks back and looks round and tries to reckon up the sorrows of childhood arising from parental folly, one feels that the task is endless. There are parents who will not suffer their children to go to the little feasts which children occasionally have, either on that wicked principle that all enjoyment is sinful, or because the children have recently committed some small offence, which is to be thus punished. There are parents who take pleasure in informing strangers, in their children's presence, about their children's faults, to the extreme bitterness of the children's hearts. There are parents who will not allow their children to be taught dancing, regarding dancing as sinful. The result is, that the children are awkward and unlike other children; and when they are suffered to spend an evening among a number of companions who have all learned dancing, they suffer a keen mortification which older people ought to be able to understand. Then you will find parents, possessing ample means, who will not dress their children like others, but send them out in very shabby garments. Few things cause a more painful sense of humiliation to a child. It is a sad sight to see a little fellow hiding round the corner when some one passes who is likely to recognize him, afraid to go through the decent streets, and creeping out of sight by back-ways. We have all seen *that.* We have all sympathized heartily with the reduced widow who has it not in her power to dress her boy better; and we have all felt lively indignation at the parents who had the power to attire their children becomingly, but whose heartless parsimony made the little things go about under a constant sense of painful degradation.

An extremely wicked way of punishing children is by shutting them up in a dark place. Darkness is naturally fearful to human beings, and the stupid ghost-stories of many nurses make it especially fearful to a child. It is a stupid and wicked thing to send a child on an errand in a dark night. I do not remember passing through a greater trial in my youth than once walking three miles alone (it was not going on an errand) in the dark, along a road thickly shaded with trees. I was a little fellow; but I got over the distance in half an hour. Part of the way was along the wall of a church-yard, one of those ghastly, weedy, neglected, accursed-looking spots where stupidity has done what it can to add circumstances of disgust and horror to the Christian's long sleep. Nobody ever supposed that this walk was a trial to a boy of twelve years old: so little are the thoughts of children understood. And children are reticent: I am telling now about that dismal walk for the very first time. And in the illnesses of childhood, children sometimes get very close and real views of death. I remember, when I was nine years old, how every evening, when I lay down to sleep, I used for about a year to picture myself lying dead, till I felt as though the coffin were closing round me. I used to read at that period, with a curious feeling of fascination, Blair's poem, "The Grave." But I never dreamed of telling anybody about these thoughts. I believe that thoughtful children keep most of their thoughts to themselves, and in respect of the things of which they think most are as profoundly alone as the Ancient Mariner in the Pacific. I have heard of a parent, an important member of a very strait sect of the Pharisees, whose child, when dying, begged to be buried not in a certain foul old hideous church-yard, but in a certain cheerful cemetery. This request the poor little creature made with all the energy of terror and despair. But the strait Pharisee refused the dying request, and pointed out, with polemical bitterness, to the child, that he must be very wicked indeed to care at such a time where he was to be buried, or what might be done with his body after death. How I should enjoy the spectacle of that unnatural, heartless, stupid wretch tarred and feathered! The dying child was caring for a thing about which Shakespeare cared; and it was not in mere human weakness, but "by faith," that "Joseph, when he was a-dying, gave commandment concerning his bones."

I believe that real depression of spirits, usually the sad heritage of after-years, is often felt in very early youth. It sometimes comes of the child's belief that he must be very bad, because he is so frequently told that he is so. It sometimes comes of the child's fears, early felt, as to what is to become of him. His parents, possibly, with the good sense and kind feeling which distinguish various parents, have taken pains to drive it into the child, that, if his father should die, he will certainly starve, and may very probably have to become a wandering beggar. And these sayings have sunk deep into the little heart. I remember how a friend told me that his constant wonder, when he was twelve or thirteen years old, was *this:* If life was such a burden already, and so miserable to look back upon, how could he ever bear it when he had grown older?

But now, my reader, I am going to stop. I have a great deal more marked down to say, but the subject is growing so thoroughly distressing to me, as I go on, that I shall go on no farther. It would make me sour and wretched for the next week, if I were to state and illustrate the varied sorrows of childhood of which I intended yet to speak: and if I were to talk out my heart to you about the people who cause these, I fear my character for good-nature would be gone with you for ever. "This genial writer," as the newspapers call me, would show but little geniality: I am aware, indeed, that I have already been writing in a style which, to say the least, is snappish. So I shall say nothing of the first death that comes in the family in our childish days, — its hurry, its confusion, its awe-struck mystery, its wonderfully vivid recalling of the words and looks of the dead; nor of the terrible trial to a little child of being sent away from home to school, — the heart-sickness and the weary counting of the weeks and days before the time of returning home again. But let me say to every reader who has it in his power directly or indirectly to do so, Oh, do what you can to make children happy! oh, seek to give that great enduring blessing of a happy youth! Whatever after-life may prove, let there be something bright to look back upon in the horizon of their early time! You may sour the human spirit forever, by cruelty and injustice in youth. There is a past suffering which exalts and purifies; but *this* leaves only an evil result: it darkens all the world, and all our views of it. Let us try to make every little child happy. The most selfish parent might try to please a little child, if it were only to see the fresh expression of unblunted feeling, and a liveliness of pleasurable emotion which in after-years we shall never know. I do not believe a great English barrister is so happy when he has the Great Seal committed to him as two little and rather ragged urchins whom I saw this very afternoon. I was walking along a country-road, and overtook them. They were about five years old. I walked slower, and talked to them for a few minutes, and found that they were good boys, and went to school every day. Then I produced two coins of the copper coinage of Britain: one a large penny of ancient days, another a small penny of the present age. "There is a penny for each of you," I said, with some solemnity: "one is large, you see, and the other small; but they are each worth exactly the same. Go and get something good." I wish you had seen them go off! It is a cheap and easy thing to make a little heart happy. May this hand never write another essay if it ever wilfully miss the chance of doing so! It is all quite right in after-years to be careworn and sad. We understand these matters ourselves. Let others bear the burden which we ourselves bear, and which is doubtless good for us. But the poor little things! I can enter into the feeling of a kind-hearted man who told me that he never could look at a number of little children but the tears came into his eyes. How much these young creaures have to bear yet! I think you can, as you look at them, in some degree understand and sympathize with the Redeemer, who, when he "saw a great multitude, was moved with compassion toward them!" Ah, you smooth little face, (you may think,) I know what years will make of you, if they find you in this world!

And you, light little heart, will know your weight of care!

And I remember, as I write these concluding lines, who they were that the Best and Kindest this world ever saw liked to have near Him; and what the reason was He gave why He felt most in His element when they were by His side. He wished to have little children round Him, and would not have them chidden away; and this because there was something about them that reminded Him of the Place from which He came. He liked the little faces and the little voices, — He to whom the wisest are in understanding as children. And oftentimes, I believe, these little ones still do His work. Oftentimes, I believe, when the worn man is led to Him in childlike confidence, it is by the hand of a little child.

CHAPTER X.

THE ORGAN QUESTION IN SCOTLAND.[1]

EPUBLICANS are born, not made," says the lively author of *Kaloolah;* and so, we have long held, are true-blue Presbyterians. A certain preponderance of the sterner elements, a certain lack of capacity of emotion, and disregard of the influence of associations, — in brief, a certain hardness of character to be found only in Scotland, is needed to make your out-and-out follower of John Knox. The great mass of the educated members of the Church of Scotland have no pretension to the name of true-blue Presbyterians: Balfour of Burley would have scouted them; under the insidious influence of greater enlightenment and more rapid communication, they have in many respects approximated sadly to "black prelacy." Dr. Candlish's book reminds us that out-and-out Presbyterians are still to be found in the northern part of this island. In arguing with such, we feel a peculiar difficulty. We have no ground in common. Things which appear to us as self-evident axioms, they flatly deny. For instance, it appears

[1] *The Organ Question: Statements by Dr. Ritchie and Dr. Porteous for and against the use of the Organ in Public Worship, in the Proceedings of the Presbytery of Glasgow*, 1807–8. With an introductory Notice, by Robert S. Candlish, D.D. Edinburgh. 1856.

to us just as plain as that two and two make four, that a church should be something essentially different in appearance from an ordinary dwelling; that there is a peculiar sanctity about the house of God; that if it be fit to pay some respect to the birthday of the Queen, it cannot be wrong to pay a greater to the birthday of the Redeemer; that the worship of God should be made as solemn in itself as possible, and as likely as possible to impress the hearts of the worshippers; that if music is employed in the worship of God, it should be the best music to be had; and that if there be a noble instrument especially adapted to the performance of sacred music, with something in its very tones that awes the heart and wakens devotional feeling, *that* is beyond all question the instrument to have in our churches. Now all this the true-blue Presbyterian at once denies. He holds that all that is required of a church is protection from the weather, with seat-room, and, perhaps, ventilation; he denies that any solemnized feeling is produced by noble architecture, or that the Gothic vault is fitter for a church than for a factory; he walks into church with his hat on to show he does not care for bricks and mortar; he taboos Christmas-day, with all its gentle and gracious remembrances; he maintains that the barest of all worship is likeliest to be true spiritual service; he holds that there is something essentially evil and sinful in the use of an organ in church; that the organ is "a portion of the trumpery which ignorance and superstition had foisted into the house of God;" that to introduce one is to "convert a church into a concert-room," and "to return back to Judaism;" and that "the use of instrumental music in the worship of God is neither lawful, nor expedient, nor edifying." [1]

[1] *The Organ Question*, pp. 108, 125, 128, &c.

We confess that we do not know how to argue with men who honestly hold these views. The things which they deny appear to us so perfectly plain already, that no argument can make them plainer. If any man say to us, "I don't feel in the least solemnized by the noble cathedral and the pealing anthem," all we can reply is simply, "Then you are different from human beings in general;" but it is useless to argue with him. If you argue a thesis at all, you can argue it only from things less liable to dispute than itself; and in the case of all these matters attached to Presbytery, though not forming part of its essence, this is impossible. Whenever we have had an argument with an old impracticable Presbyterian, we have left off with the feeling that some people are born Presbyterians; and if so, there is no use in talking to them.

But all these notions to which allusion has been made, are attached to Presbytery by vulgar prejudice; they form no part of its essence, and enlightened Presbyterians now-a-days are perfectly aware of the fact. There is no earthly connection in the nature of things between Presbyterian Church-government and flat-roofed meeting-houses, the abolition of the seasons of the Christian year, a bare and bald ritual, a vile "precentor" howling out of all tune, and a congregation joining as musically as the frogs in Aristophanes. The educated classes in Scotland have for the most part come to see this, and in Edinburgh and Glasgow, even among the Dissenters, we find church-like places of worship, decent singing, and the entire service conducted with propriety. And one of the marked signs of vanishing prejudice is, that a general wish is springing up for the introduction of that noble instrument, so adapted to church-music, the organ. Things have even gone so far that the principal ecclesiastical court of a considerable Scotch dissenting denomination, has left it to be decided by each congregation for itself, whether it will have an organ or not. And several dissenting ministers of respectable standing and undoubted Presbyterianism, are pushing the matter strongly.

We should have fancied that men of sense in North Britain would have been pleased to find that there is a prospect of the organ being generally introduced: and this upon the broad ground that church-music would thus be made more solemn, more worthy of God's worship, more likely to awaken devotional feeling. We should have fancied that there was no need for special pleading on the part of the advocates of the organ, and assuredly no room for lengthened argument on the part of its opponents. The entire argument, we think, may be summed up thus: Whatever makes church-music more solemn and solemnizing is good; the organ does this: therefore, let us have the organ. If a man denies our first proposition, he is a person who cannot be reasoned with. If he denies the second, he has no musical taste. If he admits both, yet denies the conclusion, then he is either prejudiced or yielding to prejudice. And so the discussion ends. And though we do not by any means hold that the majority is necessarily right, still in this world we have, after all, no further appeal than to the mass of educated men, and they have decided "the organ question." We believe that the Scotch Church and its offshoots are the only Christian sects that taboo the organ.

We should not have been surprised to find opposition to the organ on the part of the unreasoning crowd, who regard it as a rag of Popery, and whose hatred of everything prelatical is quite wonderful. But it startles us to find reasonable and educated Scotchmen maintaining that an organ is an idol, and that its use is not only inexpedient, but absolutely sinful and forbidden. We have read with considerable interest, and with great surprise, Dr. Candlish's publication on *The Organ Question*, elicited by " the alarm he feels at certain recent movements on behalf of instrumental music in Presbyterian worship." (p. 5.) His part in it is confined to an introductory essay, reflecting little credit upon either his logic or his taste : and instead of arguing the matter for himself, he prefers to reproduce what he regards as a complete discussion of the subject, in two documents, written nearly half a century since. The circumstances under which these were written are as follows : —

In the centre of a considerable square, opening out of the Salt Market of Glasgow (indissolubly associated with the memory of Bailie Nicol Jarvie and Rob Roy), there stands the elegant church of St. Andrew. It is a *facsimile*, on a much reduced scale, of St. Martin's-in-the-fields, at Charing Cross. Fifty years since, Dr. Ritchie, the incumbent of that church, in accordance with the wish of his entire congregation, one of the most intelligent in Scotland, introduced an organ. On Sunday, the 23d of August, 1807, the sole organ which has been used since the Reformation in any Scotch church *in Scotland*,[1] was used for the first and last time. Extreme horror was excited among the ultra-Presbyterians. Dr. Ritchie was forthwith pulled up by the Presbytery of Glasgow, and

[1] Organs are not unfrequently found in Scotch churches *out of Scotland*. The Scotch churches maintained by the East India Company at Calcutta, Madras, and Bombay, are provided with organs, which are regularly used. The case is the same with several of the Scotch churches in the West Indies, and with one long established at Amsterdam.

getting frightened at his own audacity, he declared at its meeting "that he would not again use an organ in the public worship of God without the authority of the Church." Upon this the Presbytery passed a resolution to the effect "That the Presbytery are of opinion that the use of the organ in the public worship of God, is contrary to the law of the land, and to the law and constitution of our Established Church, and therefore prohibit it in all the churches and chapels within their bounds; and with respect to Dr. Ritchie's conduct in this matter, they are satisfied with his declaration." Dr. Ritchie gave in a paper containing his reasons of dissent; and a committee of the Presbytery prepared a reply to it. These two papers form the substance of the book now sent forth with Dr. Candlish's name.

The commotion excited in Scotland by the introduction of the organ was indescribable. Dr. Ritchie was accused of "the monstrous crime of worshipping God by images, of violating the articles of the Union, of demolishing the barriers for the security of our religion, of committing a deed of perjury to ordination vows." (p. 61.) A howl of execration was directed against the man who had exhibited the flagrant insolence of introducing what John Knox had tastefully described as a "kist fu' o' whistles." Pamphlets and caricatures were numerous. Dr. Candlish thinks it worth while to preserve the remembrance of a picture "which represents Dr. Ritchie, who was about the time of these proceedings translated to Edinburgh, travelling as a street musician, with a barrel organ strapped across his shoulder, and solacing himself with the good old tune, "I'll gang nae mair to yon toun." (p. 28.) Wit and intelligence appear to have been tolerably equal in Scotland in those days.

Dr. Candlish's own sentiments are plainly enough expressed. He thinks that "cogent arguments can be urged, both from reason and Scripture, against the practice of using the organ." (p. 14.) He hopes that his present publication "will make many who have been almost led away by the plausibilities that are so easily got up on the side of organs, pause before they lend themselves to what may cause a most perilous agitation." (p. 31). This is fair enough, because there may be prejudices in the mass of the Scotch people so strong that it would be inexpedient to shock them by introducing instrumental music. But Dr. Candlish goes on, in words which bewilder us, to give his opinion on the essential merits of the question: —

> It is not that I am afraid of a controversy on this subject, or of its issue, so far as the merits of the question are concerned. I believe it is a question which touches some of the highest and deepest points of Christian theology. Is the temple destroyed, is the temple worship wholly superseded? Have we, or have we not, priests and sacrifices among us now? Does the Old Testament itself point to anything but the "fruit of the lips," as the peace-offering or thank-offering of gospel times? Is there a trace in the New Testament of any other mode of praise? *For my part, I am persuaded that if the organ be admitted, there is no barrier, in principle, against the sacerdotal system in all its fulness, — against the substitution again, in our whole religion, of the formal for the spiritual, the symbolical for the real!*

And then, remembering that this may offend Episcopalians, Dr. Candlish goes on offensively to say that the Church of England never attained light enough to reject the organ, and may therefore be permitted the use of a carnal contrivance which the more enlightened Presbyterians would be retrograding in taking up. A position at which the organ is retained, is wonderfully well for Southrons; but would be a wretched falling off in the followers of Cameron and Renwick.

Dr. Ritchie appears from his "Statement" to have been an enlightened and educated man, somewhat in advance of his age, and who had miscalculated the consequences of setting up the organ. The pear was not ripe; it is hardly so yet, after the lapse of fifty years. He adduces just such arguments in favor of instrumental music, as would present themselves to any English mind, modified somewhat by his knowledge of the prejudices of the tribunal he addressed. His statement is written with elegance, and temperately expressed. He sets out by stating that the use of instrumental music in worship has its foundation in the best feelings of human nature, prompting men to employ with reverence, according to the means they possess, all their powers in expressing gratitude to their Creator. This use cannot be traced in sacred history from the time of Moses down to that of David: but David not only employed instrumental music himself, but calls "on all nations, all the earth, to praise the Lord as he did, with psaltery, with harp, with organ, with the voice of a psalm." His psalms are constantly sung in Christian worship; "and can it be a sin to sing them, as was done by the original composer, with the accompaniment of an organ?" Christ never found fault with instrumental music, neither did Paul or John; the latter indeed tells us that he beheld in heaven "Harpers harping with their harps." During the earlier centuries, the persecutions to which Christians were exposed probably suffered no thought about a matter not essential: but the use of organs became general in the time of dawning light. At the Reformation it was felt that their use was no essential part of Popery; and thus it was retained by all the reformed churches, those of Luther and Calvin alike, except the Church of Scotland. Organs did not find favor in Scotland, because religious persecution had excited in that country a great horror of whatever had been used in popish or prelatical worship, as altars, crosses, organs. But although the organ was associated with Episcopacy, there is no necessary connection: —

> And in the use of an organ in church during public praise, I cannot, for my life, after long and serious attention to the subject, discover even an approach to any violation either of the purity or uniformity of our worship. For who will or can allege that an organ is an innovation upon the great object of worship? — we all, I trust, worship the one God, through the one Mediator. Or upon the subject of praise? — for we all sing the same psalms and paraphrases in the same language, all giving thanks for the same mercies. Or upon the posture of the worshippers? — for we all sit, as becomes Presbyterians. Or upon the tunes sung? — for we sing only such as are in general use. Or upon the office of the precentor? — for he still holds his rank, and employs the commanding tones of the organ for guiding the voices of the people. What, then, is it? It is a help, a support given to the precentor's voice, for enabling him more steadily, and with more dignity, to guide the voice of the congregation, and thus to preserve not only uniformity, but that unity of voice which is so becoming in the public service, which so pleasingly heightens devout feelings, and prevents that discord which so easily distracts the attention of the worshippers.

Such is an outline of Dr. Ritchie's argument. Our readers will, we doubt not, be curious to know what considerations, partaking of the nature of argument, can be adduced against the use of organs in church. Most people, we should think, would be more curious to know *this*, than to have arguments in favor of an usage for which common sense is authority sufficient. Now, had the committee of the Glasgow Presbytery assigned their true reason for rejecting the organ, it might have been very briefly set out: it was simply to be different from the Prelatists. A true-blue Presbyterian does not think of discussing the fitness of any observance on the ground of its own merits. He brings the matter to a shorter issue — viz.: Is it used in the Episcopal Church or is it not? If he goes beyond that, his final question would be, What did John Knox say about it? *His* infallibility is held in Scotland much more strongly and practically than the Pope's is in Italy. If any man in a Scotch Church Court should venture to impugn anything that ever was said by the Reformer, he would draw a perfect storm of indignation upon his own head. We repeat, there is no doctrine more decidedly held in Scotland than that of the infallibility of John Knox. Perhaps that of the impeccability of Calvin should be regarded as a companion doctrine. *His* vagaries as to the Sabbath preclude his reception as infallible. We have seen a paper by an eminent minister of a Scotch dissenting "body," whose purpose was to prove that Calvin was right in burning Servetus. The argument, so far as we could make it out, appeared to be that Calvin's doing so was right, because Calvin did it. Of course, had Servetus burned Calvin, it would have been quite a different thing.

As for the reply to Dr. Ritchie's Statement (which was drawn up by a certain Dr. Porteous), we shall at once say of it that it appears to us characterized by ignorance, stupidity, and vulgarity, in the very highest degree. Dr. Ritchie's paper dealt with broad principles: *this* is mainly employed in paltry personalities and misrepresentations. Its style bristles with such descriptions of instrumental music as "will-worship," "superstitious rites," "converting a church into a concert-room," "an organ *tickling* the ear of the audience" (the italics are the writer's own), "the puerile amusement of pipes and organs," &c. We shall endeavor to pick out from this very tedious lucubration whatever it contains in the nature of argument; and we believe that our readers will agree with us that the mere statement of the following objections to the organ is sufficient refutation of them. We give our references, lest we should be suspected of caricaturing Dr. Porteous's argument: —

1. Instrumental music in the worship of God is as much part of the Jewish system as circumcision: therefore, if circumcision be abolished, so is the organ. (pp. 86–7.) Instrumental music was essentially connected with sacrifice; and as sacrifice was abolished by Christ's death, so was instrumental music abolished. (pp. 87–8.) The New Testament, by prescribing a new way of worshipping God, — to wit, by singing psalms, hymns, and spiritual songs, — is to be understood as abolishing the old way, by instrumental music. (p. 91.) St. Paul, far from commending instrumental music, speaks of it with contempt — If I "have not charity, I am become as sounding brass or a tinkling cymbal." (p. 96.) True, harps are spoken of by St. John as in heaven; but St. John was drawing on his recollection of the Temple service, and is not to be literally understood. (pp. 97–8.) So much for the argument from Scripture.

2. The Christians of the early centuries would have had organs, had it been right to have them. As they had them not, "it is evident that they considered it unlawful to employ instrumental music in the worship of God. Both Arians and orthodox would have regarded themselves as returning back to Judaism, if they had permitted it in their public worship." (p. 108.) We are surprised to find the Fathers quoted by a Presbyterian clergyman, but in this case they make in favor of his views. Justin Martyr says, "Plain singing is not childish, but only the singing with lifeless organs: whence

the use of such instruments, and other things fit for children, is laid aside." (pp. 109–10.) Basil speaks of organs as "the inventions of Jubal, of the race of Cain." (p. 111.) Chrysostom says that instrumental music "was only permitted to the Jews for the imbecility and grossness of their souls: but now, instead of organs, Christians must use the body to praise God." (p. 112.) Jerome and Augustine speak in a similar strain. Thomas Aquinas, in the Schoolman age, says, "In the old law, God was praised both with musical instruments and human voices. But the Church does not use musical instruments to praise God, lest she should seem to judaize." (p. 115). And we are told, on the authority of Eckhard, that Luther (among other foolish things which he said) said that "*organs were among the ensigns of Baal!*" (p. 119.) There is no doubt that Calvin declared that "Instrumental music is not fitter to be adopted into the public worship of the Christian Church than the incense, the candlesticks, and the other shadows of the Mosaic law." (p. 121.) Our reply to all this is, that the Fathers, Schoolmen, and Reformers, might fall into error: if the question is to be decided by authority, we could adduce a thousand authorities in favor of the organ for every one against it; these eminent men had no other grounds for forming their opinion than are patent to us, and it seems manifest to common sense that neither in reason nor Scripture are there any grounds to support the opinions they express. We appeal to the common sense of mankind, even from the judgment of Chrysostom, Aquinas, Luther, and Calvin.

3. Dr. Porteous's next argument against the organ is, that the Fathers of the Scotch Church "regarded instrumental music as the offspring of Judaism, and abhorred

it as a relic of Popery, and too intimately connected with that prelatic form which our forefathers never could endure." (p. 132.) "It has been allowed by authors, foreign and domestic, that the genius of the Scotch people is much more musical than that either of the English, the Dutch, or the French. But the people of Scotland abhor the blending of the inventions of man with the worship of God. They conceive instrumental music inconsistent with the purity of a New Testament Church." (p. 134.) Then "Knox and Melville, Rutherford and Henderson, offer not one word in behalf of the organ. They allow it to perish unnoticed, as a portion of that trumpery which ignorance and superstition had foisted into the house of God." (p. 140.) "The fixed, determined opposition to instrumental music" among the Scotch Reformers "ariseth from *legal*, *political*, *moral*, and *Scriptural* grounds." (p. 140.) We admit at once that the founders of the Scotch Church had an inveterate dislike for the organ; but as they give us no reason for their dislike, except the fact that the organ had been employed in prelatic worship, and the utterly groundless assertion that instrumental music was a purely Jewish observance, we cannot regard their dislike otherwise than as an irrational prejudice. The argument from Knox's opinion may be a very good one where men believe the infallibility of Knox, but with us it has no weight whatever. We regard ourselves quite as competent to form an opinion in this matter as Knox; and the argument from mere authority will not do in a case where the authorities quoted have no special weight, and are in a minority of one to a hundred.

4. The next argument is addressed exclusive to persons belonging to the Church of Scotland. At the Re-

volution, "Prelacy was for ever abolished in Scotland;" and the organ is part of Prelacy. (pp. 144–5.) The people, at all events, regarded it as such. (p. 145.) And when it was stipulated at the union of the two kingdoms, that the established worship should continue, it was understood on all hands that this stipulation excluded instrumental music. (pp. 150–161.) Every clergyman at his ordination subscribes a formula, in which he "sincerely owns the purity of worship presently authorized and practised in this Church, and that he will constantly adhere to the same; and that he will neither directly nor indirectly endeavor the prejudice and subversion thereof." (p. 162.) But this purity of worship is destroyed by introducing an organ; for "by blending instrumental music with the human voice, the simple melody of our forefathers becomes immediately changed into a medley, composed of animate and inanimate objects." (p. 165.)

We do not think any comment is needful upon all this. We give another passage, which we presume is intended for an argument: —

> Man being a reasonable creature, and a reasonable service being demanded from him by God, that reasonable service cannot so properly be performed by man as when he useth his voice alone. This is the vehicle which God hath given him to convey to his Maker the emotions of his soul. Musical instruments may indeed tickle the ear and please the fancy of fallen man. But is God to be likened to fallen man? Organs are the mere invention of man, played often by hirelings, who, while they modulate certain sounds, may possess a heart cold and hard as the nether mill-stone. You may, if you please, style such music the will-worship of the organist; but you surely cannot, in common sense, denominate it the praise of devout worshippers, singing with grace, and making melody to the Lord in the heart.

The only passage in Dr. Porteous's argument which appears to us to partake of the nature of discussion *on the merits* of the question, is the following vulgarity: —

> Your committee have heard your *amateurs* and *dilettanti* assert that their nerves have been completely overcome with the powerful tones of the organ, and the sublime *crash* of instrumental music in the oratorios of Handel. Your committee are willing to allow this musical effect; but they believe, at the same time, that all the musical instruments that ever were used can never produce upon the devout and contemplative mind that sublime and pathetic effect which the well regulated voice of 8000 children produced, when singing the praises of God in the cathedral of St. Paul's, upon the recovery of our good old religious king. Away, then, with the cant of an organ's being so wonderfully calculated to increase the devotion of Christians! Your committee have sometimes had an opportunity of listening to instrumental music, in what is styled cathedral worship. It might for a little time please and surprise by its novelty; the effect, however, was very transitory, and sometimes produced ideas in the mind very different from devotion. Your committee believe that when the praises of God are sung by every individual, even of an unlettered country congregation, the effect is much more noble, and much more salutary to the mind of a Christian audience, than all the lofty artificial strains of an organ, extracted by a hired organist, and accompanied by a confused noise of many voices, taught at great expense to chant over what their hearts neither feel, nor their heads understand.

Now, as it appears to us, this passage is the only one in Dr. Porteous's long treatise which touches the merits of "the organ question." Here he fairly joins issue with the supporters of the organ on the question whether the use of that instrument does or does not render God's praise more solemn and affecting. He maintains that it does not. On the strongest of all evidence, our own experience, we maintain that it does. And we have no higher court to appeal to. We are just brought back to the principle with which we set out — the existence of two sorts or species of human constitution essentially different by nature. Dr. Porteous was a born Presbyterian. We are not. And we can but comfort ourselves with the belief that were the educated population of Christendom polled, we should be in a majority of ten thousand to one. We make bold to say, that were you to poll the educated people of Scotland, we should have a hundred to one in our favor.

It will amuse our readers to know that this enlightened clergyman, in closing his argument, bestows a parting kick upon the idolatrous organ, by reminding us that we read in the Book of Job, that the wicked of those days "took the timbrel and the harp, and *rejoiced at the sound of the organ*." (*Job*, ch. xxi. v. 14, 15, p. 188.) And when Nebuchadnezzar erected his golden image, the signal for its worship was "the sound of the cornet, flute, harp, sackbut, psaltery, dulcimer, and all kinds of music." (*Daniel*, ch. iii. v. 3, p. 189.) What on earth can we say to the man who could seriously write this?

We have thus set forth Dr. Porteous's argument against the organ, an argument which Dr. Candlish tells us, "impressed him, when he first studied it, with the sort of sense of completeness which a satisfactory demonstration gives; and a recent perusal has not lowered his opinion of it." (p. 30.) For ourselves, it has impressed us with absolute wonder to think that any reasonable man could have written a treatise so filled with bigotry and absurdity. We could not think of setting ourselves to answer arguments whose folly is apparent on the first glance at them; indeed, our fear is, that our readers may fancy we have intentionally caricatured them, and we beg to tender the assurance that we have set them out with scrupulous fairness. We lament to see that minds naturally powerful and candid can be cramped and cribbed by gloomy prejudices to the extent exemplified in Drs. Porteous and Candlish, and we confidently make our appeal from them to the common sense of the people of Scotland. The great mass of educated Scotch people is fast becoming extricated from the vulgar prejudice against the organ. In every circle of polished society, the wish may be heard for its introduction, on the broad ground that it would be a great improvement, and that there is no reason whatever against it, except the prejudice of the first Scotch reformers against everything which had been used in popish or prelatic worship. The feeling is gaining ground in Scotland that this spirit of mere contrariety was allowed to go to a most unreasonable length. The spirit of the Covenanters was, "Never mind if kneeling be the natural posture of prayer, and the one we ourselves always adopt in private; the Prelatists kneel in church, and therefore we shall stand. Never mind if the very necessity of using the lungs points to standing as the attitude for singing God's praise; the Prelatists stand, so we shall sit." And there can be no question that the educated classes in Scotland, in laying aside the spirit of pure contrariety to Episcopacy, and looking at observances and estimating them by their own merits, *are* in so far departing from the true Presbyterian principle; if we are to understand by *that* the principle of the gloomy fanatics who signed the Solemn League and Covenant, and thereby undertook to "endeavor the extirpation of Popery, Prelacy, superstition, heresy, schism, and profaneness."[1] No doubt the "Cameronians" and "Original Seceders" of Scotland at the present day, are a great deal more like the Covenanters than is the Church of Scotland. Holding that for many reasons Presbytery is the best form of church-government for Scotland, the great ma-

[1] *Solemn League and Covenant*, Section II.

jority of the clergy of the Scotch Church are equally persuaded that Episcopacy is the best form of church-government for England. And very many of the most influential among the elders of the Church of Scotland, say at once that they are Presbyterians in Scotland and Episcopalians in England. It would indeed be a wretched thing, if in days not over-friendly to ecclesiastical establishments, the Churches of England and Scotland, maintaining precisely the same doctrines, and differing solely in the non-essential of church-government, should ever cherish other than a spirit of mutual kindness and mutual support.

At the same time, it will take another century of railway communication and intercourse with England to rub off the horror of Prelacy and all its belongings which exists among the humble classes — at least, in country-places. A cross over the gable of a church, or a window of stained glass, must still be introduced, in country-parishes, with great caution. We observe from a Scotch newspaper, that a country clergyman, within the last six months, introduced a choir of trained singers into his church, in the hope of improving the psalmody. Whenever the choir began the psalm, most of the congregation closed their books, and refused to join in the singing, and many rose and left the church. A choir was introduced in the parish church of a considerable town in the north of Scotland. Some of the people listened in wonder to its first notes, and then hurried out to escape the profanation, exclaiming, " They'll be bringing o'er the Pope next ! " If a country minister wishes his *precentor* or clerk to appear in a gown and a white neckcloth, instead of entering the desk in a sky-blue coat and scarlet waistcoat, some of his parishioners are sure to trace in the arrangement an undue leaning towards Episcopacy. The minister of a remote parish was presented with a pulpit gown by his people. The people naturally expected to see it next Sunday, and a larger congregation came to see the gown than would have assembled to hear the sermon. The minister, however, wore no gown. Some of the chief contributors to its expense called at the manse, to express the hope of the parish that the gown might be worn.

"I cannot wear it," said the minister; "it is too large for me."

"Too large!" was the reply; "it fits elegantly."

Upon which the enlightened and cultivated gentleman answered —

"No, it is far too large: the tail of it reaches a' the way to Rome!"

No doubt this man would have judged an organ a blasphemous, Satanic, Jewish, Popish, and Prelatic device. But we do not believe that at the present day such a person could be found among the clergy of the farthest presbytery of the Hebrides.

We do not think that the time has come for the general introduction of the organ in Scotland. There is no use in running in the face of the prejudices of a whole people; and while the opponents of the organ regard the question as one of principle, its supporters cannot regard the organ as more than a luxury. It is a step in advance that there should be in Scotland such a thing as "The Organ Question." The matter is now in debate: at one time the Presbyterian who raised it would have been knocked on the head. With the increasing enlightenment of the age, and the rapid communication that now exists between this country and

Scotland, it is a mere matter of time till the organ shall be employed wherever its expense can be afforded. It would be highly inexpedient to press it upon the people now. It would retard the period of its general reception. All that can be looked for at present is, that permission should be granted to each congregation to act upon its own judgment in the matter of the organ. It will be introduced first in the churches in the fashionable parts of Edinburgh and Glasgow, next in country parishes where the squire has been educated at Oxford, and ultimately, we doubt not, it will excite as little wonder in Scotland as it does in England now. The tide is flowing surely. But we shall not live to see that time.

Half-material beings as we are, and often the worse for the material things which surround us — which by their very solidity make spiritual things seem shadowy and unreal in the comparison — it is well when we can make (so to speak) a reprisal on the hostile territory, and get a material thing to conduce to our spiritual advantage. We cannot but think that in all the reasonings of ultra-Presbyterians on the immorality of organs, there is woven a thread of the old Gnostic heresy of the essential evil of matter; as though the same God who made our spirits capable of being impressed, had not made the material sights and sounds which are capable of impressing them. We are not afraid to argue "The Organ Question" with Dr. Candlish on the highest and farthest-reaching grounds, though we think it quite sufficiently decided by the ready appeal to common sense. But what greater harm is there in using the organ's notes to waken pious thought and feeling, than in learning a lesson of our decay from the material emblem of the fading leaf, or from the lapse of the passing river? If it be not wrong to avail ourselves of the natural pensiveness of the departing light, and to go forth like Isaac in the eventide to meditate upon our most solemn concerns, — why is it sinful or degrading to turn to use the native power which the Creator has set in the organ's tones to stir tender and holy emotion? When we *can* get the Material to yield us any impulse upward, in God's name let us take its aid and be thankful! And as Dr. Candlish likes authorities, we shall conclude with a better authority than that of Dr. Porteous. *He* tells us that the organ may " tickle the ear," but denies its power to touch the heart. Milton thought otherwise: and we believe that *his* words describe the normal influence of the organ on the healthy human mind: —

But let my due feet never fail
To walk the studious cloister's pale;
And love the high embowered roof,
With antique pillars massy proof,
And storied windows richly dight,
Casting a dim religious light;
There let the pealing organ blow
To the full-voiced quire below,
In service high and anthems clear,
As may with sweetness, through mine ear,
Dissolve me into ecstasies,
And bring all heaven before mine eyes.

CHAPTER XI.

THORNDALE; OR, THE CONFLICT OF OPINIONS.[1]

AUTHORS, moral and political, have of late years been recognizing the fact, that abstract truths become much more generally attractive when something of human interest is added to them. Most people feel as if thoughts and opinions gain a more substantial being, and lose their ghost-like intangibility, when we know something of the character and history of the man who entertained them, and something of the outward scenery amid which he entertained them. Very many persons feel as if, in passing from fact, or what purports to be fact, to principle, they were exchanging the firm footing of solid land for the yielding and impalpable air; and a framework of scenes and persons is like a wing to buoy them up in traversing that unaccustomed medium. And there are few indeed to whom a peculiar interest does not result when views and opinions, instead of standing nakedly on the printed page, are stated and discussed in friendly council by individual men, seated upon a real grassy slope, canopied by substantial trees, and commanding a prospect of real hills, and streams, and valleys. It is not entirely true that argument has its weight and force in

[1] *Thorndale; or, the Conflict of Opinions.* By William Smith. Edinburgh: Blackwoods. 1857.

itself, quite apart from its author. In the matter of practical effect, on actual human beings, a good deal depends on the lips it comes from.

The author of "Thorndale" has recognized and acted upon this principle. Mr. William Smith is a philosopher and a poet, as the readers of his tragedy, "Athelwold," are already aware; and whoever sits down to read his new book as an ordinary work of fiction to be hurried through for its plot-interest, will probably not turn many pages before closing the volume. The great purpose of the work is to set out a variety of opinions upon several matters which concern the highest interests of the individual man and of the human race; but instead of presenting them in naked abstractness, Mr. Smith has *set* them in a slight story, and given them as the tenets or the fancies of different men, whose characters are so drawn that these tenets and fancies appear to be just their natural culmination and result. If we were disposed to be hypercritical, we might say that the different characters sketched by Mr. Smith are too plainly built up to serve as the *substrata* of the opinions which they express. There is hardly allowance enough made for the waywardness and inconsistency of human conclusion and action. Given any one of Mr. Smith's men in certain circumstances, and we are only too sure of what he will do or say. The Utopian is always hopeful; the desponding philosopher is never brightened up by a ray of hope. But this, it is obvious, is a result arrived at upon system; for we shall find abundant proof in the volume that Mr. Smith has read deeply and accurately into human nature, in all its weaknesses, fancies, hopes, and fears. It is long since we have met with a more remarkable or worthy book. Mr. Smith is always thoughtful and suggestive: he has been entirely successful in carrying out his wish to produce a volume in reading which a thoughtful man will often pause with his finger between the leaves, and muse upon what he has read. We judge that the book must have been written slowly, and at intervals, from its affluence of beautiful thought. No mind could have turned off such material with the equable flow of a stream. We know few works in which there may be found so many fine thoughts, light-bringing illustrations, and happy turns of expression, to invite the reader's pencil. A delicate refinement, a simple and pathetic eloquence, a kindly sympathy with all sentient things, are everywhere apparent: but the construction of the book, in which the most opposite opinions are expressed by the different characters without the least editorial comment, approval or disapproval, renders it difficult to judge what are truly the opinions of the author himself. Mr. Smith's English style is of classic beauty: nothing can surpass the delicate grace and finish of many passages of description and reflection; and although it was of course impossible, and indeed not desirable, that equal pains should be bestowed upon the melody of all the pages of the book, still the language is never slovenly; the hand of the tasteful scholar is everywhere. Nor should we fail to remark the author's versatility of power. Everything he does is done with equal ease and felicity: — description of external nature, analysis of feeling and motive, close logic, large views of men and things. There is not the gentle and graceful humor of Mr. Helps: the book is serious throughout, with no infusion of playfulness. The author evidently thinks that in this world there is not much to smile at, — unless it be at everything. Let us remark, that in this volume the characters come and go as in real life. There is nothing of the novel's artificial working up of interest, deepening to the close. Mr. Smith may say of his book, as Mr. Bailey of his grand but unequal poem: —

"It has a plan, but no plot: — Life has none."

But Mr. Smith's men, after all, are not such as one commonly meets. They are all greatly occupied, and for the most part perplexed and distressed about speculative and social difficulties. Now in ordinary life such distresses are little felt. Are we wrong in saying that they are never felt at all, except in idleness; — or by minds far above the average of the race? How little are the perplexities of speculation to the busy man, anxious and toiling to find the means of maintaining his wife and children, of paying his Christmas bills, and generally of making the ends meet at the close of the year! *That*, whether we admit the fact or deny it, is, with the great majority even of cultivated men, the practical problem of life. And indeed it is sad to think how, long before middle age, in many a man who started with higher aspirations, *that* becomes the great end of labor and of thought. But it seems to be a law of mind, that as the grosser and more material wants are supplied, other wants of a more ethereal and fanciful nature come to be felt. And thus perhaps many a man, whom circumstances now compel to bestow all his energies on the quest of the supply of the day that is passing over him and his, is by those very circumstances saved from feeling wants more crushing, and from grappling with riddles and mysteries that sit with a heavy perplexity upon the heart. Let us be thankful if we are not too independent of work: let us be thankful that we are not too thoughtful and able.

Mr. Smith's book sets out with a charming description of a secluded dwelling to which a young philosophic thinker, smitten by consumption, had retired to die. On a little terrace, near the summit of Mount Posilipo, there stands a retired villa, looking from that height over the Bay of Naples. Overlooked by none, it commands a wide extent of view. Myrtle and roses have overgrown its pillared front. The rock descends sheer down from the terrace. Charles Thorndale, the hero of the book, had been charmed by the *Villa Scarpa* in the course of a continental tour, made while still in health; and when stricken with the disease of which he died, and when the physicians spoke of the climate of Italy, he chose this for his last retreat. It would not be long he would be there, he knew; and in its quiet he had much to think of.

It is a spot, one would say, in which it would be very hard to part with this divine faculty of thought. It seems made for the very spirit of meditation. The little platform on which the villa stands is so situated, that, while it commands the most extensive prospect imaginable, it is itself entirely sheltered from observation. No house of any kind overlooks it; from no road is it visible; not a sound from the neighboring city ascends to it. From one part of the parapet that bounds the terrace you may sometimes catch sight of a swarthy, bare-legged fisherman, sauntering on the beach, or lying at full length in the sun. It is the only specimen of humanity you are likely to behold: you live solely in the eye of nature. It is with difficulty you can believe that within the space of an hour you may, if you choose it, be elbowing your way, jostled and stunned, amongst the swarming population of Naples — surely the noisest hive of human beings anywhere to be found on the face of the earth. Here, on these heights, is perfect stillness, with perfect beauty. What voices come to you from the upper air — the winds and the melody of birds; and not unfrequently the graceful sea-gull utters its short, plaintive cry, as it wheels round and back to its own ocean-fields. And then that glorious silent picture for ever open to the eye! Picture! you hastily retract the word. It is no dead picture; it is the living spirit of the universe manifesting itself, in glorious vision, to the eye and the soul of man.

Thorndale was a studious man, but had not been attracted by either of the learned professions. His modest competency relieved him from the necessity of choosing a decided path in life. Like many meditative idlers, he intended, vaguely, to write a book; and, indeed, he did finish a philosophical treatise more than once; but he always became dissatisfied with it and destroyed it. But in his retirement at Villa Scarpa, a large manuscript volume lay on his table, in which, "the habit of the pen" clinging to him to the last, he was accustomed to write down his thoughts upon whatever topic interested him for the time. This book was autobiography, essay, diary, record of former conversations with friends, as the humor of the moment prompted; and we are invited to believe that this book, having fallen into the hands of Mr. Smith, is now given to the world: —

> It is precisely this manuscript volume, note-book, memoir, diary, whatever it should be called, which we have to present to the reader. In it, Thorndale, though apparently with little of set purpose or design, gives us a description of himself and of several friends, or rather sketches out their opinions and modes of thinking. Amongst these two may be at once particularly mentioned: *Clarence*, who might be called a representative of the philosophy of hope; and *Seckendorf*, his complete contrast, and who, especially on the subject of human progress, takes the side of denial or of cavil.

The author, or editor, sets before us the character of his hero, less by one complete description, than by many touches, given here and there, as he exhibits Thorndale to us in various combinations of circumstances, and at several critical points in his life. Our impression of Thorndale is being retouched, modified, lightened, and shadowed, on to the close of the book. He was a meditative and melancholy man, of little pith or active energy: he was shy and retiring; overshadowed by a settled despondency; but always kind and gentle, with no trace of fret fulness or irritability. Although his character is an interesting and truthful one, it is essentially morbid; and we may be glad that men like him must always be few. We should have no railroads, no Great Easterns, no ocean telegraphs, in a world peopled by Thorndales. The weakly physical constitution which he bore from birth, had much to do with the tone of his thought and feeling. The remark is in the main just and sound, though it was made by Boswell: —

The truth is, that we judge of the happiness and misery of life differently at different times, according to the state of our changeable frame. I always remember a remark made to me by a Turkish lady educated in France: *Ma foi, monsieur, notre bonheur dépend de la façon que notre sang circule.*

Nor ought we to forget that deeply philosophic remark of Sydney Smith, that little stoppages in the bodily circulation are the things which, above all others, darken our views of life and of man. A friend, said the genial physiologist, comes to him in a most depressed condition. He declares that his affairs are getting embarrassed; that he must retrench his establishment and retire to the country; that his daughter's cough has settled upon the lungs; that his wife is breaking up, and his son going to the mischief. But Sydney only asks on what he supped the evening before; and finds that he then partook of lobster to an undue degree. "All this," he says, "all these gloomy views are the lobster." Instead of seeking directly to minister to a mind diseased, he does so indirectly, but not the less effectually. He suggests medicine, not philosophy. And next day the world is a capital world, after all; the income is ample, the cough is gone, the wife is in rude health, and the son all that a father's heart could wish. Now in the case of Thorndale, there was an entire deficiency of healthy animalism; and if, as a Scotch divine lately declared in a sermon published by royal command, it is easier for a camel to go through the eye of a needle than for a dyspeptic man to be kind, gentle, and long-suffering; not less true is it that a well-knit, vigorous, sinewy mind, is oftentimes trammelled and hampered all through life, by being linked to a weakly, puny, jaded body. How much of Sydney Smith's wit, how much of Christopher North's reckless abandonment of glee, was the result of physical organization! How incomprehensible to many men must such despondency as Thorndale's seem! No worldly wants or anxieties, no burden of remorse, kind friends around him, what right had he to be unhappy?[1] Thorndale, in short, is a less energetic and passionate form of the nameless hero of *Maud.* Shall we confess that a less happy association at certain points in his history suggested itself to our mind? We thought of Mr. Augustus Moddle, of whom his historian records as follows: —

> He often informed Mrs. Todgers that the sun had set upon him; that the billows had rolled over him; that the car of Juggernaut had crushed him; and also that the deadly upas tree of Java had blighted him.[2]

Young men, who at five-and-twenty profess that they have lost all interest in life, and that they have done with time, are by no means uncommon. But Byron's influ-

[1] We remember a review of *Maud* which we read in a certain provincial journal. The writer evidently thought the gloomy hero an ungrateful and querulous fellow for making such a moan. "Why," said the reviewer, "the man was in very comfortable circumstances: he was able to have two servants ('*I keep but a man and a maid*'): and what earthly right had he to be always grumbling? If a man has two servants, ought he not to be content?"

[2] Dickens's *Martin Chuzzlewit.*

ence is wearing out; and they are pretty generally laughed at. Yet where a lad at college can say sincerely, as Thorndale said —

> For me, there was more excitement to be got out of any dingy book, thumbed over by a solitary rushlight, than from fifty ball-rooms —

his mind is taking a morbid growth, which bodes no good to himself; nor are things better when he goes on a tour to the Cumberland lakes, and instead of cheerfully enjoying the scenes around him, goes on as follows: —

> Forgetful of lake and mountain, my eyes fixed perhaps on the topmost bar of some roadside gate which I had *intended* to open, or pausing stock-still before some hedgerow in the solitary lane, apparently intent upon the buds of the hawthorn, as if I were penetrating into the very secrets of vegetable life, I have stood for hours musing on the intricate problems which our social condition presents to us.

We need not say that such a man is out of his place in England in the nineteenth century. In this age we want, not visionaries, but actors; healthy, robust men, like Arnold, who can think and reason, and who can likewise walk five miles in the hour. Perhaps, indeed, the cry for "muscular Christianity" is passing into cant; and we know of noble minds which, notwithstanding the clog of physical debility and suffering, bear a kindly sympathy towards all mankind, and make the race their debtors for the gift of elevating thoughts. But as for Thorndale — sensitive as the mimosa, ever watching with introverted eye the lights and shadows of his own mind — how could he be happy? A certain amount of insensibility is in this world needful to that. We must not bear a nervous system so delicately appreciative of external influences as to keep us ever on the flutter or on the rack. Above all, let us have the equable mind, though it should live in a light which is uniformly subdued, rather than that which is ever alternating between April sunshine and April gloom. Justly and thoughtfully did Wordsworth make this equanimity a marked characteristic of the happiness of a higher life: —

> He spake of love, such love as spirits feel,
> In worlds whose course is equable and pure:
> No fears to beat away, no strife to heal,
> The past unsighed for, and the future sure:
> Spake of heroic arts in graver mood
> Revived, with finer harmony pursued.[1]

We may have faults to find with the character of Thorndale, regarded as that of a representative man: but we feel at once with what delicate accuracy the author maintains its keeping. From first to last, he never speaks or acts otherwise than he ought, under the given conditions. The malady that killed him had marked him from his birth; and he is always the same kindly, tender-hearted, meditative, unenergetic, spiritless being. Mr. Smith shows us the whole man by one happy touch. Thorndale had chosen the shores of Loch Lomond as his autumn retreat one year. He had been there only a day, when he suddenly resolved that he would return and seek the hand of a gentle cousin whom he loved, and who appears not to have been indifferent to him. He had hitherto kept silence, because her worldly position was higher than his own. He left Loch Lomond on the instant; he travelled on day and night; he seemed never to have drawn breath till he stood at the gate of the shrubbery that surrounded Sutton Manor, her home and his: —

Then indeed I paused. Leaning on the half-opened gate, I saw again my own position in its true and natural light. Was it not al-

[1] *Laodamia.*

ways known and understood that *such a thing was not to be?* One after the other, all my fallacious reasonings deserted me. What madness could have brought me there? I hoped no one had seen me. Slowly and softly the half-opened gate was closed again. I walked away, retracing my steps as unobserved as possible through the village.

Here was Thorndale himself. Like most thoughtful men, he had much of the irresolution of Hamlet, — the irresolution that comes of thinking too much. There can be no doubt that in order to act slap-dash, with promptness and decision, it is best not to see a case in all its bearings. It is best to see one side clearly and strongly: — and then no lurking irresolution will retard the arm in its descent. Here was the secret of poor Thorndale's creeping away, with a sinking heart, from the only presence he cared for in this world. There is not invariable truth in the lines of Montrose, —

He either fears his fate too much,
  Or his desert is small,
Who dares not put it to the touch,
  And win or lose it all.

We need not relate how the author explains his chancing upon Villa Scarpa in wandering about Naples. The villa was then deserted; all was over. We have no particulars recorded of Thorndale's death. We confess we feel in this omission something of cruelty on the author's part towards his hero. There is something pitiful in the story of the neglected manuscript-volume, found after the poor visionary was gone, hidden away in the roof of the abandoned house; and in the picture which rises before us of the tender-hearted youth, lying down to die alone. He had a kind servant, indeed; and an old friend, with his little adopted daughter, who reappeared as evening was darkening down, may be supposed to have tended and soothed the last agony. But Mr. Smith, in his careful avoidance of whatever might seem a clap-trap expedient to excite interest and feeling, is entirely silent as to the close. However, he chanced on the deserted Villa Scarpa: he found a despatch-box, bearing the name of Charles Thorndale, whom he had known, though not intimately. This despatch-box contained the manuscript volume already mentioned, which Thorndale seemed to have bequeathed to the first finder and the good-natured Italian to whom the villa belonged, willingly gave up box and manuscript to one who said he had been Thorndale's friend. We quote a single sentence, for its graceful beauty, from the picture of Thorndale called up to the mind's eye of his editor, on thus chancing on his last retreat: —

> His eye was not that of which it is so often said that it looks through you, for it rather seemed to be looking out beyond you. The object at which it gazed became the half-forgotten centre round which the eddying stream of thought was flowing; and you stood there, like some islet in a river which is encircled on all sides by the swift and silent flood.

The manuscript volume now published has been divided by its editor into five books, and each of these into several chapters. Book I. is called "The Last Retreat:" it is given to many reflections, mostly thrown out with little arrangement, upon the Sentiment of Beauty, and upon the two Futurities, the one on this side and the other beyond the grave. In Book II., which is called "The Retrospect," the current of thought has set away into the past; and we have an autobiographical sketch. Book III., called "Cyril, or the Modern Cistercian," gives an account of the conflict of thought by which a companion passed from an Evangelical Anglican to a

Roman Catholic monk. Book IV., "Seckendorf, or the Spirit of Denial," sketches the character and views of a friend who cavilled at the possibility of all human progress. In Book V., "Clarence, or the Utopian," we first read how, as strength and life had well-nigh ebbed away, Thorndale met once more with an old friend of hopeful views, who seems to have stayed by him to the last: and when Thorndale's weak hand had laid down the pen for the last time, Clarence wrote out, in the last two hundred pages of the volume, his *Confessio Fidei*; — a connected view of his theory of man, the growth of the individual consciousness, and the development of the human race.

The earlier part of the book is very desultory; and the book as a whole appeals to a limited class of readers. There will never be a rush for it to the book-club in the county town. Young-lady readers will for the most part vote it a bore; and solid old gentlemen of bread-and-butter intellect will judge Thorndale and his friends a crew of morbid dreamers, — though the book, amid sublimer speculations, sets out here and there much common sense on the affairs of practical life. But we trust that Mr. Smith may find an audience fit, and not so few. It elevates and refines the mind to hold converse with an author of his stamp. And how much the world must have gone through before such a character as Thorndale's became possible! No appliance of modern luxury, no contrivance of modern science, says so much as the conception of such a character for the civilization and artificiality of our modern life. Although the book is mainly dissertational, the reader will find in it much exquisite narrative, and much skilful delineation of character, in the history of the hero and his friends, their views and fates. Yet, while we cordially acknowledge in Mr. Smith a man of refined and pathetic genius, we should not be doing justice to ourselves if we did not say, that in all the views of life and society, whether hopeful or desponding, which are set out in the book, we have felt strongly a great blank and void. We believe, and we humbly hope we shall never cease believing, that Christianity shows us the true stand-point from which to look at man, and the true lever by which to elevate him. We believe that the same influence which has raised our hopes to "life and immortality," must and will elevate and purify this mortal life. We believe that it is false philosophy to ignore the existence, power, and teaching of the Christian faith; and to take pains, before looking into the framework and the prospects of society, to exclude the only light which can search out the dark recesses, and dissipate the gloom that hangs before. Why should a man persist in wading through Chat Moss on a drenching December day, when the means are provided of flitting over it, light and warm and dry? Why should we go up to Box-hill, and declare we shall dig our way through it with our own nails and fingers (being in haste); when we know that it has been nobly tunnelled for us already?

The first book, entitled "The Last Retreat," consists of disjointed fragments of thought, cast upon the page with little effort at arrangement. *All* these fragments are well worthy of preservation: many of them are of striking originality and force. The dying man becomes aware that a peculiar beauty has been added to the beautiful scenes around him by the close approach of death. He says, —

I owe to death half the beauty of this scene, and altogether owe to him the constant serenity with which I gaze upon it. . . . Strange! how the beauty and mystery of all nature is heightened by the near prospect of that coming darkness which will sweep it all away! — that night which will have no star in it! These heavens, with all their glories, will soon be blotted out for me. The eye, and that which is behind the eye will soon close, soon rest, and there will be no more beauty, no more mystery for me. . . . What an air of freshness, of novelty, and surprise, does each old and familiar object assume to me when I think of parting with it for ever!

There is no more of ennui *now*. Time is too short, and this world too wonderful. Everything I behold is new and strange. If a dog looks up at me in the face, I startle at *his* intelligence. "I am in a foreign land," you say. True, all the world has become foreign land to me. I am perpetually on a voyage of discovery.

Very true, very real, is this feeling, drawn from the much-suggesting Νυξ γαρ ερχεται! We really do enjoy things intensely, because we know we are not to have them long. And how well does experience certify that the most familiar scene grows new and strange to us when we are forthwith to leave it. The room in which we have sat day by day for years, — rise to quit it for the last time, and we shall see something about its proportions, its aspect, that we never saw before. The little walk we have paced hundreds of times, — how different every evergreen beside it will seem, when we pace it silently, knowing that we shall do so no more!

Here is an apt and happy comparison: —

When the lofty and barren mountain, says a legend I have somewhere read, was first upheaved into the sky, and from its elevation looked down on the plains below, and saw the valley and the less elevated hills covered with verdure and fruitful trees, it sent up to Brahma something like a murmur of complaint, "Why thus barren? Why these scarred and naked sides exposed to the eye of man?" And Brahma answered, "The very light shall clothe thee, and the shadow of the passing cloud shall be as a royal mantle. More verdure would be less light. Thou shalt share in the azure of heaven, and the youngest and whitest cloud of a summer day shall nestle in thy bosom. Thou belongest half to us."

So was the mountain dowered. And so too have the loftiest minds of men been in all ages dowered. To lower elevations have been given the pleasant verdure, the vine, and the olive. Light, light alone, and the deep shadow of the passing cloud, — these are the gifts of the prophets of the race.

Thorndale felt strongly what every reflective man must feel, that the ordinary arguments for the immortality of the soul, drawn from the light of nature, are quite insufficient and unsatisfactory. It is upon entirely different grounds, and these grounds partaking often but little of the nature of argument, that the belief in the doctrine really rests. Still the argument fills the page; and is appended to the doctrine much as in cheap Gothic buildings a buttress is added to a wall which does not need its support, because it at least looks as if it supported the wall. Thorndale's illustration is this: —

In old wood-cuts one sometimes sees a vessel in full sail upon the ocean, and perched aloft upon the clouds are a number of infant cherubs, with puffed-out cheeks, blowing at the sails. The swelling canvas is evidently filled by a stronger wind than these infant cherubs, sitting in the clouds, could supply. They do not fill the sail; but they were thought to fill up the picture prettily enough.

In truth, the usual arguments for immortality are quite futile: none more so than that founded upon the immateriality of the soul. The soul's immateriality is assumed to be proved by a manifest *petitio principii*, to use the logician's phrase. The soul is immaterial, we are told, because it thinks and feels; and matter cannot think and feel. But if the soul be material, why then matter *can* think and feel. Thorndale indicates as follows the foundation of his own belief: —

I think the contemplation of God brings with it the faith in immortality. The mere imperfections of our happiness here, our blundering lives and inequitable societies, our unrewarded virtues and unavenged crimes, our present need of the great threat of future punishments,— these do not, in my estimation, form safe grounds to proceed upon. They enter largely as grounds of a popular faith; but it would be unwise to build upon them: because to rest on such arguments would lead us to the conclusion, that in proportion as society advances to perfection, and men are more wise and just, in the same proportion will they have less presumption for the hope of immortality.

We confess that we stand in no great fear of this last suggestion. There is little prospect, as yet, of this world becoming too good to need another. We need now, and we shall need for many a year, all the comfort and help we can draw from "the world that sets this right."

Our readers will thank us for extracting the following passage: —

A fond mother loses her infant. What more tender than the hope she has to meet it again in heaven? Does she really, then, expect to find a little child in heaven? some angel-nursling, that she may eternally take to her bosom, fondle, feed, and caress? Oh, do not ask her! I would not have her ask herself. The consolatory vision springs spontaneously from the mother's grief. It is nature's own remedy. She gave that surpassing love, and a grief as poignant must follow. She cannot take away the grief: she half transforms it to a hope.

It is indeed quite true, that in the attempt to define with precision the consolations and hopes which Christianity affords us with respect to our departed friends, we sometimes only destroy what we desired to grasp. And it would be hard for us to say exactly how and in what form we hope to meet again the dear ones who have gone before us. Perhaps Archbishop Whately is right, when he suggests as one possible reason why revelation leaves the details so little *filled in* of the picture of immortality which it draws, that some margin may be left for the weakness of human thought and wish; and that in matters beside the great essential centre-truth, each may believe or may hope that which he would love the best. And in the matter of a little child's loss, we know that two quite opposite beliefs have been cherished. For ourselves, it seems more natural to think of the little thing as it left us; we believe that, in the case of most of us, the little brother or sister that died long ago, remains in remembrance the same young thing forever. Many years are passed, and we have grown older and more careworn since our last sister died; but *she* never grows older with the passing years; and if God spares us to fourscore, we never shall think of her as other than the youthful creature she faded. Still there is pathos and nature in Dickens's description, how the father and mother who lost in early childhood one of two twin sisters, always pictured to themselves, year after year, the dead child growing in the world beyond the grave, in equal progress as the living child grew on earth. And Longfellow, in his touching poem of *Resignation*, suggests a like idea: —

Day after day, we think what she is doing
 In those bright realms of air:
Year after year, her tender steps pursuing,
 Behold her grown more fair.

Thus do we walk with her, and keep unbroken
 The bond which nature gives,
Thinking that our remembrance, though unspoken,
 May reach her where she lives.

Not as a child shall we again behold her;
 For when, with raptures wild,
In our embraces we again enfold her,
 She will not be a child.

It is worthy of notice, how the death of little children has formed the subject of several of the most touching poems in the language. Only those could have written them who have children of their own; and few but parents can fully enter into their pathos. We may remind our readers of Mr. Moultrie's best poem, "The Three Sons;" of Mrs. Southey's (Caroline Bowles) beautiful picture of an infant's death-bed; and in a volume lately published by Gerald Massey, natural feeling has kept affectation from spoiling a most touching piece, called "The Mother's Idol Broken." And no one needs to be reminded of what it is that has afforded scope for the most pathetic touches of Dickens and Mrs. Beecher Stowe.

Thorndale puts a somewhat startling question as to the *extent* of the gift of immortality.

> Why must I except the alternative — all or none? Why every Hun and Scythian, or else no Socrates or Plato? Why must every corrupt thing be brought again to life, or else all hope be denied to the good and the great, the loving and the pious? Why must I measure my hopes by the hopes I would assign to the most weak or wicked of the race? Let the poor idiot, let the vile Tiberius, be extinct forever: must I too, and all these thoughts that stir in me, perish?

Probably Thorndale was not aware that this notion, which he throws out on merely philosophical grounds, is one which, in a modified form, has been suggested, if not maintained, upon theological principles, by the most independent and original theologian of the age — we mean the Archbishop of Dublin. Dr. Whately has proposed it as a subject for inquiry, whether those passages of Scripture which describe the everlasting destruction of the finally impenitent, may not be justly interpreted as signifying their total annihilation; and thus, whether evil and suffering may not entirely cease to be in God's universe, not by an universal restoration of all things to the good and right, but by the total disappearance of that which has been marred past the mending? No doubt, there is something unutterably appalling in the thought of a soul in everlasting woe; no doubt, to our finite minds, it appears the most consistent with the divine glory and happiness, that a time should come when there should be no more pain, sin, and death, anywhere; but the Christian dares not add to or take from *that which is written;* and few, we think, can read the words even of the Saviour himself as bearing any other meaning than one. And as for the difficulty suggested by Thorndale, we confess we can discern in it very little force. It is a humble thing, always and everywhere, to be a man: whether the man be Plato or the Hun. We do not look for immortality on the ground that we deserve it, or that we are fit for it. And although there may be truth in Judge Haliburton's bitter remark, that there is a greater difference between some men and some other men, than there is between these other men and some monkeys; still, in looking down from the divine elevation, we believe that the distances parting the lowest and highest, the worst and best, must seem very small. Look down from the top of Ben Nevis, and the tuft of heather which is a dozen inches higher than the heather round it, differs not appreciably from the general level. Nor should it be forgotten, that in the lowest and the worst, there is a potentiality of becoming good and noble under a certain influence which philosophy does not know of, but whose reality and power we are content to test by the logic of induction. The coarse lump of ironstone is in its essence the self-same thing as the hair-spring of a watch.

We pass to the second part of Thorndale's manuscript, the *Retrospect*, which will be much more interesting to ordinary readers than the first book. And here we find a graceful and beautiful sketch of the history of his life, from the dawn of consciousness down to the time when he came to Villa Scarpa to die. He was the happy child of a gentle and loving mother, over whom early widowhood had cast a shade of melancholy. His father he never knew. A poor lieutenant in the navy, he died of fever caught as his ship lay rotting off the coast of Africa The mother's piety was deep, and her faith undoubting; she knew nothing of the world beyond her own little daisied lawn. And the remembrance of the prayer she early taught her child to utter, has inspired one of the most beautiful passages in English literature: —

> Very singular and very pleasing to me is the remembrance of that simple piety of childhood; of that prayer which was said so punctually night and morning, kneeling by the bedside. What did I think of, guiltless then of metaphysics, — what image did I bring before my mind as I repeated my learnt petition with scrupulous fidelity? Did I see some venerable Form bending down to listen? Did He cease to look and listen when I had said it all? Half prayer, half lesson, how difficult it is now to summon it back again! But this I know, that the bedside where I knelt to this morning and evening devotion became sacred to me as an altar. I smile as I recall the innocent superstition which grew up in me, that the prayer must be said *kneeling just there*. If, some cold winter's night, I had crept into bed, thinking to repeat the petition from the warm nest itself, it would not do! — it was felt in this court of conscience to be 'an insufficient performance:' there was no sleep to be had till I had risen, and, bedgowned as I was, knelt at the accustomed place, and said it all over again from the beginning to the end. To this day, I never see the little clean white bed in which a child is to sleep, but I see also the figure of a child kneeling in prayer at its side. And I, for the moment, am that child. No high altar in the most sumptuous church in Christendom could prompt my knee to bend like that snow-white coverlet tucked in for a child's slumber.

The mother early died; and her brother, a baronet,

who dwelt in a noble house standing in a fine old English park, adopted the desolate child as his own. Grand were the trees and fair the shrubberies of Sutton Manor; but its great attraction to Thorndale was his little cousin Winifred. He loved her, he tells us, before he knew what love was, and long before he knew the vast worldly distance that parted even such near relations. Lady Moberly, Winifred's mother, was a lady at once ultra-fashionable and ultra-evangelical. She was one of those of whom the sarcastic *Saturday Review* declared that the names of their great men must be written alike in the *Peerage* and in the Book of Life. Thorndale was shortly placed under the charge of a country clergyman, to be prepared for Oxford. Here he had one fellow-pupil, Luxmore, a youth passionately devoted to poetry. And his tutor's library furnished an endless store of poetry, theology, and philosophy, which were all devoured with equal avidity. When the vacation approached, Thorndale was somewhat surprised by receiving from Lady Moberly a formal invitation to Sutton Manor. He had counted, as a matter of course, upon spending the vacation there. But her ladyship was cautious; and her letter contained a postscript, cautioning Thorndale to beware of a certain fairy who haunted the shrubbery in which he was accustomed to walk. He learned the meaning of the postscript too soon. His cousin was more charming than ever; but his love, hopeless, yet unconquerable, was on his part "a mere worship, where even the prayer was not to be spoken." And this passion served to extinguish all ambition. He entered the cloisters of Magdalen, he tells us, —

as indifferent to the world as any monk of the fourteenth century could have been. Academical honors, or the greater distinctions in life to which they prepare the way, had no sort of charm for me. The 'daily bread' was secured; and neither law, physic, nor divinity could have given me my Winifred.

A life of mere reflection, then, was to be his portion. His over-sensitive mind never recovered the frost of that early disappointment. Is it too much to say that it results from the morbid body, from the weakness of physical nature, when trouble and sorrow, no matter how heavy, borne in early youth, cast their shadow over all after-years? What a vast deal a healthy man can "get over!" True, as beautiful, are the words of Philip van Artevelde, in Mr. Taylor's noble play:—

Well, well, — she's gone,
And I have tamed my sorrow. Pain and grief
Are transitory things, no less than joy,
And though they leave us not the men we were,
Yet they do leave us. You behold me here,
A man bereaved, with something of a blight
Upon the early blossoms of his life,
And its first verdure, — having not the less
A living root, and drawing from the earth
Its vital juices, from the air its powers:
And surely as man's health and strength are whole,
His appetites re-germinate, his heart
Re-opens, and his objects and desires
Shoot up renewed.[1]

How many twice-married men and women can testify to the truth of Artevelde's philosophy! Out of a romance, it takes very much to kill a man, — unless, indeed, consumption has marked him from his birth, and his physical constitution lacks the reacting spring. But Mr. Smith has made his hero feel and act just as it was fit under the conditions given. He became a solitary dreamer; and though feeling the attraction which draws

[1] Taylor's *Philip van Artevelde*, Second Part, Act iii., Scene ii.

the moth to the flame, yet at vacation times, instead of going to Sutton Manor, he betook himself to Wales or Cumberland, to "read." There he read, thought, wrote, destroyed. He mused deeply on the constitution of society: he longed for a time when manual labor should not be deemed inconsistent with refinement and intelligence. But he found his theory crumble at the touch of fact.

As I marched triumphantly along, I came to a field where men were ploughing. I had often watched the ploughman as he steps on steadily, holding the share down in its place in the soil, and felt curious to try the experiment myself. This time, as the countryman who approached me had a good-natured aspect, I asked him to let me take his place within the stilts. He did so. I did not give him quite the occasion for merriment which I saw he anticipated; I held down the share, and kept it in its due position. But I had no conception of the effort it required — which, at least, it cost me. When I resigned my place, my arms trembled, my hands burned, my brain throbbed; the whole frame was shaken. And something, too, was shaken in the framework of my speculations. The feasibility of uniting with labors such as these much of the culture we call intellectual, was not so clear to me as it was an hour ago. I walked along less triumphantly, maintaining a sort of prudent silence with myself.

Thorndale all over! Easily driven by some little jar, even from a cherished purpose or belief. All physical constitution again. In the days when manual labor and mental cultivation are combined, men like Thorndale must be watchmakers and printers: men with more bone and sinew must go to field-work. But who does not remember the diary of Elihu Burritt, when teaching himself half a dozen languages, with its constantly recurring entries of "Forged twelve hours to-day" — "Forged fourteen hours to-day" — the brawny blacksmith, with his fore-hammer and his Hebrew lexicon side by side?

Very frankly and without reserve, Thorndale shows

us how his opinions on society swayed to and fro. He went to see Manchester. and mourned to think how, " for leave to live in habitations, where air and light, beauty and fragrance, are shut out for ever, men and women are toiling as no other animal on the face of the earth toils." And, caring little for conventional proprieties, he sits down in London on the steps of a church — it was in Regent-street — amid the offscourings of the population, and contemplated society from this new point of view. It looked very different! He heard the stifled mutterings of the deadly hate which the very lowest class bear to those above them. The ground underneath us, in truth is mined: the mine is charged. Is not the hatred *natural?* We do not ask whether it is right.

Without a doubt, we of the pavement, if we had our will, would stop those smooth-rolling chariots, with their liveried attendants (how we hate those clean and well-fed lackeys!), would open the carriage-door, and bid the riders come down to us! — come down to share — good heaven! what? — our ruffianage, our garbage, the general scramble, the general filth.

Walking another day down Regent-street, he passes an open carriage standing at a shop-door. Seated alone in it is — Winifred! He avoids recognition, and hurries away. Soon he slackens his speed — stops — turns, walks back, slowly, rapidly, breathlessly! The carriage was gone. True to the life!

He left Oxford at last, and returned to Sutton Manor. " It was the old story of the moth and the flame." He resolved that for a month his heart should have its way; and rowing with Winifred on the river, wandering with her in the shrubbery, watching the sun go down, he had his "month of elysium." All his philosophy was in those days full of hope. He wondered at the greatness of the human *capacity for happiness.* At length he broke hurriedly away, and hastened to Loch Lomond. We have already seen how he returned, and with what result.

Then he became a wanderer. He tells us he never ceased to think, but "a despondency crept from his life into his philosophy." He went to Germany, Switzerland, Italy — the accustomed route — and learned to appreciate the diversity there is in human life. On the banks of the lake of Lucerne he met his Utopian friend, Clarence, whom he had known at Oxford; and they spent long days in varied talk together. Clarence dwelt much upon the misery of the better or the middle classes. He thought it exceeds that of the poor wretches on the Regent-street steps. What ceaseless and life-wearing anxiety and care there are in the hearts of most educated men! Clarence did not wonder that men go mad. As life goes against them, as the income proves insufficient, as the expenses increase, as impending calamity ever jars miserably upon the shaken nerves, and as the mind is day by day racked by ceaseless fears, the only wonder is that Reason does not oftener forsake her seat, totter, and fall!

On some futile pretence of seeing his friend, Luxmore, the poet, Thorndale returned to England. Luxmore had published, and failed. Thorndale found him in a Special Pleader's office, studying for the bar. Luxmore held steadily to his books of Practice, till, in an evil hour (he had parted with all his poets), he bought at a stall a cheap edition of Shelley. It wakened the old spirit. He would emigrate. He would clear the forest and the jungle. He would grow corn by the Mississippi. But he must see the South American mountains first; and so he sailed for Rio Janeiro. Thorndale greatly doubted to the last whether he had ever "worked his way round" to the farm he had talked of. Luxmore's character and career are ably and skilfully sketched; but we cannot say that we are especially struck by the specimens given of his poetry.

In the great steamer, as it lay off Southampton, Thorndale bade his friend farewell. He had loved him he tells us, as a brother, and an elder brother. Thorndale's pliant nature was plastic in those robust hands. Sadly depressed, he betook himself to a little cottage at Shanklin, once more alone but for the old companion — the box of books. It was Thorndale's especial misfortune that, with a native craving for some attached companion to dwell under the same roof, he was by circumstances always doomed to days of solitude. But a new interest now arose. Symptoms of disease, disregarded in the excitement of the last days with Luxmore, now forced themselves on his attention. Some business matter compelled him to write to his uncle, thus informing his relations at Sutton Manor, for the first time, that he had returned to England. Kind messages and regrets came in reply: Winifred especially chiding him for his unsocial habits. It seemed "a wild strain of irony." Yet the few lines she wrote wakened old feelings, never quite asleep. Surely she would come and see the poor invalid? So strong did the impression grow, that, catching sight one day of a female figure in the garden, bending over the flowers, he felt sure it must be Winifred; and watched breathlessly, with violently-beating heart, till she turned her face, and the delusion was dispelled. Still, for days he cherished the vain expectation that she would come, and restore him, by her very presence, to life, and hope, and faith. *That* was all he needed.

If I could see thee, 'twould be well with me!

Now there came consultations with this and that great physician: and soon the death-warrant decidedly expressed. Then was a first moment of confusion and agony; and then followed an indescribable calm. It was now all smooth water before him. He betook himself to his last retreat at Villa Scarpa; but he did not see Winifred before he left England for ever. Kind letters followed him from her mother. Lady Moberly would come over to take care of him, with a doctor in either hand. Of course she never came. And now the last days are gliding over swiftly: —

The day is never long. I have, indeed, ceased to take note of the measurement of time. One hour is more genial than another; thought flows more rapidly, or these damaged lungs breathe somewhat more freely at one time than another: but where the present hour stands in the series which makes up day and night, what the clock reports of the progress of time, I have ceased to ask myself. There is but one hour that the bell has to strike for me.

Yet life is not quite over, even after Thorndale has found his last harbor of refuge. Present incident proves the completion of past remembrance. The Third Book of the manuscript volume is entitled "Cyril, or the Modern Cistercian."

In watching a little point of beach which was visible from his terrace, Thorndale had often been struck by the figure of a youthful monk, wearing the white habit of the Cistercian order, who passed slowly by the sea-margin, and sometimes paused in thought. Thorndale had constructed a whole theory of his thinking and history, and began to feel towards him as towards a friend. At length, in his ride, Thorndale passed two monks, one of whom had sunk exhausted by the wayside. He conveyed the monk to the monastery in his carriage, and recognized in him the Cistercian so often watched. A further surprise awaited him. On entering the Cistercian's cell, he recognized in him an old acquaintance — Cyril. Cyril had entered the Roman Catholic Church, through the gate of the monastery. He had sought a peaceful, pious, and harmonious life within those walls; and he assured Thorndale that he had found all he sought. His history had been a tragical one. Brought up in a pious family, he had been assailed by sceptical doubts. His father was an enthusiast for reformatory punishment. The house was full of books on the subject. And from these Cyril imbibed the notion that one grand end of all punishment should be the reformation of the criminal himself. To punish for mere revenge was unchristian and irrational. How, then, of God's punishments inflicted in a future life? The pious father appeared to claim for the human legislator principles more noble and enlightened than those he attributed to the Divine. *Eternal punishment* aims not at the reformation of the guilty. Cyril was plunged into all the miseries of doubt. And brought up in the conviction that unbelief was the extremest sin, his anguish was indescribable. He became restless, gloomy, morose. And so, leaving Oxford, Thorndale left him.

Thorndale was at Dolgelly, in Wales, when he learned that Cyril was at Barmouth, and rode over to see him. He met him, just come off the water. Cyril's joy at the meeting was extreme. They sat cheerfully down to supper. Cyril never had been so gay. At length, absently, he drew from the pocket of his rough greatcoat a large mass of iron, the fluke of an old anchor. At the sight of it, suddenly recollecting himself, he burst into a violent flood of tears. He confessed to his friend that an accident only had prevented him from throwing himself into the sea, during the sail from which he had just returned. He had gone out with that purpose, driven to it by his agony of doubt, and (strange as it may seem) by the fear of death. His fear of death was such, that he longed to make a plunge and have it over. And amid all the misery of his scepticism, he says, surely with sad truth: —

> I am quoted by my family and my friends as a monster of impiety and guilt. I am frowned upon, avoided, expostulated with, — and pious ministers reprove me — for intellectual pride!

We can well believe that a pious father or mother, deeply loving their son, would yet rather see him laid in his coffin than see him turn doubtful of their own simple faith. What malady makes a breach so total — what leads to a doom so fearful — as unbelief? But let it be remembered that in many cases it is a malady, a disease for which a man is no more guilty than for consumption or for typhus. No doubt there is a wilful blindness, a preference of falsehood to truth, a flippant, hateful self-sufficiency, in the case of some: and let these be held responsible. But surely there *are* earnest spirits, battling for the truth — shedding tears of blood because they cannot believe, though they long to do so. Let us be thankful that in almost every such case the disease is a temporary one. It will wear away. "Unto the upright there ariseth light in darkness." Unbelief is a crisis which must be passed through by the thinking human mind, as certainly as measles and whooping-cough by the human body. Of course a blockhead, who never thinks at all, will not be troubled by it. The humble and earnest man comes out of it, with a faith grounded so deeply that it can never be shaken more. Let us pity, then, the young doubter: let us aid him by God's blessing: let us not accuse him, and so perhaps drive him to despair. The guilty unbelief is that of the man who knows in his conscience that he would rather not believe. There is another kind of want of faith which the Almighty will not condemn. It is that which utters the creed and the prayer together: "Lord, I believe: help Thou mine unbelief."

The next morning Thorndale and Cyril were to have breakfasted together. But when Thorndale went to his lodgings, he was gone, without a word; and they met no more till they met in the Cistercian monastery.

After this meeting, Cyril sometimes visited Thorndale at the Villa Scarpa. Thorndale did not seek any account of the process by which the youth who could believe nothing, had passed into the monk who believed everything. No doubt it would have been the usual story of reaction commenced, and then a positive *appetite for belief* growing upon the man. In any case, belief had brought Cyril peace and rest. And the doctrine of purgatory had been to him a favorable distinction of the Church of Rome. *It* represented a reformatory nature even in punishment beyond the grave; and the young enthusiast fancied that a special revelation had been vouchsafed to him by the Saviour, that every soul that God has made should in some way be saved at last. And coming not frequently, stealing quietly up to the terrace with his *pax vobiscum*, Cyril visited Thorndale to the last. But Thorndale saw the Cistercian on the strip of beach no more.

Cyril had felt the difficulty which most thoughtful men

must feel, as to what conception should be formed of God : —

> How personify the Infinite? I said to myself. Does not the notion of personality itself imply contrast, limitation, and must not a Person be therefore Finite? or how personify at all, but by borrowing from the creature, and framing an ideal out of human qualities?
>
> At one moment my conception of God seemed grand and distinct, and my whole soul was filled and satisfied with it. Suddenly I was startled and abashed when I traced in it too plainly the features of humanity. These I hastened to obliterate; and the whole image was then fading into terrible obscurity. I remember one day our common friend Luxmore saying, in his wild poetic manner, that the ordinary imagination of God was but the shadow of a man thrown upwards, — the image of our best and greatest, seen larger on the concave of the sky.

We remark upon this, that Luxmore, after all, was only stating in a poetical and somewhat exaggerated form, a great and fundamental religious truth. We are "created in the image of God:" and it is only because there is something in us which resembles God, that we are able to form any conception of Him and his character. But for this, we could no more conceive of God's attributes than a blind man, who never saw, can conceive of color. We, of course, are fallen creatures ; and our blurred and blotted qualities bear only the faintest and farthest likeness to that Divine Image in which we were made. And further, it is true enough that when we kneel down to pray, we should only distract and dishearten ourselves by trying to form a conception of a Being in whose nature there are such elements as eternity, omnipresence, omnipotence, invisibility ; and by trying to feel that we are addressing *Him*. But was Luxmore entirely wrong when he said that the Hearer of prayer, to our weak minds, draws personality from a sublimed humanity? It is not a fable, that we know the picture of a man's character and life set out in a certain simple story, Glad Tidings to all to whom it comes:—a man towards whom we can feel kindly sympathy and warm affection: a human being like ourselves: and we are told that He is "the image of the invisible God:" that when we picture Him to our hearts, we picture God — softened, but not degraded. We can see "the glory of God in the face of Jesus Christ:" and in praying to God, we can feel as though the kind face were bent over us as we pray, — as though we were telling of our wants and sorrows to that kind and gentle heart. Do we desire to think clearly to whom we speak when we pray? We are chilled and overwhelmed when we think of infinite space and infinite time: it is not to an aggregate of such qualities as *these* that we can address heartfelt pleading. Let us think we are speaking to a sympathizing Man; and child-like, we can bend down our head upon the knee of Jesus of Nazareth, and breathe into His ear the story of our wants and woes. We have all that the grossest idolatry ever gave of clear conception; and yet our worship is not degraded, but sublimed.

Not so pleasing is the Fourth Book of Thorndale's manuscript, entitled "Seckendorf, or the Spirit of Denial." Long ago, in Switzerland, Thorndale found Seckendorf in the studio of Clarence, the Utopian artist. Seckendorf was a tall man, with gray hair and keen gray eyes, and advanced in years. He was by birth a German baron; but he was known in England as Doctor Seckendorf, an eminent physician and physiologist. In philosophy, he was just the opposite of Clarence: sceptical, sarcastic, hoping nothing. His philosophy was "firm as a rock, and as hard and barren." He held that what is excellent never can be common, because "higher excellence is greater complication, and its manifestation must be more restricted, because a larger number of antecedent conditions are necessary for that manifestation." The Utopian's "good time coming," of universal goodness and happiness, could therefore never be. And Thorndale thought out a sad induction of facts in corroboration of the thing: —

> There is more sea than land; three fourths of the globe are covered with salt water.
>
> There is more barren land than fertile; much is sheer desert, or hopeless swamp; great part wild arid steppes, or land that can only be held in cultivation by incessant toil.
>
> Where nature is most prolific, there is more weed and jungle than fruit and flower.
>
> Of the animal creation, the lowest orders are by far the most numerous. The *infusoria*, and other creatures that seem to enjoy no other sensations than what are immediately connected with food and movement (if even these), far surpass all others in this respect. The tribes of insects are innumerable; the mammalia comparatively few.
>
> Of the human inhabitants of the earth, the ethnologist tells us that the Mongolian race is the most numerous, which is not certainly the race in which the noblest forms of civilization have appeared. As in the tree there is more leaf than fruit, so in the most advanced nation of Europe there are more poor than rich, more ignorant than wise, more automatic laborers, the mere creatures of habit, than reasoning and reflective men.

We do not know whether the celebrated anonymous work, entitled *The Plurality of Worlds*, was published before Thorndale's death. If he had read it, he might have gathered from its eloquent and startling pages one instance more for his induction. He might have stated that there seems strong reason to believe that of all the orbs which have (if we may say so) blossomed in immensity, only one has arrived at fruit: that this earth is the only inhabited world in all the universe. The Creator works with a lavish hand. But as his works grow nobler, they grow fewer. Scarcity, we all know, makes a thing more valuable: the converse holds as truly, that value makes a thing scarce.

The second chapter in this Fourth Book treats ingeniously and strikingly of the power of money; and also furnishes proof that Thorndale, like many men of his make, was not minutely accurate. The chapter is called "The Silver Shilling;" and over and over again we have *the silver shilling* repeated, as the type of money. Seckendorf tells us where he got the name: it was from "a poem by one Phillips, 'On the Silver Shilling.'" We know, of course, what Seckendorf is referring to; but there is no such poem as that he quotes. Most men who are tolerably well read in the poetry of the seventeenth century, have at least heard of John Phillips's poem, *The Splendid Shilling*, an amusing parody of the style of Milton: it sets out thus: —

> Happy the man, who, void of care and strife,
> In silken or in leathern purse, retains
> A Splendid Shilling: he nor hears with pain,
> New oysters cried, nor sighs for cheerful ale.

Our shortening space forbids our offering our readers any account of Seckendorf's career, which Mr. Smith sketches with great liveliness and interest; or our noticing the topics which were discussed in council by Thorndale, Clarence, and Seckendorf. Seckendorf thought there is a general movement in England towards the Roman Catholic Church; and that it is not unlikely that the ragged urchin who is chalking up "No Popery" on the walls of London, may live to see High Mass performed in St. Paul's Cathedral. He maintained that fear is the root of all religion; the unseen root, even in the happiest Christians: — that "the pillars of heaven are sunk in hell." We differ from him. We think that love and hope, rather than fear, are the guiding influences in the Christian life. We believe that though a great fear may be the thing that wakens a man up from total unconcern about religion, yet that the race once entered on, he treads "the way to Zion with *his face thitherward;*"—looking towards the home he seeks; and drawn by the hope before, rather than driven by the fear behind him.

Thorndale's Fifth Book is called "Clarence, or the Utopian." As the invalid was wearing down from day to day, one morning he was sitting in the gardens of the Villa Reale. There a group drew his attention, — a father, and, as it seemed, his little daughter. The father was evidently an Englishman: the little girl, with fair complexion and light hair, had the dark eye of the Italian. Thorndale recognized his old friend Clarence; but with characteristic reserve, he shrunk from making himself known. But he looked with kind feeling upon the little child; and mused, as Dr. Arnold had done before him, on a child's power to reawaken a parent's flagging interest in life. The beaten track is no longer monotonous: the circle of the year looks new. Thorndale thus mused: —

What beautiful things there are in life! joys that have come down to us pure and unstained from the times of the patriarchs. It is to me an eternal miracle to see the same roses year after year bloom as freshly as they did in Paradise. Plant this wedded happiness, plant these roses, in every rood of ground, ye who would improve the aspect of this world! but do not think you can change a single leaf of the plant itself.

Thorndale's idea had been anticipated. James Hedderwick thus excuses a new poem on the old theme of *Love:* —

The theme is old, — even as the flowers are old,
  That sweetly showed
Their silver bosses and bright-budding gold
  Through Eden's sod; —
And still peep forth through grass and garden mould,
  As fresh from God!

Happily Thorndale and Clarence met at last. The little girl, compassionating the wan look of the consumptive, offered him another day some flowers. Clarence followed her; and suddenly recognizing his old companion, "burst into tears like a woman." He and his little Julia were afterwards constant visitors at the Villa Scarpa; and all the beauty of the scene, which had been paling to the dying man's languid eye, suddenly revived. Morning after morning Clarence spent, painting the view from Thorndale's terrace. Julia was not his daughter: she was his adopted child. She was the daughter of an exiled Italian patriot who had come to England, married an English woman, settled down quietly in a little cottage on the borders of the New Forest, and supported himself as a sculptor. We trust that all our readers will make a point of perusing the chapter called "Julia Montini," in which the story of the exile, his wife and child, is related with exquisite grace and pathos. Very beautifully did the simple and untaught English girl tell Clarence how, as there gradually grew upon her the sense of the genius and refinement of the man she had married, she feared that he would cease to love her, so much above her as he was. She read and studied, hoping to make herself more worthy of him: but her fear proved idle; he never loved her less. It is indeed something of a disappointment for a husband to feel there are realms of thought to which *he* has access, but into which a gentle and loving wife cannot enter with him: but solitude is the penalty which attaches of necessity to elevated thought. The man who climbs too high, leaves common sympathy behind him. Our readers may remember how beautifully the author of *In Memoriam* has anticipated the poor young wife's thoughts and fears: —

> He thrids the labyrinth of the mind,
> He reads the secret of the star:
> He seems so near and yet so far:
> He looks so cold: she thinks him kind.
>
> For him she plays, to him she sings,
> Of early faith and plighted vows;
> She knows but matters of the house,
> And he, he knows a thousand things.
>
> Her faith is fixt and cannot move,
> She darkly feels him dark and wise:
> She dwells on him with faithful eyes,
> "I cannot understand: I love."

Suddenly the sculptor and his wife died of fever; and Clarence found the little child all alone in the deserted cottage. The quiet home, that had looked so happy, was obliterated at a stroke. Is it a morbid thing, if we find it for ourselves impossible to look at any happy home, without picturing to our mind a day sure to come? We look at the cottage in the sunshine, amid its clustering roses, and with children's voices by. Ah, some day there will be an unwonted bustle, — straw flying about the neat walks — empty, echoing rooms — the children gone — and the peaceful home broken up for ever. It is well for those who can feel themselves secure even if they be not safe.

And now Clarence and Julia soothe the dying man's solitude. Thorndale lies on his sofa under the acacia-tree ; Clarence stands near, painting ; Julia is busy gardening. And as Thorndale's hand turns too feeble to hold the pen, Clarence takes up his abandoned manuscript volume, and fills the remaining leaves with his own confession of faith. To notice *that* at all adequately would demand an article of itself; and we shall not attempt to do so. But we see our last of Thorndale as we have just described him. We leave him, now with very little to come of life, under the acacia-tree. There is now only the stillness of expectation upon that terrace that looks down upon the bay.

We should have been happier, we confess, had we left him with something better to support him at the last than philosophy, whether cynical or Utopian. Surely he had within himself, too sacred for common talk, a hope and a belief not to be paraded for Seckendorf's sarcasm! Surely, when, in the last hours, the pictures of childhood came back, the perplexed and tempest-driven man was again the child that prayed by the little white bedside. We do not care if our readers should complain that the sermon peeps through the article — that the disguise of the reviewer does not quite conceal the gown and band. Let it be so : but in treating of such grave matters as those which this book suggests, we could not have forgiven ourselves had we failed to notice the book's essential defect. Holding the belief which we hold, we could not have written of the mystery of life, without reference to that which alone can read it.

CHAPTER XII.

CONCERNING A GREAT SCOTCH PREACHER.[1]

MR. CAIRD'S name is already known to the English public as that of the author of a sermon on *Religion in Common Life*, which was published two or three years ago by her Majesty's command. Every Sunday during her autumn sojourn at Balmoral, the Queen and court worship at the little parish church of Crathie; and at various times several of the most popular preachers of the Church of Scotland have there preached in the presence of royalty. Dr. Norman McLeod of Glasgow, Dr. Cumming, Mr. Stuart, of St. Andrew's, Edinburgh, and other eminent Scotch clergymen, have officiated at Crathie Church, and in more than one instance with so favorable an impression, that the manuscripts of the discourses have been required for the Queen's private perusal. But Mr. Caird was the first Scotch minister who received a royal command to give his sermon to the public; and indeed, with the exception of the Bishop of Oxford, the first preacher who had been so distinguished during her Majesty's reign. Many circumstances, apart from the merit of the discourse, contributed to secure for it a very large circulation in England as well as in Scot-

[1] *Sermons.* By the Rev. John Caird, M. A., Minister of the Park Church, Glasgow, Author of *Religion in Common Life.* Edinburgh and London: Blackwoods. 1858.

land; and we have been informed that no single sermon published in modern times has been so extensively read. Somewhere about a hundred thousand copies of it were exhausted in Britain: a still greater number were required for the United States, where our friends were eager to know what sort of religious instruction was approved by a queen; and the sermon being translated into the German tongue, was republished in Germany with a recommendatory preface by the Chevalier Bunsen. At that period it became known for the first time to the English public that there had arisen in Scotland a new luminary; a great pulpit orator who was held by many to be equal to any who had preceded him, Chalmers and Guthrie not being excepted. And the published sermon seemed almost to justify the enthusiasm of Mr. Caird's warmest admirers. We believe that among intelligent readers there was but one opinion of it, as an ingenious, eloquent, sensible, and interesting exposition of an important practical subject. Still, we have been told that some readers thought Mr. Caird's theology very defective; and it is not long since we read a letter in a newspaper which is the organ of a small religious sect, in which Mr. Caird was sadly torn to pieces as lacking all spiritual insight and knowledge of the gospel doctrines. And the ingenious writer of that letter stated that nothing could be more mistaken than the popular belief that the Queen, in commanding the publication of Mr. Caird's sermon, intended to express her approval of it. On the contrary, her Majesty's purpose was (so the writer of the letter assures us) to make an appeal to the sympathies of the religious public, and to say, — "Pity me, my subjects; here is a specimen of the kind of thing that I have to listen to in Scotland in autumn!"

Mr. Caird made his reputation as a preacher while minister of a church in Edinburgh, but about ten years since he retired from the bustle of a city clergyman's life to the country parish of Errol, in Perthshire. From his seclusion there he occasionally emerged to preach in the large towns of Scotland, and far from being forgotten or lost sight of in his country retirement, his popularity appeared ever on the increase. Whenever he preached in Edinburgh or Glasgow, the crowds that followed him had hardly been equalled since the great days of Dr. Chalmers; and the fame to which *Religion in Common Life* attained did not surpass the expectations of his Scotch admirers. A few months since Mr. Caird, now a clergyman of thirteen years' experience, was transferred from his country parish to the beautiful church recently erected in the West-end Park at Glasgow, to which we are sorry to see its builders were too Protestant to give a saint's name. There, with undiminished fire and unslackening popularity, Mr. Caird preaches twice every Sunday. The stranger in Glasgow, if he wanders on Sunday afternoon in the direction of the Park, will see a well-dressed eager crowd hurrying towards the Park Church; and we understand that so overcrowded was the building at Mr. Caird's first coming, that it has been found necessary to furnish the congregation with tickets, no one being admitted without producing one. Mr. Caird, we believe, is of opinion that in order to produce its full impression, a sermon ought not to be read, but to be delivered as if given *extempore;* but as the labor of committing a discourse to memory is great, he reads his forenoon discourse, and delivers without any manuscript that which he preaches in the afternoon. The afternoon appearance is thus the great one, and it is to that service that strangers who wish to hear the eminent preacher generally go. And although it is in the nature of things impossible that a great orator should be always at his best, we believe that hardly any one who goes to hear Mr. Caird of an afternoon, however high his expectations may have been, returns disappointed.

Let us suppose that by the kindness of some Glasgow acquaintance we have succeeded in procuring tickets of admission to the Park Church. In the midst of a throng which has converged from many points to the steep ascent which leads up to it, we approach the stately Gothic building, with its massive tower, which, standing on an elevated ridge of ground, looks on either hand over the distant din of thronging streets beneath to the quiet country hills far away. We find our way into the church, and we have time to look around us, for there is still half an hour before service begins. Is this really a Presbyterian church? What would John Knox say to it? For all the light within is the "dim religious light" of the cathedral, mellowed in its passage through the windows of stained glass: there is the lofty vaulted roof of richly carved oak, and the double line of shafts parting the side aisles: far up, the amber-tinted clerestory windows throw shafts of sunset color upon the oaken beams; and in the distance — for the church is a very long one — there is nothing less than a spacious chancel, parted from the church by a lofty pointed arch, partly filled up by a traceried screen of stone. And at the extremity of the chancel, but (something lacking still) at the *west* end of the church, there is an altar-window, whose fair proportions and rich tracery might have been designed by Pugin. No galleries cut these graceful shafts, and the seats are not pews, but open benches of oak. There is no organ, and no altar; but directly in front of the chancel a plain pulpit of oak.

It is just two o'clock. Every seat is crowded, and the passages have gradually filled with people who are content to stand. And as the last tones of the bell have died away Mr. Caird ascends the pulpit, wearing, as Scotch ministers do, the black silk preaching-gown and cassock. His appearance is natural and unaffected. Of the middle size, with dark complexion and long black hair, good but not remarkable forehead, a somewhat careworn and anxious expression, and looking like a retiring and hard-wrought student of eight-and-thirty — there we have Mr. Caird. He begins the service by reading the psalm which is to be sung, and we are struck at once by the solemnity and depth of his voice, and we feel already something of the indescribable charm there is about the whole man. The psalm is sung by a choir so efficient that the lack of the organ is hardly felt. Then the minister rises, and, the whole congregation standing, offers a prayer. The Church of Scotland has no liturgy, and every clergyman has to prepare his own prayers. These are commonly understood to be given extemporaneously, and generally they are extemporaneous; but as we listen to those sentences, uttered with so much feeling, solemnity, quietude, and fluency, we soon know that the prayers, filled with happy turns of expression, containing many phrases and sentences borrowed from the Liturgy, and some (or we are much mistaken) translated from the Missal, and all conceived and expressed in the simple, beautiful liturgical spirit, have been, if not written, at least most carefully thought over at home. At one time Mr. Caird's prayers were ambitious and oratorical; but now their perfect simplicity tells of more mature judgment and taste. We cannot say whether the congregation has so far mastered the essential difficulty of unliturgical common prayer as to be properly joining in those petitions; but the perfect stillness, the silence and stirlessness that prevail in church, testify that the congregation is at all events intently listening. The prayer is over — only a quarter of an hour. Then a lesson from Scripture is read, chosen at the discretion of the clergyman; then a psalm is sung; then comes the sermon. You cannot doubt, as you see the people arranging themselves for fixed attention, what portion of the worship of God is thought in Scotland the most important. The service in that country is essentially one of instruction rather than one of devotion. The text is read; it is generally such as we feel at once to be a suggestive one; it is sometimes striking, but never odd or strange. Then Mr. Caird begins his sermon. He has no manuscript before him, not a shred of what the humbler Scotch call *paper*, and abhor as they abhor a vestige of Rome; but who could for a moment be misled into imagining those felicitous sentences extemporaneous, or that masterly symmetrical discussion of the subject, so ingenious, so thoughtful, so rich in fine illustration, rising several times in the course of the sermon into a fervid rush of eloquence that you hold your breath to listen to — the excogitation of the moment? In hearing Mr. Caird you have nothing to *get over*. There is nothing that detracts from the general effect; none of those disagreeable peculiarities and awkwardnesses in utterance, in gesture, in appearance, in mode of thought, which grievously detract from the pleasure with which we listen to many distinguished speakers till we get accustomed to them, and learn to forget their defects in their merits and beauties. He begins quietly, but in a manner which is full of earnestness and feeling; every word is touched with just the right kind and degree of emphasis; many single words, and many little sentences which when you recall them do not seem very remarkable, are given in tones which make them absolutely thrill through you: you feel that the preacher has in him the elements of a tragic actor who would rival Kean. The attention of the congregation is riveted; the silence is breathless; and as the speaker goes on gathering warmth till he becomes impassioned and impetuous, the tension of the nerves of the hearer becomes almost painful. There is abundant ornament in style — if you were cooler you might probably think some of it carried to the verge of good taste; there is a great amount and variety of the most expressive, apt, and seemingly unstudied gesticulation: it is rather as though you were listening to the impulsive Italian speaking from head to foot, than to the cool and unexcitable Scot. After two or three such climaxes, with pauses between, after the manner of Dr. Chalmers, the preacher gathers himself up for his peroration, which, with the tact of the orator, he has made more striking, more touching, more impressive than any preceding portion of his discourse. He is wound up often to an excitement which is painful to see. The full deep voice, so beautifully expressive, already taxed to its utmost extent, breaks into something which is almost a shriek; the gesticulation becomes wild; the preacher, who has hitherto held himself to some degree in check, seems to abandon himself to the full tide of his emotion: you feel that not even his eloquent lips can do justice to the rush of thought and feeling within. Two or three minutes in this impassioned strain and the sermon is done. A few moments of startling silence; you look round the church; every one is bending forward with eyes intent upon the pulpit; then there is a general breath and stir. You think the sermon has lasted about ten minutes; you consult your watch — it has lasted three quarters of an hour. If you are an enthusiastic Anglican you say to yourself, "Well, that comes to the mark of Melvill or Bishop Wilberforce." If an enthusiastic Scotch churchman, you say to yourself, "Well, I suppose Chalmers was better; but *I* never heard preaching like it, save from Guthrie or Norman McLeod."

Then follow a brief collect, a hymn, and the benediction; and you come away, having heard the great Scotch preacher. We may very fitly call him so; for except Dr. Guthrie and Dr. McLeod, there is no one whom the popular judgment of Scotland in general places near Mr. Caird. And though every district of Scotland and every town has its popular preacher — and though many congregations have each their own favorite clergyman whom they prefer to all others — still the very best that the warmest admirers of other Scotch ministers can find to say of them is, that they are better than Mr. Caird. He is the Scotch Themistocles. Even those who would place another preacher first, place Mr. Caird second.

It is rarely indeed that we find such a remarkable combination in one individual of the qualities which go to make an effective pulpit orator. Mr. Caird's mind has the knack of producing the precise kind of thought which shall be at once worthy of the attention of the best educated and most refined, and effective when addressed to a mixed congregation. And *that* is the practical talent for the preacher, after all. No depth, originality, or power of thought will make up in a sermon for the absence of general interest. No thought or style is good in the pulpit, which is tiresome. There is an insufferable but lofty order of thought, which you listen to with an effort, feel to be extremely fine, and cease listening to as soon as possible. John Foster, who scattered congregations, was beyond doubt an abler preacher than Mr. Caird; but he *did* scatter congregations, and therefore he was not a good preacher, finely as his published discourses read. There are other preachers who attract crowds by preaching sermons which revolt every one who possesses good sense or good taste; but in distinction alike from the good unpopular preacher and the bad popular preacher, Mr. Caird has the talent to produce at will an order of thought elevated enough to please the most cultivated, and interesting enough to attract the masses. He has a good foundation of metaphysical acumen and power; strong practical sense; then great powers in the way of happy and striking illustration; indeed, he traces analogies between the material and the spiritual with a felicity which reminds us of Archbishop Whately. Mr. Caird has also that invaluable gift of the orator — a capacity of intense feeling; he can throw his whole soul into what he says, with an emotion which is contagious. Further, he has a remarkably telling and expressive voice, and a highly effective dramatic manner. Add to all these qualifications that, from natural bent, fostered and encouraged by unequalled success from his first entering the church, he has devoted himself steadfastly to the single end of becoming a great and distinguished preacher. That end he has completely attained. For at least ten years he has held in Scotland the position which he now holds; and the fortunate incident of his preaching at Crathie extended his reputation beyond the limits of Scotland. Mr. Caird is certainly the most generally popular preacher in the Scotch Church, and he deserves his popularity. We cannot, of course, go into the question of mute inglorious Miltons, and of flowers born to blush unseen. It is possible enough that among the Cumberland hills, or in curacies like Sydney Smith's on Salisbury Plain, or wandering sadly by the shore of Shetland fiords, there may be men who have in them the makings of better preachers than Bishop Wilberforce, Mr. Melvill, Dr. McLeod, or Mr. Caird. Of course there may be Folletts that never held a brief, Angelos that never built St. Peter's, and Vandycks who never got beyond their sixpence a day. There may be, of course, and there may not be; and what *is known* must for practical purposes be taken for what *is*.

It may readily be supposed that the announcement of a forthcoming volume of sermons by so distinguished a preacher did not fail to excite much interest in the district where he is best known. Little Tom Eaves, who at different times has given Mr. Thackery so much valuable information, assured us, on his return from a recent visit to Edinburgh, that the eminent publishers who have sent forth this volume, were content to give for its copyright a sum which, for a volume of sermons, was quite extraordinary — as much, in fact, as Sir Walter Scott received for *Marmion*. Mr. Caird's book is sure to have many readers. Many educated people in England will feel curious to know what sort of preaching is at a premium in the Scotch Church, where many things are so different from what they are among us. And we think we have been able to trace one or two indications in the volume, that Mr. Caird had an English audience in view. On at least two occasions we find the word *Sunday* ("a *Sunday* meditation," "*Sunday*-school teachers,") where we are mistaken if most Scotch preachers would not have employed the word *Sabbath*, which is in almost universal use north of the Tweed. But in Scotland, no doubt, Mr. Caird will find the great majority of his readers. Numbers of people who have listened to the fiery orator will be anxious to find whether the discourses which struck them so much when aided by the accessories of a wonderfully telling manner, will stand the severer test of a quiet perusal at home. So here is Mr. Caird's volume.

Here, then, we have the spent thunderbolts, motionless and cold. Here we have the locomotive engine, which tore along at sixty miles an hour, with the fire raked out and the steam gone down. Here, in short, we have the sermons of the great Scotch pulpit orator, stripped of the fire, the energy, the eloquent voice, the abundant gesticulation, which did so much to give them their charm when delivered and heard. There is but one story told as to the share which *manner* has always had in producing the practical effect which has been felt in listening to all great orators, from Demosthenes to Chalmers. Manner has always been the first, second, and third thing; and Mr. Caird could not publish his manner. We can examine his sermons calmly, and make up our mind about their merits deliberately, now. To do so was quite impossible while we were hurried away by the rushing eloquence of the living voice.

No doubt, then, this volume will disappoint the less intelligent class of Mr. Caird's admirers, who expect to be as deeply impressed in reading these discourses as they were in hearing them. No words standing quietly on the printed page can possibly have the effect of the same words spoken by the human voice, with immense feeling, and with all the arts of oratory. To expect that they should have an equal effect is to expect that the sword laid upon the table should cut as deeply as it did when grasped in a strong and skilful swordsman's hand. Mr. Caird's manner we know is a remarkably effective one; and of course the better the speaker's manner, the more his speech loses by being dissociated from it.

Still, after making every deduction, they are noble sermons; and we are not sure but that, with the cultivated reader, they will gain rather than lose by being read, not heard. There is a thoughtfulness and depth about them which can hardly be appreciated, unless when they are studied at leisure; and there are many sentences so felicitously expressed that we should grudge being hurried away from them by a rapid speaker, without being allowed to enjoy them a second time. And Mr. Caird, we feel as we read his pages, has succeeded in attaining a great end: he has shown that it is possible to produce sermons which shall be immensely popular, and popular with all classes of people: while yet all shall be so chaste and correct that the most fastidious taste could hardly take exception to a single word or phrase. In Mr. Caird's sermons there is nothing extravagant or eccentric either in thought or style. There is nothing unworthy of the clergyman and the scholar. There are no claptrap expedients to excite attention; nothing merely designed to make an audience gape; nothing that could possibly produce a titter. The solemnity of the house of God is never forgotten. Mr. Caird has no peculiar views, no special system of theology: he preaches the moderate and chastened Calvinism of the Church of Scotland, — precisely the doctrine of the Thirty-Nine Articles. He does not tell his hearers that the world is coming to an end; he finds nothing about

Louis Napoleon in the Book of Revelation; he does not select queer texts, or out of the way topics for discussion. It is no small matter to have proved in this age of pulpit drowsiness on the one hand, and pulpit extravagance on the other, that sound and temperate doctrine, logical accuracy, and classical language are quite compatible with great popularity. It is pleasant to find that discourses which are thoroughly manly and free from sentimentalism or cant prove attractive to a class which is too ready to run after such preachers as Mr. Charles Honeyman; and that sensible and judicious views, set forth in a style which is always scholarly and correct, and enforced by a manner in which there is no acting, howling, ventriloquizing, or gymnastic posturing, can hold vast crowds in a rapt attention, which would please even that slashing critic of the pulpit, *Habitans in Sicco.* Wide as the poles apart is such popularity as that of Mr. Caird from such popularity as that of Mr. Spurgeon and his class. It is very often with contempt and indignation that people of sense and taste listen to "popular preachers." No doubt such preachers may be well fitted to please and even to profit the great multitude who have little sense and no taste at all; but it is a fresh and agreeable sensation to the reviewer when he discovers a man whose eminence as a preacher is the sequel to a brilliant career at the University; whose sermons indicate a mind stored with the fruits of extensive reading and study; who shrinks instinctively from whatever is coarse or grotesque; who abhors all claptrap; who is perfectly simple and sincere without a trace of self-consciousness; in whose composition there is nothing spasmodic, nothing aiming to be subtle and succeeding in being unintelligible; and who seems, so far as it is possible to judge, to be actuated by an earnest desire to impress religious truth upon the minds of his hearers. And, indeed, when we think what is the great end of the preacher's endeavors, we feel that all mere literary qualities and graces are of no account whatever when compared with the presence of that efficacious element in the sermon which makes it such as that it shall be the means of saving souls. For ourselves, we should prefer a thousand times the magic spell which Miss Marsh (all honor to the name) exercised at Sydenham over *English Hearts*, to the church-crowding eloquence of Chalmers. And in that solemn sense, perhaps the greatest of all English preachers is the homely, pithy, earnest Mr. Ryle.

We confess that we do not think sermons, generally speaking, by any means attractive reading; and we have not read a sufficient number of them to be able to institute a comparison between the printed sermons of Mr. Caird and those of other distinguished preachers. Still, we may say that we do not find in Mr. Caird the originality of Mr. Melvill, or the talent of that eminent divine for eliciting from his text a great amount of striking and unexpected instruction. There is nothing of the daring ingenuity and the novel interpretations of Archbishop Whately. Mr. Caird will never found a school of disciples, like Dr. Arnold; nor startle steady-going old clergymen, like Mr. Robertson of Brighton. He is so clear and comprehensible that he will not, like Mr. Maurice, make many readers feel or fancy the presence of something very fine, if they could only be sure what the preacher would be at. He hardly sets a scene before us in such life-like reality as does Dr. Guthrie. And although people may go to hear him for the intellectual treat, they will never go to be amused, as by Mr. Spurgeon. He will never point a sentence at the expense of due solemnity, like a great Scotch preacher who contrasted men's profession and their practice by saying, "Profession says, 'On this hang the law and the prophets;' Practice says, 'Hang the law and the prophets!'" He will not, like Mr. Cecil, arrest attention by beginning his sermon, "A man was hanged this morning at Tyburn;" nor like Rowland Hill, by exclaiming "Matches! matches! matches!" — nor like somebody or other by saying as he wiped his face, "It's damned hot!" — nor like Whitefield, by vociferating "Fire! fire — in hell!" He will not imitate Sterne, who read out as his text, "It is better to go to the house of mourning than to go to the house of feasting;" and then exclaimed, as the first words of his discourse, "That I deny!" — making it appear in a little while that such was not the preacher's own sentiment, but what might be supposed to be the reflection of an irreligious man. He will never introduce into his discourses long dialogues and arguments between God and Satan, in which the latter is made to exhibit a deficiency in logical power which is, to say the least, remarkable in one who is believed not to lack intellect. He will not appear in the pulpit with his shirt-sleeves turned back over his cassock, in ball-room fashion; and after giving out his text, astonish the congregation by bellowing, "Now, you young men there, listen to my sermon, and don't stare at my wrists!" All such arts for attracting or compelling interest and attention Mr. Caird eschews.

And when we read his sermons, though we feel their interest, we find it hard to say in what it lies. They are admirable sermons: but we should scarcely, *à priori*, have ventured to predict their vast popular effect. The finely-linked thought, the completeness and symmetry of the discussion, the beautifully appropriate illustrations, none stuck in for ornament, but all *bonâ fide* illustrating the subject; the general sobriety and good sense: — these are literary characteristics which we should say would prove hardly discernible, and certainly not appreciable, save by people of considerable cultivation. Must we, then, fall back upon Manner, and suppose that the charm which gives these sermons their popular effect lies in a great measure in the touching and thrilling tones, the tears in the voice, the enchaining earnestness, with which they are poured forth by an orator who, like Whitefield, could almost melt an audience to tears by saying *Mesopotamia?* Or may we not rather ask whether Mr. Caird, in his elaborate and fastidious preparation of these discourses for the press, has not cut out, or smoothed down, much which was most striking when the sermons were preached, but which might have appeared of doubtful taste when they were carefully and critically read over? Perhaps these sermons, while gaining in *finish* and perfection of literary construction, have lost some of the salient points, the roughness and raciness, which added to their piquancy when delivered. We have heard Mr. Caird preach two of those now published; and we find he has drawn his pen through several of those phrases which had stuck longest and most vividly in our memory. We think he has erred here. He has been over-cautious, over-fastidious. It is on the very borderland of good taste that the deepest popular impression is made: and there was no fear of Mr. Caird's crossing the border. And we believe that upon ordinary Sundays, by discourses of much less elaborate preparation, he produces even a greater effect upon his congregation than could be produced by any sermon in this volume, were it preached exactly as it is printed.

The published discourses are certainly very ambitious in thought and style. There is a want of repose in them; and when two or three are read successively, the effect upon the mind is a little wearisome. But no doubt they were written to be preached; and when they are listened to one at a time, and at intervals of a week, this result will not follow. It is well to have the attention riveted and the nerves tightened for half an hour in the week: but the process becomes painful when it lasts too long. We remark a little mannerism here and there. An extraordinary number of paragraphs begin with the word *Now:* and the term *yearning* is, we think, of much too frequent occurrence. The result of the abundant use of this word, and of the occasional heaping up of adjectives unconnected by any copulative, and of nearly the same meaning, is to leave an occasional impression of an excess of the *gushing* element. There is the least shade here and there of the cant of the present day about "the response of our deepest nature," — its "instinctive throb," and its "instinctive yearnings," — phrases which to plain folk mean just nothing at all. We confess that we do not like the word *fair* several times applied to the Almighty — "the alone Infinitely True and Holy and Fair." The word suggests ideas which are not in harmony with so solemn an application of it. And as we are fault-finding at any rate, we may here state that in all the volume there is but a single passage which appears to us to be in glaringly and painfully bad taste: so much and so disagreeably so that we wonder that Mr. Caird should have published it. It is that passage in which heaven is described as a place —

where, *heart to heart with God*, happy souls *revel* unsated, undazzled, in the Essential Element of Love.

The description appears to us most irreverent, and its entire strain most unbecoming. Mr. Spurgeon could hardly have said anything worse. We have drawn the pen through it in our copy, that our pleasure in reading the volume may not be interrupted by its jarring and irritating effect; and we trust that in the future editions which are sure to be wanted, Mr. Caird will strike the entire passage out. It is most unworthy of him.

We do not know whether Mr. Caird was accustomed to preach such sermons as those now published to his country congregation. There are many phrases and sentences in them which to rustics would be quite unintelligible. What could a ploughman make of the following question: —

What elements must we eliminate from suffering caused by sin in forming our ideal of suffering purity? — (p. 171.)

But as we know that Madame Rachel, by her wonderfully expressive gesticulation, succeeded, while in Russia, in making her meaning intelligible to people who did not understand the language which she spoke, so Mr. Caird may have been able to get country folk to understand the general drift of sentences containing many words whose sense they did not know. And indeed the late Hugh Miller maintains that sermons which are in a considerable degree *over the heads* of a rural congregation, are the most likely both to interest and improve them.

By this time, we doubt not, our readers are impatient of our remarks, and would like to hear Mr. Caird speak for himself. We proceed to give a more specific account of the contents of the volume.

It contains eleven sermons, the fourth being divided into two parts, intended, we presume, to be preached at different times; and a glance at the Table of Contents at once makes us suspect that the sermons have, with a view to publication, been materially changed from what they were when they were preached. Sermons in Scotland, as in England, have a sort of average length, from which they do not deviate materially except on extraordinary occasions. But while Mr. Caird's first sermon occupies forty pages, the second occupies only twenty-five, the fourth twenty, and the fifth thirteen. The first sermon is thus three times as long as the fifth, and twice as long as the fourth. So if the fifth sermon be of the standard Scotch length of three quarters of an hour, the first would occupy in the delivery two hours and a quarter. Or if the first sermon is to be taken as the standard, the fifth would crumple up into the "just fifteen minutes."

The subject of the first sermon is *The Self-evidencing Nature of Divine Truth;* its text is, "By manifestation of the truth commending ourselves to every man's conscience in the sight of God." (2 Cor. iv. 2.) It is a scholarly and masterly production; but the thought which forms its staple is more severe than is usual in Mr. Caird's discourses. It is, in short, a view set out with consummate tact and ingenuity, of the internal evidence of the truth of the Christian religion. We should ask our university men and our clergy to read this sermon the first. They will find in it a strict and unerring logic, great skill in simplifying and illustrating abstract ideas, and a style which could scarcely be improved. But when we pass to the discourse which stands next in order we find much clearer indications of the power of the popular orator.

It is on *Self-Ignorance;* the text, "Who can understand his errors." (Psalm xix. 12.) We almost wonder in reading the former sermon how Mr. Caird can be so popular; but when we read this, more especially if we have heard Mr. Caird preach, and can imagine the fashion in which he would deliver many passages, we have less difficulty in understanding the matter. Here is the introduction, which would arrest attention at once: —

Of all kinds of ignorance, that which is the most strange, and, in so far as it is voluntary, the most culpable, is our ignorance of self. For not only is the subject in this case that which might be expected to possess for us the greatest interest, but it is the one concerning which we have amplest facilities and opportunities of information. Who of us would not think it a strange and unaccountable story, could it be told of any man now present, that for years he had harbored under his roof a guest whose face he had never seen — a constant inmate of his home, who was yet to him altogether unknown? It is no supposition however, but an unquestionable fact, that to not a few of us, from the first moment of existence there has been present, not beneath the roof, but within the breast, a mysterious resident, an inseparable companion, nearer to us than friend or brother, yet of whom after all we know little or nothing. What man of intelligence amongst us would not be ashamed to have had in his possession for years some rare or universally admired volume with its leaves uncut? or to be the proprietor of a repository filled with the most exquisite productions of genius, and the rarest specimens in science and art, which yet he himself never thought of entering? Yet surely no book so worthy of perusal, no chamber containing objects of study so curious, so replete with interest for us, as that which seldom or never attracts our observation — the book, the chamber of our own hearts. We sometimes reproach with folly those persons who have travelled far and seen much of distant countries, and yet have been content to remain comparatively unacquainted with their own. But how venial such folly compared with that of ranging over all other departments of knowledge, going abroad with perpetual inquisitiveness over earth and sea and sky, whilst there is a little world within the breast which is still to us an unexplored region. Other scenes and objects we can study only at intervals: they are not always accessible, or can be reached only by long and laborious journeys; but the bridge of consciousness is soon crossed — we have but to close the eye and withdraw the thoughts from the world without in order at any moment to wander through the scenes and explore the phenomena of the still more wondrous world within. To examine other objects delicate and elaborate instruments are often necessary: the researches of the astronomer, the botanist, the chemist, can be prosecuted only by means of rare and costly apparatus; but the power of reflection, that faculty more wondrous than any mechanism which art has ever fashioned, is an instrument possessed by all — the poorest and most illiterate alike with the most cultured and refined have at their command an apparatus by which to sweep the inner firmament of the soul, and bring into view its manifold phenomena of thought and feeling and motive. And yet with all the unequalled facilities for acquiring this sort of knowledge, can it be questioned that it is the one sort of knowledge that is most commonly neglected, and that, even amongst those who would disdain the imputation of ignorance in history or science or literature, there are multitudes who have never acquired the merest rudiments of the knowledge of self?

By no means a far-fetched or difficult idea, the reader must see; and turned in many lights and brought out by a throng of illustrations; but a good and natural introduction to a sermon on self-ignorance, and quite sure, if given with a sort of *extempore* air, as if each successive comparison struck the speaker just at the moment, to get the people to listen with great stillness.

Then, restricting his view to the matter of a man's moral defects, Mr. Caird goes on to point out several reasons why the sinful man does not "understand his errors." The first is, that sin can be truly measured only when it is resisted. This principle indeed holds good of all forces: —

The rapid stream flows smooth and silent when there are no obstacles to stay its progress; but hurl a rock into its bed, and the roar and surge of the arrested current will instantly reveal its force. You cannot estimate the wind's strength when it rushes over the open plain; but when it reaches and wrestles with the trees of the forest, or lashes the sea into fury, then, resisted, you perceive its power. Or if, amid the ice-bound regions of the north, an altogether unbroken continuous winter prevailed, comparatively unnoticed would be its stern dominion; but it is the coming round of a more genial season, when the counteracting agency of the sun begins to prevail, that reveals, by the rending of the solid masses of ice, and by the universal stir and crash, the intensity of the bygone winter's cold.

The second reason is, that sin often makes a man afraid to know himself. The third, that sinful habits steal on men slowly and gradually. The fourth, that as character gradually deteriorates, there is a parallel deterioration of the standard by which we judge it. Such are the "heads" of the sermon, as they are called in Scotland. They are all very clearly brought out and abundantly illustrated, and the sermon ends with a stirring "practical application."

It is possible now to seek the peace of self-forgetfulness, — to refuse to be disturbed, — to sink for a little longer into our dream of self-satisfaction; but it is a peace as transient as it is unreal. Soon, at the latest, and all the more terrible for the delay, the awakening must come. There are sometimes sad awakenings from sleep in this world. It is very sad to dream by night of vanished joys, — to revisit old scenes, and dwell once more among the unforgotten forms of our loved and lost, — to see in the dreamland the old familiar look, and hear the well-remembered tones of a voice long hushed and still, and then to wake with the morning light to the aching sense of our loneliness again. It were very sad for the poor criminal to wake from sweet dreams of other and happier days, — days of innocence, and hope, and peace, when kind friends, and a happy home, and an honored or unstained name were his, — to wake in his cell on the morning of his execution to the horrible recollection that all this is gone for ever, and that to-day he must die a felon's death. But inconceivably more awful than any awakening which earthly daybreak has ever brought, shall be the awakening of the self-deluded soul when it is roused in horror and surprise from the dream of life — to meet Almighty God in judgment!

Of course all this has been very often said before; but probably those who heard Mr. Caird declaim these sentences, thought that it had never before been said so forcibly.

The third sermon is upon *Spiritual Influence.* Its text is that passage in the Saviour's speech to Nicodemus, "The wind bloweth where it listeth," &c. (S. John iii. 7, 8.) Here the preacher argues in defence of the Christian doctrine of Regeneration, maintaining that whatever difficulties surround that doctrine have their parallel in Nature. The "heads" here are three. The analogy between Nature and Revelation is traced in regard to *Supernaturalness*, *Sovereignty*, or *apparent Arbitrariness*, and *Secrecy.* The gist of the first head is given in a sentence towards its close: —

If not the slightest movement of matter can take place without the immediate agency of God, shall we wonder that His agency is needed in the higher and more subtle processes of mind?

The burden of the second head is given thus: —

Marvel not nor be disquieted at your inability to explain the laws that regulate the operations of an infinite agent; for in a province much more within the range of human observation there are familiar agents at work, the operations of which are equally inscrutable, arbitrary, incalculable. Think it not strange that the ways of the Spirit of God are unaccountable to a mind by which even the common phenomena of the wind are irreducible to law.

Then, under the third division of the discourse, Mr. Caird shows that the fact that the Holy Spirit works unseen is no reason for doubting that he does really act: —

As you have surveyed the face of nature in some tranquil season, — the unbreathing summer noon or the hushed twilight hour, — every feature of the landscape has seemed suffused with calmness, every tree hung its motionless head, every unrippled brook crept on with almost inaudible murmuring, every plant, and flower, and leaf seemed as if bathed in repose. But anon you perhaps perceived a change passing over the scene, as if at the bidding of some invisible power; — a rushing sound, as of music evoked by invisible fingers from the harp of nature, began to fill your ear; the leaves began to quiver and rustle, the trees to bend and shake, the stream to dash onward with ruffled breast and brawling sound, and from every wood, and glade, and glen, there came forth the intimation that a new and most potent agent was abroad and working around you. And yet while you marked the change on the face of nature, did you perceive the agent that effected it? Did the wind of heaven take visible form and appear as a winged messenger of God's will, hurrying hither and thither from object to object? Do you know and can you describe the way in which he worked, — how his touch fell upon the flowret and bade it wave, or his grasp seized the sturdy oak and strove with it till it quivered and bent? No, you cannot. You have not penetrated so far into the secrets of nature. You have seen only the effects, but not the agent or the process of his working. You have seen the wind's influences, but not itself. But do you therefore marvel, or hesitate to believe, that it has indeed been abroad and working over the face of the earth? or do you ever doubt whether there be any such agent as the wind at all? No; you have heard the sound thereof, you have witnessed the stir and commotion of nature that told of its presence, and so you believe in its existence, though you "cannot tell whence it cometh or whither it goeth."

The three "heads" having been illustrated, the sermon is wound up by various practical inferences, given at considerable length.

The fourth sermon is from the text, "No man hath seen God at any time; the only-begotten Son, which is in the bosom of the Father, He hath declared him." (S. John i. 18.) It is divided into two parts, the subject of the former being *The Invisible God*, and that of the latter *The Manifestation of the Invisible God.* The preacher, having dwelt upon the fact that God is invisible to human eyes, and shown that not without destroying the character of our present state of being as a state of trial and training could the case be otherwise; goes on to show that the Saviour, by his person, his life and character, his sufferings and death, is a visible manifestation of the invisible God.

We believe that this sermon, when preached, was a

very effective one; and probably the view which it sets out struck many ordinary hearers as novel and original. It is not, however, necessary to tell the well-informed reader that Mr. Caird has here done nothing more than present, in a somewhat more popular and rhetorical form, the substance of a sermon upon the same text by Archbishop Whately, which, being detached from its text, is now published in the first series of the Archbishop's Essays.[1] The reader will find it interesting to do what we have done since writing the last sentence, — to peruse the two sermons together, and compare them. The Archbishop's sermon was addressed to a learned audience: it was preached before the University of Oxford; and accordingly it is the more critical and philosophical. Mr. Caird intended his sermon to be preached to ordinary congregations, and accordingly he quotes no Greek, and lengthens out his remarks upon those parts of his subject which most admit of popular illustration. Some observations early in the discourse, on the Invisibility of the Almighty, appear to have been suggested by Letter VI. in Foster's Essay, *On a Man writing Memoirs of Himself*, in which that topic is discussed with a power unparalleled in theological literature. And whoever wishes to find *The Manifestation of the Invisible God* through the personal Redeemer set out in a very interesting fashion, may find it in the first two chapters of a book of so popular a character as Jacob Abbott's *Corner-Stone.* The view taken by Abbott is precisely that of Archbishop Whately, as may be inferred from the motto prefixed to the first chapter, which is, "The glory

[1] *Essays on some of the Peculiarities of the Christian Religion.* Essay II. "On the Declaration of God in His Son," pp. 98–118. Edition of 1856.

of God in the face of Jesus Christ." It does not appear, however, that Abbott was acquainted with the Archbishop's discourse.

Although we cannot give Mr. Caird the credit of having thought out the idea which is pressed in this sermon, still he is entitled to the praise of having grasped it with great force, and of having set it forth in a discourse which would produce a strong popular effect. It must be said, however, that the style of this sermon is ambitious to a somewhat extravagant degree; in taste and accuracy it is very inferior to several of the other sermons in the volume. We should judge it to have been a comparatively juvenile production, which its author has got so fond of that he cannot now try it by the same severe standard as his recent compositions. And we are not sure if the phrase, *a woe that Deity could feel*, contains very sound theology. Deity can feel nothing like woe.

The sermon which comes next is, we think, one of the most eloquent in the book: it contains, perhaps, finer passages than any other. And although it is highly wrought up in several parts, there is not a word in it to which the severest critic could take exception. It is on *The Solitariness of Christ's Sufferings:* the text, "I have trodden the wine-press alone." It sets out with the following beautiful and natural introduction: —

There is always a certain degree of solitude about a great mind. Even a mere human being cannot rise preëminently above the level of his fellow-men without becoming conscious of a certain solitariness of spirit gathering round him. The loftiest intellectual elevation, indeed, is nowise inconsistent with a genial openness and simplicity of nature, nor is there anything impossible or unexampled in the combination of a grasp of intellect that could cope with the loftiest abstractions of philosophy, and a playfulness that could condescend to sport with a child. Yet whilst it is thus true that the possessor of a great mind may be capable of sympathizing with, of entering kindly into the views and feelings, the joys and sorrows of inferior minds, it must at the same time be admitted that there is ever a range of thought and feeling into which they cannot enter with him. They may accompany him, so to speak, a certain height up the mountain, but there is a point at which their feebler powers become exhausted, and if he ascend beyond that, his path must be a solitary one.

What is thus true of all great minds must have been, beyond all others, characteristic of the mind of Him who, with all his real and very humanity, could "think it no robbery to be equal with God." Jesus was indeed a lonely being in the world. With all the exquisite tenderness of his human sympathies, — touched with the feeling of our every sinless infirmity, — with a heart that could feel for a peasant's sorrow, and an eye that could beam with tenderness on an infant's face, — he was yet one who, wherever he went, and by whomsoever surrounded, was, in the secrecy of his inner being, profoundly *alone*. You who are parents have, I dare say, often felt struck by the reflection, what a world of thoughts, and cares, and anxieties are constantly present to *your* minds into which your children cannot enter. You may be continually amongst them, holding familiar intercourse with them, condescending to all their childish thoughts and feelings, entering into all their childish ways, — yet every day there are a thousand things passing through your mind, with respect, for instance, to your business or profession, your schemes and projects, your troubles, fears, hopes and ambitions in life, your social connections, the incidents and events that are going on in the world around you, — there are a thousand reflections and feelings on such matters passing daily through your mind, of which your children know nothing. You never dream of talking to them on such subjects, and they could not understand or sympathize with you if you did. There is a little world in which the play of their passions is strong and vivid, but beyond that their sympathies entirely fail. And perhaps there is no spectacle so exquisitely touching as that which one sometimes witnesses in a house of mourning — the elder members of the family bowed down to the dust by some heavy sorrow, whilst the little children sport around in unconscious playfulness.

The bearing of this illustration is obvious. What children are to the mature-minded man, the rest of mankind were to Jesus.

The preacher goes on to say that he intends to follow out the thought of Christ's solitariness with particular reference to his *sorrows*. And he does so with eloquence so impressive that we regret we can find room for no further specimens of it.

We have not space to do more than mention the subjects of the remaining sermons which make up the volume. The sermon which follows that on *The Solitariness of Christ's Sufferings*, is a sort of companion piece, on the text " Rejoice, inasmuch as ye are partakers of the sufferings of Christ." (1 Peter iv. 13.) There is a discourse on *Spiritual Rest* which we think less happy; a very able one on the text, " I wish that thou mayest prosper and be in health even as thy soul prospereth," (3 John 2); another admirable sermon on " All things are yours," which Mr. Caird preached before the Queen last autumn. There is a temperate and judicious sermon on *The Simplicity of Christian Ritual*, in which the author cautions us against attaching too much consequence to such things as church architecture and stately church services. At the same time Mr. Caird describes these perilous delights with such manifest gusto, that it is quite obvious he would have no serious objections to the cathedral worship and to York Minster. It is indeed quite true that —

There is a semi-sensuous delight in religious worship imposingly conducted, which may be felt by the least conscientious even more than by the sincerely devout. The soul that is devoid of true reverence towards God may be rapt into a spurious elation while in rich and solemn tones the loud-voiced organ peals forth his praise. The heart that never felt one throb of love to Christ may thrill with an ecstasy of sentimental tenderness while soft voices, now blending, now dividing, in combined or responsive strains, celebrate the glories of redeeming love. And not seldom the most sensual and profligate of men have owned to that strange, undefined, yet delicious feeling of awe and elevation that steals over the spirit in some fair adorned temple on which all the resources of art have been lavished, where soft light floods the air and mystic shadows play over pillar and arch and vaulted roof, and the hushed and solemn stillness is broken only by the voice of prayer or praise.

All quite true; but though no doubt such feeling as Mr. Caird describes is not religion, it may prepare the way for receiving impressions which are properly religious. Nor can we evade the grand principle, that we ought to consecrate to the Almighty our very best in architecture and in melody as in everything else, by the reflection that such things, like all others in this world, may be abused. And, by the way, Mr. Caird appears to have forgotten to tell his hearers that if worshippers in the south may mistake their æsthetic enjoyment of beautiful church-worship for true devotion, there is at least as much risk that worshippers farther north may confuse their enjoyment of the intellectual treat of listening to impassioned and brilliant pulpit-oratory with a real reception of the great truths which are in such oratory set forth. If Anglicans must smash their stained-glass, board over their vaulted roofs, and turn off their cathedral choristers, then ought Mr. Caird to cut out his imagery, to destroy the rhythm of the last sentences of his paragraphs, and to cultivate a chronic sore-throat. If it be right for a clergyman to labor day and night to make his sermon beautiful, why not his church as well? And if the church must be only moderately beautiful, then the preaching must not be obtrusively so. Does Mr. Caird mean to insinuate a covert assurance, that however pleasing and admirable his discourses may be, he could, were it not for fear of exciting æsthetic emotion, make them a great deal better?

The last sermon in the volume is on *The Comparative Influence of Character and Doctrine.* The text is "Take heed unto thyself, and unto the doctrine." (1 Tim. iv. 16.) And Mr. Caird, not perhaps with very critical accuracy, maintains that St. Paul, in writing that text, placed the two matters to be attended to in the order of their importance: thus signifying that the life was of more moment than the instruction; that it was the preacher's duty to take heed, first to himself, and secondly to his doctrine. Whether the general principle be implied in the text or not, there is no doubt it is a sound one; and the sermon enforces the old story, that example is better than precept, with extraordinary ability and eloquence.

Thus have we endeavored, as regards these discourses of Mr. Caird, to do what we used to do every Sunday evening when we were children at home: to wit, to "give an account of the sermons." It was rather wearisome work then, we remember; we trust our readers have not found it so now. Let us add, that fine as are these published sermons, we are not sure that they are Mr. Caird's best. Authors are proverbially bad judges of their own productions, and preachers are no exceptions to the rule. And we have heard from some of the author's warm admirers fond recollections of sermons on the texts, *Every man shall bear his own burden*, *Surely I come quickly*, *There shall be no more pain*, *All things are become new*, *They have Moses and the prophets, let them hear them*, — which are said to contain passages which for telling effect upon a congregation are not equalled by anything in the printed volume. Perhaps the great preacher thought it as well not to give his followers the opportunity of examining the red-hot shot after it had grown cold.

An amusing proof of Mr. Caird's great popularity is afforded by the number of young preachers who try to imitate him. And indeed it cannot be denied that several have succeeded in brushing their hair very like him. Others can walk up the pulpit-stair very much as Mr.

Caird does. Several have a happy knack of wiping their face like him at the close of each "head," and more have successfully imitated some tones of his voice, and the manner in which he pronounces certain words which he pronounces ill. The general impression left on the mind by any imitator of Mr. Caird, is that of a very fat goose attempting to fly like an eagle. It may be supposed that only the weakest of the aspirants to the clerical office will join the class of direct imitators. But Mr. Caird's success has had a powerful influence upon young men of a higher stamp, in leading them to cultivate a highly animated and impassioned kind of pulpit oratory. The calm unexciting elegance of a former age is at a discount in the North. Dr. Blair would preach to empty benches now. And it must be admitted that the standard of Scotch preaching is at this time a very high one. The sermon is so completely the great thing in the Scotch service, that extraordinary labor is often spent upon it. It would be easy to mention the names of a score of preachers who, if they were to sink as far as the Surrey Music Hall, could, without claptrap or buffoonery, completely eclipse Mr. Spurgeon in the arts of popular oratory. Poor as is the worldly remuneration of the Scotch clergy, it is wonderful how the most able and accomplished students in the Universities of Scotland are found to devote themselves to that ill-paid ministry. A, who was first all through the classes, goes into the church, fills several important charges with great ability, and dies at the age of fifty, worn down by labor and excitement, an Edinburgh minister with six hundred a year. B, whom he easily beat in every competition, goes to the Scotch bar, does pretty fairly, is made (by the Whigs) a judge, draws his three or four thousand *per annum*, and by judiciously husbanding his bodily and mental energies, is able to adorn that high station to the age of eighty-six. In six months after A dies, the crowds he thrilled by his eloquence have entirely forgotten him. Yet possibly the work he did is remembered somewhere: and crowds of clever young lads in the academic shades of Edinburgh and Glasgow aim rather to be A than B.

A great deal has of late been said and written about preaching. It seems to be agreed on all hands that it will no longer do to have sermons such that people cannot listen to them. Assuming sound instruction as present in all sermons, the highest of all remaining qualities of the sermon is *interest.* Whatever literary characteristics tend to make a sermon *interesting,* are good; and the very highest, if they make it uninteresting, are bad. Yet how great a proportion of the sermons one hears, — however deserving in other respects, — are utterly devoid of the grand quality, interest. The sermons are able, well-thought, and well-written compositions, but they are very *dry.* Yet Sydney Smith's saying of literature in general holds especially good of pulpit literature, that every style is good, *except the tiresome.* We believe that church is the only place where people do not listen to what is said to them. "I like so much," said the laboring man in Southey's *Doctor,* "to go to church on Sunday: when the sermon begins I lean back in the corner, and lay up my legs, and *think of nothing.*" We sympathize with that poor man. It is the clergyman's business to make his sermon such that while it is going on no one shall be able to "think of nothing."

There are two things which from our earliest youth have in our mind stood out together as equally desirable, and in the nature of things equally impossible. The one is, to bring matters to such a point that it shall be possible to get out of our snug warm bed on a cold winter morning without a very great effort; the other is, that the service of the Church should be made such that it shall not be tiresome to be present at it. We believe that in the case of men in general the most insufferably tedious and wearisome hours they have ever spent, have been many of those which they have spent at church.

As to the prayers of the Anglican ritual, no doubt they are very beautiful, though with a calm scholarly beauty which makes no impression upon children or uneducated people. There are likewise by far too many of them; and we are persuaded that if the truth were told, most of our readers have experienced that sense of relief we used to feel in our youth, when our worthy pastor and master of those days reached that prayer of St. Chrysostom which signified that the long service was nearly over. We are not going to say anything of the devotional part of the Church service; because we fear that no beauty and no brevity will ever make that portion of it interesting except to the sincerely devout; and there we must leave the matter. But there is another part of the usual public worship which we really think need not be so horribly tedious as it is in most cases, — we mean the sermon. When Edward Irving published a volume of discourses, instead of designating them by the usual name of sermons, he preferred to describe them on his title-page as *Orations;* mentioning as his reason the well-ascertained fact, that there is something in the very name of *sermon* that makes people grow sleepy, and that suggests dulness, yawning, and tediousness to the last degree.

We quite believe that in the nature of things it is

properly impossible to render serious instruction as interesting as light amusement. Disguise it as we can, work will never be made so attractive as play. Boys are instantly aware when it is intended to benefit them under the pretext of amusing them ; and the revulsion is instant and complete. When Dr. Chalmers said that the thing which above all others has tended to make *Robinson Crusoe* such a favorite book with boys is, that no book combines to such a degree instruction with amusement, he made a statement just as absurd and false as if he had said that black was white. But while we admit all this, we believe that the pill may be gilded so far, and that sermons need not be nauseous as medicines are, and never to be listened to but by a conscious effort and as an irksome task.

He would be a benefactor of his race who should succeed in laying down a code of rules, by obeying which men of ordinary ability might succeed in preparing and preaching sermons, which should be interesting to an ordinary congregation, and at the same time characterized by good sense and good taste. These two ends have hardly ever been attained together. There are numbers of sensible and correct preachers, whom no one can listen to for ten minutes without becoming aware of that peculiar pricking of the veins, and disposition to fidget uneasily, which are associated with the last degree of weariness. There is really such a thing as *acute* tediousness. And of the much smaller number of pulpit orators who succeed systematically in keeping the attention of their congregations thoroughly alive from the beginning to the end of their discourses, most, if not all, deal to a great degree in what may be termed claptrap. Their sermons are often outrageously revolting to men of refined taste, or filled with views which are extravagant and absurd.

It is a great end to get an entire congregation to listen with interested attention from first to last of a sermon; but this end may be attained at too considerable an expense. One can easily think of various expedients that would for a time attract a crowd, and get it to gaze stupidly for an hour. A person from America preached some time since in some dissenting meeting-house in this country, arrayed in skins and feathers as an Indian chief. He was described as a war-chief of the Somethingorotherawaws, and vast crowds, with visions of scalping-knives and wampum-belts, came to hear him, till it was understood that he was only a porter at a steamboat wharf on the Mississippi, and that his strange attire would have excited much more surprise in his native place than it did at Manchester. A small boy of nine or ten years old was advertised to preach in a large building in Glasgow; and to the disgrace of that town some three or four thousand people crowded to hear him on more occasions than one. An individual calling himself the Angel Gabriel, held large assemblages of the Modern Athenians in breathless attention by preaching with a trumpet in his hand, which he sounded at the end of each paragraph of his sermon. The usual tedium of a church would be dissipated were the officiating clergyman to turn a somersault at intervals. Any wretched mountebank may keep attention alive by shrieks and yells, rushings about his platform, imitations of the Yankee snuffle or the gibberish of Cockayne, — in short, by degrading the pulpit beneath the level of the stage of a minor theatre. But the question is, how may a man, without sinking the clergyman, the scholar, and the gentleman, — without becoming a buffoon or a melodramatic actor, — without eccentricity in the choice of texts and topics, in illustration or gesture, — make a sermon as interesting and attractive as in the nature of things religious instruction can be made.

There is one obvious rule which is very generally violated: a preacher should take some pains to make his meaning intelligible. Many a clergyman who would not think of giving orders to his man-servant in terms which that person could not by possibility understand, is yet accustomed every Sunday to address a rustic congregation in discourses which would be just as intelligible *to it* if they were preached in Hebrew. Let a preacher be direct and straightforward: let him avoid roundabout sentences; they are much more puzzling to the dull brain of a country bumpkin than are mere big words: let him put his meaning sharply and clearly. We believe that this is a great secret of interest. We might suggest the abundant use of illustration *which really illustrates* the subject; but every preacher has not the faculty which enables him to use this arm. Comparisons drawn from daily life are a tower of force. And we strongly recommend to all young clergymen whose pulpit manner is not yet hopelessly formed, the reading of a good deal of light literature. They should read *that* to see what kind of matter interests the majority of minds. Most preachers have a thoroughly mistaken notion on that point. A man who has brought himself to feel a deep interest in dry tomes of old Theology, or even in the more flimsy popular theological literature of the day, forgets that the human race in general takes no interest in such things; and fancies that when producing thought which he knows or thinks would interest *himself*, he is all right. He is far mistaken! Who reads Theology by choice? Ask the publisher of ordinary sermons. Let the preacher, then, make himself familiar with the kind of thought and style which people read because attracted and interested by it. We do not say that he should take that for his model, or imitate it in any way. But let him see there what sort of *pabulum* suits the common appetite; and let him aim at making his sermons if possible as easy and pleasant to be listened to as *that* is to be read. We believe that the main cause why sermons are so dull is that their writers do not seriously set it as a worthy aim to make them interesting. Most preachers — if we except those whose end is simply to cover their paper with the least possible trouble — aim at completeness of treatment, at elegance of style, at scholarly tone and finish, — all ends quite apart from the great end of *interest*. If interest were systematically made the great object of endeavor; if clergymen remembered that unless they get their congregation to listen to them, they might as well not preach at all, — we are convinced, with average talent and average industry on the preacher's part, there would be fewer dry sermons and fewer sleepers in church.

CHAPTER XIII.

OULITA THE SERF.[1]

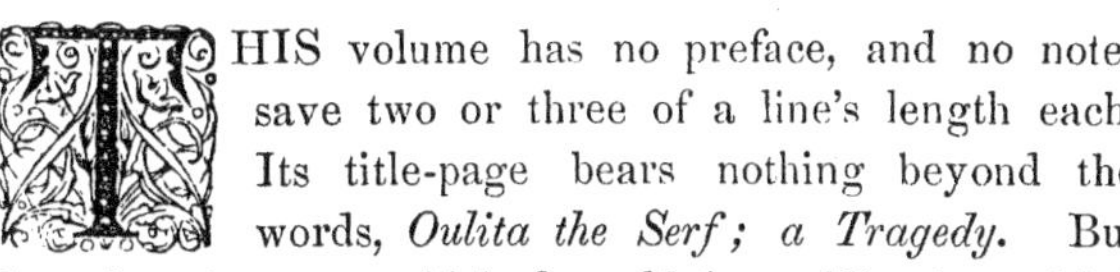

THIS volume has no preface, and no notes save two or three of a line's length each. Its title-page bears nothing beyond the words, *Oulita the Serf; a Tragedy.* But the advertisements which foretold its publication, added a fact which made us open the book with a very different feeling from that with which we should have taken up an ordinary anonymous play, — a fact which at once excited high expectations, — and which, we doubt not, has already introduced *Oulita* to a wide circle of readers, each prepared to gauge its merits by a very severe test and a very high standard. The forthcoming volume was announced as *Oulita the Serf; a Tragedy: by the Author of* "*Friends in Council.*"

The disguise of the author of that work is becoming ragged. We have found, in more than one library, where a special glory of binding was bestowed upon the book and its charming sequel, that though the title-page bore no name, the volumes were marked with a name which is well and honorably known. And indeed there are few books which are so calculated as *Friends in Council* to make the reader wish to know who is their author:

[1] *Oulita the Serf.* A Tragedy. London: John W. Parker and Son. 1858.

and surely the language has none which affords its writer less reason for seeking any disguise. Yet it is not for us to add the author's name to a title-page which the author has chosen to send nameless into the world: though we may be permitted to say, that in common with an increasing host of readers, we cannot think of him as other than a kindly and sympathetic friend.

Accordingly, we expected a great deal from this new work. We were not entirely taken by surprise, indeed, when we saw it announced; for Ellesmere, in *Friends in Council*, makes several quotations from the works of "a certain obscure dramatist," which are likely to set the thoughtful reader inquiring. And whoever shall carefully collate the advertisements of the late Mr. Pickering's publications, will discover that the author of *Oulita* published fifteen years ago a historical drama, entitled *King Henry the Second;* and a tragedy entitled *Catherine Douglas*, whose heroine is the strong-hearted Scottish maiden who thrust her arm into the staple of a door from which the bolt had been removed, in the desperate hope of thus retarding for a moment the entrance of the conspirators who murdered James the First. But these plays are comparatively unknown; and probably very many readers who have been delighted by that graceful, unaffected prose, were quite unaware that its writer was endowed with the faculty of verse. We could not fail, indeed, to discern in his prose works the wide, genial sympathy, the deep thoughtfulness, the delicate sensitiveness, of the true poet. And his talent, we could also discover from these, is essentially dramatic. The characters in *Friends in Council* have each their marked individuality; while yet that individuality is maintained and brought out, not by coarse caricature, but by those delicate and natural touches which make us feel that we are conversing with real human beings, and not with mere names in a book. It is an extremely easy thing to make us recognize a character when he reappears upon the stage, by making him perpetually repeat some silly and vulgar phrase. Smith is the man who never enters without roaring "It's all serene:" Jones is the individual who always says, "Not to put too fine a point upon it." Nor is it difficult for an author to *tell us* that his hero is a great man, a philanthropist, a thinker, an actor: it is quite another matter to make him speak and act so that we shall find *that* out for ourselves. Most characters in modern works need to be labelled; — like the sign-painter's lion, which no one would have guessed was a lion but for the words *This is a lion*, written beneath it.

Let us say at once, that this tragedy has surpassed our expectation. It is a noble and beautiful work. It is strongly marked with the same characteristics which distinguish its author's former writings. Its power and excellence are mainly in thoughtfulness, pathos, humor. There is a certain subtlety of thought, — a capacity gradually to surround the reader with an entire world and a complete life: we feel how heartily the writer has thrown himself into the state of things he describes, half believing the tale he tells, and using gently and tenderly the characters he draws. We have a most interesting story: we see before us beings of actual flesh and blood. We do not know whether the gentle, yet resolute Oulita, — the Princess Marie, that spoiled child of fortune, now all wild ferocity, and now all soft relenting, — the Count von Straubenheim, that creature of passion so deep yet so slow, so calm upon the surface, yet so impetuous in its under-currents, — ever lived save in the fancy of the poet: but to us they are a reality, — far more a reality than half the men who have lived and died in fact, but who live on the page of history the mere bloodless life of a word and an abstraction. We find in this tragedy the sharp knowledge of life and human nature for which we were prepared: a certain tinge of sadness and resignation which did not surprise us: a kindly yet sorrowful feeling towards the very worst, which we are persuaded comes with the longer and fuller experience of the strange mixture of the lovable and the hateful which is woven into the constitution of the race. Here and there, we find the calm, self-possessed order of thought with which we have elsewhere grown familiar, gradually rise into eloquent energy, and vigor of expression which startles. But the hero is not one who raves and stamps. And indeed the fastidious taste of the writer, shrinking instinctively from the least trace of coarseness or extravagance, has perhaps resulted in a little want of the terrible passion of tragedy: for we can well believe that many an expression, and many a sentiment, which, heard just for once from eloquent lips, would thrill even the most refined, would be struck out by the remorseless pen, or at least toned down, when calmly, critically, and repeatedly read over by such an author as ours, when the fever of creative inspiration was past. We remark, as a characteristic of the plot, and a circumstance vitally affecting the order of its interest, that the catastrophe is involved in the characters of the actors. It is not by the arbitrary appointment of the author, that things run in the course they do. There is something of the old Greek sense of the inevitable. We feel from the beginning that the end is fixed as fate. Like Frankenstein, the poet has bodied out beings whom he has not at his command: and not without essentially changing their natures, could he materially modify what they say and do, or materially alter the path along which they advance to the precipice in the distance. Given such beings, placed in Russian life and under Russian government: and not without a jarring sacrifice of truthfulness could the story advance or end otherwise than as it does.

The language of the tragedy is such as might have been expected from its author. There is not a phrase, not a word from first to last, to which the most fastidious taste could take exception. So much might be anticipated by readers familiar with the author's prose style: but we felt something of curiosity as to how it might adapt itself to the altered conditions of verse. Even those readers who were not aware that the author of *Friends in Council* had ever before published poetry, might well judge that surely these lines, so easy, so flowing, so little labored, so varied in their rhythm, so uncramped by metrical requirements, are not the production of an unpractised hand. Parts of the dialogue are in prose; the larger portion is in blank verse; and some graceful lyrics occur here and there. A peculiarity of the author's blank verse is, that the lines frequently end in three short syllables. Our readers are of course aware that both in rhymed and blank verse, double endings of lines are very common: in dramatic blank verse, indeed, we find line after line exhibiting this formation:[1] but we are not aware that any author has

[1] To be, or not to be, that is the *question:*
Whether 'tis nobler in the mind, to *suffer*
The slings and arrows of outrageous *fortune,*
Or to take arms against a sea of *troubles,* &c.

employed the triple ending to the same degree, or indeed has employed it at all except on very rare occasions. In the first page, we find it said that the end of government should be, not to govern overmuch, but

> To make men do with the least show of *governing.*

Other examples are,

> In foreign Courts 'tis everything, this *precedence.*
> From trappings overgreat for poor *humanity.*
> E'en to yourself must be unknown your *benefits.*
> Alone and undisturbed, upon her *loveliness.*

And there is one instance of an ending in four short syllables: —

> In evidence against us, marking *preparation.*

We have been interested by finding here and there, throughout the tragedy, several thoughts upon matters more or less important, with which we had become acquainted in the writer's former works. It is plain that the writer thinks the discomfort arising from fashions of dress a not insignificant item in the tale of human suffering: he would agree with Teufelsdröckh himself as to the undeserved neglect in which men have held the "philosophy of clothes." We find the men-servants at a Boyard Prince's chateau busily engaged in trying on their new liveries, which have been prepared for a grand occasion. The Prince enters, and finds but little progress made. He rates his domestics for their slowness; whereupon the "Small Wise Man," a dwarf attached to his establishment, thus excuses his fellows: —

> Oh! the happy peasants are so uncomfortable, my little father, in their happy new clothes, that they put off the squeezing themselves into them to the last moment. It's a nice thing a new shoe, now; and not so very unlike a marriage, my little mother.

The author had thought upon this subject before: —

My own private opinion is, that the discomfort caused by injudicious dress, worn entirely in deference to the most foolish of mankind, would outweigh many an evil that sounds very big. Tested by these perfect returns, which I imagine might be made by the angelic world, if they regard human affairs, perhaps our every-day shaving, severe shirt-collars, and other ridiculous garments, are equivalent to a great European war once in seven years; and we should find that women's stays did as much harm, *i. e.* caused as much suffering, as an occasional pestilence, — say, for instance, the cholera.[1]

In graver mood, we find something of the philosophy of worldly progress and quietude, in words which suggest (how truly) that the man who would *get on* in life had better not think to carve out a way for himself, but should rather keep to the track which many other feet have beaten into smoothness and firmness. The hero of the tragedy says, —

> To preserve one's quietude,
> It needs that one should travel in the ruts
> That form the ordinary road, for else
> The wheels stick fast.

The analogy is so apt and true, that it had previously suggested itself: —

Get, if you can, into one or other of the main grooves of human affairs. It is all the difference of going by railway, and walking over a ploughed field, whether you adopt common courses, or set one up for yourself. You will see very inferior persons highly placed in the army, in the church, in office, at the bar. They have somehow got upon the line, and have moved on well with very little original motive power of their own.[2]

We find that the author, very naturally, makes his hero express tastes which he himself feels strongly. One of

[1] *Companions of my Solitude.* Chap. III. And see the same subject discussed in the essay on *Conformity*, in Chap. II. of *Friends in Council.*

[2] *Ibid.* Chap. IV.

these tastes, which appears repeatedly in his former writings, is for woodland scenery. "There is scarcely anything in nature," he says, "to be compared with a pine-wood." Once, in approaching a certain continental city, the author passed through what the guide-books described as a most insipid country. But the guide-books did not know what were his personal likings; leaving his carriage at the little post-house, he walked on, promising to be in the way when it should overtake him.

The road led through a wood, chiefly of pines, varied, however, occasionally by other trees. Into this wood I strayed. There was that almost indescribably soothing noise (the Romans would have used the word *susurrus*), the aggregate of many gentle movements of gentle creatures. The birds hopped but a few paces off as I approached them: the brilliant butterflies wavered hither and thither before me: there was a soft breeze that day, and the tops of the tall trees swayed to and fro politely to each other. I found many delightful resting-places. It was not all dense wood; but here and there were glades (such open spots I mean as would be cut through by the sword for an army to pass); and here and there stood a clump of trees of different heights and foliage, as beautifully arranged as if some triumph of the art of landscape had been intended, though it was only Nature's way of healing up the gaps in the forest. For her healing is a new beauty.[1]

Thus speaks the author in his own person: and his hero passing alone through a wood, speaks as follows: —

I ever loved a wood; and here I 've mused,
Pressing with lightest footfall the crisp leaves,
In boyhood's days, when life seemed infinite,
And every fitful sound a song of joy.
Great is the sea, but tedious; rich the sun,
But one gets tired of him, too; joyous the wind,
But boisterous and intrusive; — while, the wood
Divides the sun, and air, and sky; and, like
A perfect woman, naught too much revealed,
Nor aught too much concealing.

[1] *Companions of my Solitude.* Chap. VI.

We shall be content to quote one other instance of parallelism, in the notice given to a matter which every one who lives in a wooded district must often have remarked in his woodland wanderings. The hero of the tragedy is asked to tell of what he has been thinking, as he has been traversing the wood which he enjoys so much: here is his reply: —

> Mere melancholy thoughts, fit for a servitor:
> How this tree here hemmed in its puny neighbor,
> Drinking the air and light from it; how that,
> The vagrant branches into shapes grotesque
> Constrained, insisted yet on being beautiful,
> And like a homely girl with one charm only,
> Took care to make that charm discernible.

In saying this, the hero of the play is repeating what had before been said by its author. And it appears to us an indication of the lifelike reality with which the author depicted to himself the man whom he drew as he paced along, looking at the gray stems and the long grass below, and the green leaves and blue glimpses of sky above: —

> Yes, Ellesmere, my love for woods is unabated. There is so much largeness, life, and variety in them. Even the way in which the trees interfere with one another, the growth which is hindered, as well as that which is furthered, appears to me most suggestive of human life; and I see around me things that remind me of governments, churches, sects, and colonies.

We should not be doing justice to *Oulita*, if we failed to remark, as something singular in these days, that it is a purely and perfectly original work. Its author has constructed his own plot, and imagined his own characters It is very well for writers who have no higher aim than to supply the immediate exigencies of the stage, to quarry in the abundant mine of French invention; and to copy, borrow, or *adapt*, as the phrase now runs. But we should have been greatly surprised had the author of *Friends in Council* resorted to that cheap method of producing a dramatic work. It cannot be denied that several dramatic writers of the day have shown considerable tact in toning French characters and modifying French plots, till they should hit the English taste, and not sound absurdly upon English ground. But to do *that* is a *knack*, a sort of intellectual sleight of hand: it argues no invention, no dramatic genius: it comes rather of much practical acquaintance with the tricks and effects of the theatre. The author of this play has essayed a higher flight. He has resolved to give the English stage a really original work: and holding firmly, as we know from his former writings, that some kind of amusement is a pure necessary of life, and that there is in human nature an instinctive leaning to the dramatic as a source of amusement, he has sought to show, by example, that without becoming namby-pamby, — without making the well-intentioned degenerate into the twaddling, — and without making the great school-boys of mankind scent the birch-rod and the imposition under the disguise of cricket-bats and strawberry tarts, — it is possible to make a play such as that in amusing it shall also instruct, refine, and elevate. It is not by coarsely tacking on a moral to a tragedy that you will enforce any moral teaching. You must so wrap up the improving and instructive element in the interesting and attractive, that the mass of readers or listeners shall never know when they have overstepped the usually well-marked limit that parts work and play. And we think that the author of *Oulita* has succeeded in this. A refreshing and elevating influence sinks into the mind, like a shower upon a newly-mown lawn, as we read his pages. You feel, but cannot define it. But many worthy people would cram improvement, a thick porridge, down their humbler neighbors' throats, — like Mrs. Squeers's treacle and sulphur.

As the reader would expect from the title of the book, the scene of the tragedy is in Russia. Its time is the beginning of the present century. And the author has, in virtue of his hearty sympathy with humanity under all conditions, thrown himself completely into Russian life, and brought his readers into an entire world of scenes, things, and men and women. Yet, though the scene be in Russia, and though we know from his other works how much the author hates slavery, we find proof of the calm balance of his mind in the fashion in which he represents serfdom. His honesty will not permit him to coarsely daub his picture for the sake of popular effect, or to represent the "peculiar institution" as more glaringly bad than he has ground for believing it practically is, in order to render it more abhorrent to our feeling. Nor do we find any violent exhibition of despotic sway. We do not believe that the author would sympathize in the least with the childish cry for Imperialism which lately arose in this country. We trust the nation has passed through that crisis, like a child through the cow-pox, and that we are fairly done with it. Still, in the play, the Emperor of Russia is represented in a very favorable light, as kind-hearted, accessible, willing to listen to reason, and even to accusation of himself; and though autocratic, yet enchained by an overmastering and tyrannic sense of what is right and just, which drags him against his dearest wishes. We have said that there is no putting of serfdom in its coarser and more repellent features. *Oulita, the Serf,* is the pride and pet of the old Prince to whom she belongs; and the chosen companion and friend of the Princess his daughter. No cruelties are described as actually inflicted upon any serf in the course of the action of the drama: — we can imagine that the sensitive nature of the author would shrink from any such description: yet we feel keenly the hard iron links which are present beneath the soft velvet surface. We never entirely forget the difference that parts the serf, however indulged, from the freeman, however degraded. The gentle confidante is liable to be handed over, at the capricious word of her spoiled-child mistress, to the executioner's lash. And the naturally noble heart of the Princess is well-nigh ruined by the long possession of unlimited power. We are not sure but that to the thoughtful reader, serfdom is made as incurably bad in this volume, as it could have been in the picture of a Legree. The way to make us feel that a thing is hopelessly bad, is to show us that it is bad at its very best. If it be a sad thing to be in bondage to a mild, silly old gentleman who would not hurt a fly, and to a warm-hearted girl who kisses more than she scolds, — what must it be when the whip is in the hand of a coarse, brutal, swearing, drunken reprobate!

The first scene of the tragedy shows us Baron Grübner, the Russian Minister of Police, seated at his desk in his bureau at St. Petersburg. He is inveighing against the Count Von Straubenheim, who is on terms of intimate friendship with the Emperor, and who has been instilling into the autocrat's mind certain political doctrines of much too advanced a character for Grübner's taste. Grübner is the type of the old Continental politician: the Count belongs to the school of progress; and Grübner, fearing lest the Count's influence with the Emperor should bring to an end the reign of police administration, has organized a system of *espionage*, in the hope of detecting the Count in some proceeding which may lead to his downfall. We feel, at once, that the ground is mined beneath our feet, and that we are in a region over which broods the unseen but all-seeing presence of a secret police. We never escape the feeling on to the end of the play. A spy enters, and informs Grübner that the Emperor again receives the obnoxious Count that evening. The vulgar spy has his information from a certain baroness, a spy of a higher class. The spy leaves, and Grübner thus goes on: —

> Far into
> The distant future this wise man looked forward,
> And saw a time, he told the Emperor,
> When half the world would not employ itself
> In worrying the other half. Great sage!
> He meant that for a sneer at the Police;
> And when good honest men would not sit down
> At meat with titled spies — that means the Baroness;
> Or with the men who pay them — that means me.

Another spy enters, one Ermolaï, whom Grübner has got into the Count's employ as his secretary, to maintain a constant watch over his private doings. Ermolaï complains that his post is a sinecure. There is nothing to report. The Count spends all his time in reading. He reads theology. *That*, Grübner thinks, is an important point. If the Count succeeds in indoctrinating the Emperor with his theories, down goes Grübner, and with him (of course he is a most disinterested man) Russia. The Count, Grübner says, is to be married: so the Emperor and he have resolved: then he is to go as ambassador to England, where he will probably make some mistake that will ruin him, or at least where he will be beyond the Emperor's reach. Grübner dismisses Ermolaï, ordering him to maintain a most minute watch, and chuckles at his own skill in getting the Count to take a police tool for his secretary.

The second scene carries us to the Count von Straubenheim's library. He is among his favorite books. He lays down his volume, and muses as follows: —

One reads, and reads, and reads: one seldom gets
Right into the heart of things — there's so much floss
And fluff; and few can tell what they do know.
Long histories: weary biographies:
They only teach us what I partly guessed
Before — that men were most times miserable,
And simple thoroughly, wasting their souls
In plaguing other men, and seldom living
What I call life — an ugly dream it is;
And yet, with all my faculty for sarcasm,
I must confess that men, the worst of men,
This scoundrel horde of conquerors, for instance,
Have something very lovable about them.
The deeper that one goes, the more one's pity
Falls like a gentle snow upon the plain
Flooded with blood, and strewed with cruel carnage
Leaving the outlines beautiful, and just
Concealing what 'twere better never had
Been done — concealing only, not erasing:
'Tis a mixed brood.

We speedily find that the recluse student is not so simple after all. He knows all about Ermolaï being a spy upon him. He sends for Ermolaï: says he is about to marry the beautiful daughter of Prince Lanskof. Ermolaï discourages the marriage, and says, —

I've heard a saying
Of some sagacious world-versed man, — that marriage
Must be pronounced a thing so hazardous,
The odds so much against one, that it were
As if a man should dip his hand within
A bag of snakes, where one eel lies concealed;
And mostly he draws back his injured hand
Without the innocent eel.

The Count is anxious to repudiate any notion save of a prosaic marriage of convenience; but at the same time he beautifully depicts what he says he never had felt: —

> I have a distant notion of what love
> Might be. I know the dreams about the thing.
> That there is one whose every look and word
> Is fascination, graceful as the clouds,
> Bright as the morn, and tender as the eve, —
> Whose lightest gesture, as she moves across
> The room, seems like a well-known melody, —
> And whom you need not talk to much, for that's
> The touchstone, — to whom you've nothing to explain,
> Because she always thinks too well of you.

In answer to the Count's question where he shall find such a paragon, the Secretary mentions the name of the singing-girl at Moscow, Oulita. The Count remembers her well. But he speedily passes to talk of the embassy to England; and then bids Ermolaï prepare a sumptuous retinue for his visit to the chateau of Prince Lanskof, the father of his intended bride. Ermolaï goes: and then we learn from a speech of the Count's that he is quite aware that the marriage and embassy are a design of Grübner's to compass his ruin. But he will fight Grübner with his own weapons. He will pluck from his bosom the remembrance of Oulita, wed the Princess, come back with credit from his embassy, and do good to his country. If he shall succeed, well. And if not, life is already as dull as it well can be.

We next find ourselves in the hall of Prince Lanskof's chateau. The servants are trying on their new liveries: the dancing-girls are practising their steps. The "Small Wise Man," a dwarf belonging to the Prince, a jester of more than usual jest, and deeper than ordinary wisdom, makes his first appearance. All is bustle: the Count is to arrive in three hours. Oulita appears along with the Princess, the latter promising her that she shall not have to join in the dances. The Prince drills his domestics in a manner that reminds us of Mr. Hardcastle in *She Stoops to Conquer*. He is a fussy, silly old gentleman, proud of his daughter, and picturing the grand figure she is to make at the English Court as the Russian ambassadress.

Meanwhile Oulita has strayed into a wood near the chateau; and there the Count, who has chosen to dismiss his retinue and walk through the wood alone, hears her well-remembered voice as she sings. The Count accosts her with some light badinage, of which Oulita has the best. Then they talk more gravely. Mitchka, the executioner at the chateau, watches them from behind a tree. Oulita recognizes in the Count the man who followed her about at Moscow. He tells her that he came in the Count's train.

Then we are carried to the hall at the chateau, where the Small Wise Man is addressing the servants. He speaks from a barrel, on which he is seated: —

> The illustrious Count Von Straubenheim, who, with our permission, is about to marry into our family, intends to give to every member of the household — something which shall be good for him: great guerdon, liberal largesse. For you Melchior, Nicholas, and Petrovitch (pointing out three fat men), he intends to ask for a week's fast, and three weeks' out-of-door's work in the woods. For you, Theodore, a sound scourging at the hands of gentle Mitchka, that you may know how to manage your horses better, and what are the feelings of an animal when it is whipped. For you, Dimitri, our illustrious son-in-law has thought deeply, and intends to ask the Prince to have your wife brought home from his other estate, because you always lived so happily together.

No wonder that the Small Wise Man held his own in

that household. We doubt not the servants feared his tongue nearly as much as Mitchka's scourge.

The Prince, Princess, and their attendants enter; as do the Count, Ermolaï, and their people. The Small Wise Man catechizes the Count in a jocular manner as to his qualifications for marrying and becoming ambassador; and when the Count and Prince go together to the banquet, he muses in a very different strain. He is pleased with the Count's appearance: —

> A noble presence and a thoughtful eye,
> But sad.

And Oulita entering, he speaks to her wisely and kindly, in a fashion which reveals strongly to us the grand want which every thoughtful serf must never cease to feel. "Study to get free, girl," he says; "free, free, free, free!" We now overhear a conversation between the executioner Mitchka, and Vasili Androvitch, Prince Lanskof's steward; from which we find that the steward has promised to pay Mitchka three thousand roubles if he can catch Oulita in any fault which may bring her under his lash. The steward's hope is, that in such a case he may compel Oulita to become his wife, as the reward of his procuring her pardon. Vasili is quite aware that Oulita hates him; but that does not matter, in his estimation. In the crowd of dancers in the hall, the Count again meets Oulita: a confidence has grown up fast between them, and she tells her longing to be free. The Count declares that she shall be, and gives Oulita his ring as a pledge. He has mingled unnoted with the throng in the hall, and Oulita is still unaware who he is. But she tells us she feels entranced and bewildered.

Meanwhile the Count seeks Ermolaï, and has an explanation with him. Ermolaï is startled to find that the Count has been quite aware that he was a spy of Grübner's, and is penetrated with remorse at the thought that, while aware of all this, the Count saved him from drowning in the Neva. He always loved the Count; and from this time forward he is his faithful ally and friend. The Count tells him he loves Oulita, and is determined to make her free. He has thought of several plans. An adroit serf, Stépan, disguised as a merchant, will come to buy her. That scheme failing, the Count's servants are to create some great alarm, and bear her off in the tumult. Meanwhile there is to be a great hunt of several days' duration. Ermolaï is to remain behind: to send for Stépan, for money, for horses of the Ukraine breed: to watch Mitchka, to grow familiar with every corner of the huge chateau. And then the Count, left alone, soliloquizes. He is determined to go through with his design, but he is not in the least blinded to the wrong he is doing:—

I am a knave, a double-dealing scoundrel,
To woo one girl the while I love another,
For I do love her —
What should I say of any other man?
But then our own misdeeds are quite peculiar,
White at the edges, shading into darkness,
Not wholly black like other men's enormities.
Theirs are the thunder-clouds; ours but the streaks
Across the setting sun — No, no! I'm not
A fool like that. I know full well 'tis base,
Supremely base; natheless it shall be done.
If there were time, some other course we might
Devise; but that's what scoundrels always say —
If there were time, they would replace, repay,
In Virtue's silvery path they would walk leisurely.
I am not duped by that. Seeing it all,
Foreseeing all the misery, the mischief,
I'll do't, I say, and take the guilt upon me.
She shall be free.

Thus ends the First Act. It has indeed wrought an extraordinary change on the Count's feelings and position. The cool, pensive, unenergetic student of theological books, whose great aim was the progress of Russia, has had the latent fire of his nature touched at last.

In the Second Act we have the working of the Count's scheme. The hunt is over: the Prince and Count have returned to the chateau. The Small Wise Man has preceded them: cautioned the Princess that a merchant has arrived to buy Oulita and her fine voice for the Imperial Opera: advised that Oulita should not sing her best in his presence. Stépan, a shrewd fellow, appears: tells the Prince he has heard of Oulita, and with many disparaging remarks, desires to hear her sing. The Count, consulted by the Prince, speaks slightingly of Oulita, and artfully suggests that the Prince's hunting-ground was somewhat hemmed in by an adjoining property, which might be bought. Oulita sings: but she has overheard the Count's remarks: she now knows who he is, and she wilfully sings to the very best of her power. She sings two songs: we extract the former as a specimen of the author's lyric art. It gives us the story of *The End of the Rebel Stenko-Razin's Love:* a story which is exactly true.

The barge was moored on Volga's shore, the stream
  Went murmuring sorrowfully past,
The water-lilies played amidst the gleam
  Their golden armor, moon-lit, cast.

Mute sat the Persian captive by her mate,
  And gazed at her lover askance;
A little of love and something of hate
  Were couched in that dubious glance.

"Base that I am," he cried, "dear stream, to thee,
  Who, rebel too, with willing waves

Hast borne my armies up to victory,
  And floated down the gold and slaves."

He mused; he turned; and smiling on her charms,
  He met that look of love and hate;
Lightly he took her in his mailèd arms,
  And casting, left her to her fate.

One lily more went shimmering 'midst the gleam
  Their golden armor, moon-lit, cast;
That lily slowly sank beneath the stream;
  Volga went sadly murmuring past.

"Murmur no more," the chief replied, "no more;
  What I loved best to thee I gave."
His fierce men shuddered, but from fear forbore
  The Persian lady's life to save.

The songs are received with great applause, and when silence follows Stépan criticizes in true musical cant: —

There is a something, and there is not a something. There is a feeling and there is not a feeling. But there are makings, makings, makings. The G is better than the Freduccini's G.

And after more in the like tone, he offers the Prince thirty thousand roubles. But the old gentleman is so vain of Oulita's triumph, that he absolutely refuses to part with her on any terms: and thus fails the Count's first idea.

But instant action becomes necessary. The Princess upbraids Oulita severely for singing so well, contrary to her arrangement; and goes on to speak of her meeting the Count in the wood. Oulita replies sharply: the Princess sentences her to Mitchka's lash in the morning. The Count upon this determines to rescue her that night. He is well aware of the risk he runs in the hands of the old Prince's vassals; but will brave it all. Oulita comes to him, and begs his intercession for her. He replies coldly: but conveys in whispered interjected sentences his plan for her rescue. A striking scene follows, in which Vasili, who thinks he has Oulita in his power, tries entreaties and threats with equal unsuccess to gain her consent to be his wife. The Count and Ermolaï deliberate. They have arranged to fire the chateau in the night, and carry Oulita away. Ermolaï, with his tastes formed under Grübner, is delighted with the tact exhibited in the Count's plan: and when he leaves to arrange with the men, the Count thus speaks: —

We shall succeed — I will not let a doubt
Intrude upon my mind, — we shall succeed.
This one injustice may be remedied.
But then the things that have been — why they come
Upon me now I wot not: hideous deeds
Long numbered with the past. The Earth may smile,
And deck herself each May, vain thing! with flowers,
And seem forgetful of the cruelties
Enacted on her ever-changing stage,
Till every spot upon the storied surface
Is rank with tragic memories: beauteous slaves,
Like dear Oulita, forced to endure, half-crazed,
Caresses which they loathe — and children slain
Before their mother's eyes — and women murdered
(Happy if murdered soon) in the dear presence
Of those who till that moment ever looked at them
With reverent tenderness, and now dare not look;
Whose corded limbs, straining in agony,
Have lost — the wretch's last resort — the power
To give them death. . . .
The earth may smile, I say,
But like a new-made widow's mirth, it shocks one.
And she, the earth, should never quit her weeds;
And should there come a happier race upon her,
Ever there'll be a sighing of the wind,
A moaning of the sea, to hint to that
More favored race what we poor men have suffered.
There must have been a history, they'll say
To be interpreted by all these sighs
And moans.

It is indeed a strange inconsistency, between the beauty and gayety of external nature, and the wickedness and misery of man. And it has existed ever since the Fall. The Vale of Siddim was "as the garden of the Lord," — fair as another Eden: the black blot there was man. And the natural beauty and the human wickedness had to be dashed from Creation together. "At that one spot, it is far towards four thousand years, since Nature bloomed and Man sinned, — for the last time."[1] We remember, too, what thought it was that came sadly to the mind of Bishop Heber, as he breathed the spicy air of Ceylon. Many a sad heart must have felt the sunshine and the green leaves a dreary mockery of the gloom within. And how hard it is to feel, that beyond that cheerful veil, there is hidden a Being of infinite power and infinite justice, who looks down quietly on the scene, and lets the world go on! Well, things will be set right some day.

His plans being thus arranged, the Count proceeds to the Hall, where there is a grand banquet. The Governor of the province proposes the health of the Count and his affianced bride, in a speech which is a happy imitation, by no means caricatured, of the speeches common in England after public dinners. In the middle of the banquet, somewhat prematurely, the flames break out. Great confusion follows, amid which Stépan bears off Oulita. But he is intercepted and brought back by Mitchka, who, as well as Vasili, had suspected the Count's design. The Count kills Mitchka: then he and Stépan bind Vasili, whom the latter must now take with him, as a refractory serf. Then the Count hurries Oulita off, with the words which close the Second Act.

[1] Foster.

I said you should be free, and free you are.
Your horses wait; the road is clear to Moscow.
He goes with you (*pointing to Stépan*), and will insure your safety,
Nearer: a word! I loathe this hateful marriage.
'Tis forced upon me by the Czar. Escape
I may, and then —
No! this is not the time —
When you are wholly free, you can reject me.

In the Third Act we are at Moscow. Grübner has guessed correctly as to the share the Count had in the fire at the Prince's chateau, about which the Prince has been constantly complaining to the police. Neither the Prince nor Princess has had the slightest suspicion. Oulita has been safely conveyed to Moscow, and is under the Count's care. The Count is maintaining appearances with the Princess; but is afraid of Siberia, to which the arson and homicide at the chateau would certainly send him, if brought home to him; and is perplexed how to deal honorably with the Princess, whose nature, with its fierce mixture of good and evil, is not one to be trifled with. Grübner has stated his suspicions to the Princess, who resolves to have an explanation with the Count. Accordingly, we have a striking scene, in which the Princess tells the Count that the police are on Oulita's track, and threatens fearful vengeance upon her when taken. The Count manfully avows what he has done, and leaves the Princess in a whirl of rage. But she admires and loves the Count still; and it is on Oulita that she determines her vengeance shall be wreaked.

However, she relents. A little later, while the Count is with Oulita, the police enter the house and seize her, to carry her back to Prince Lanskof. But their plans are disconcerted by Stépan producing a bill of sale, signed in due form by the Prince, which shows that Oulita has been fairly sold to Stépan. The Princess, at a masked ball in the Kremlin, had placed this in the Count's hand. The police have to give up their prey. And when Grübner enters after a while with a file of soldiers, he finds that he is duped, and that Oulita is beyond his reach.

At the beginning of the Fourth Act, we find that the Count feels the meshes of the police closing round him. He is in his house at St. Petersburg, when Stépan enters to tell him that spies are now watching his house on every side. The Count feels that the odds against him are too great, and he must be beaten at last. The Czar, too, is becoming cold.

We next find Oulita in a room at St. Petersburg, working at embroidery. She is perfectly happy; but change is near. The Small Wise Man has found out her retreat, and comes to tell her of the Princess's wrath, and the storming and vaporing of her father. And now it breaks on poor Oulita's mind what peril the Count is incurring for her sake. She resolves to leave him, lest she should bring him to ruin; and as a last resort, asks the Small Wise Man to give her poison which she might have within her reach. Then a most beautiful scene follows between Oulita and the Count. Her eyes, now awakened, see the traces of ceaseless anxiety and alarm on his altered face; and he, wearied out, falls into deep sleep as he is telling her of his travels in other lands. Half-awaking, he thinks he is speaking to the Czar, and tells him that "if he but knew her, he would pardon all." He sinks to sleep again; and Oulita, resolute, though broken-hearted, leaves her farewell written, and hastens away.

She has taken a desperate resolution. We next find the Princess in her chamber, brooding upon her wrongs, and wrought up to a tigress-fury. Even as she is declaring what fearful vengeance she would take of Oulita, Oulita enters and kneels at her feet. The scene which follows is one of the most striking in the play; and the more so that our extracts have been only of detached speeches, we shall quote this dialogue entire.

OULITA.

Madam, an outcast girl implores the pardon
She dares not hope for.

PRINCESS.

Ha! He has left you then:
And you return, in those becoming robes,
To penitence and virtue — rather late,
Methinks.
Speak, girl, unless you wish me to call Mitchka.
Mitchka is dead, you think; there lives another.
Say, has the Count forsaken you?

OULITA (*rising*).

The Count!
What Count?

PRINCESS.

Why this surpasses patience! What Count, minx, —
That Count who was to be my husband, wretch;
That Count who, to his eminent dishonor,
Stole you away — set fire to his friend's palace —
Slew that friend's servants — decked you out, great lady
In this fine garb — who broke his plighted word
For you, — the Count von Straubenheim.

OULITA.

You know, then?

PRINCESS.

There is no thread of his and your intrigues
Unknown to me. He told me of your love.

OULITA.

Permit me now to speak. Of a return,
You spoke, to virtue. There is no return.
A woman might have thought more charitably,
Of any sister-woman, though a serf:
Madam, there's no return, I say, to virtue,
And none to penitence, though much to sorrow.
I loved the Count, 'tis true, yet not to love
I fled, but to escape a shame one maiden
Should hardly have inflicted on another.
I saw the Count again. I listened — who
Would not? — to his fond words and vows repeated
To make this slave in other climes his wife.
But soon the bloodhounds were upon the track.
I heard, or seemed to hear, the avenger's baying,
Marked the ignoble lines of care — his care
For me — indenting that majestic brow:
'Twas then that I divined his danger, sought
To save his life, myself surrendering
To all your sternest cruelty might do.
I am too late, and am prepared to bear
The now most thriftless, useless penalty.
But hear: men are most wayward in their fancies;
He should have worshipped at your shrine, great Princess.
Perhaps it was your very excellence
Made him decline to such a thing as me.
He ever spoke of you with tenderest homage.

PRINCESS.

He did?

OULITA.

He did; and one there was who sat beside him,
Who joyed to hear your praises, for the Count
Said ever you were most magnanimous, —
Great as a foe, and splendid as a friend.

PRINCESS.

And nothing else, the while he played with those
Fair tresses, said the Count, — nothing about
My furious temper, and the difference 'twixt
Mine and the soft Oulita's, — nothing, girl?
Sealing his pretty sayings with a kiss —
The false, the perjured man.

OULITA.

Not false, nor perjured.

PRINCESS.

Ah, now we stir the meek one.

OULITA.

What he said
In rare disparagement of your great charms,
Was such indeed as might make any woman
Desire the more to win the man who said it. —
By that dread suffering image that looks down
On us this moment, I would die to win
His love for you; would worm myself into
His heart, to find an entrance there for you,
And thus insure his safety and your joy:
That safety being — for I'll not deceive you, —
The chiefest aim in life for me. Dear Princess —
[*Puts her arm round the* PRINCESS.
You used to let me call you dear, — be true
To your great mind. Let's set our women's wits
To work, to make the man love you. There only
His safety lies — and there his happiness.
'Tis you alone are worthy of the Count.
With you to aid his plans, to fix his purposes,
Partake success with him, console in failure,
Cheering with your bright wit his melancholy,
He will become the greatest man in Russia.

PRINCESS.

How blind is pride! The Count was right, Oulita,
Were I a man I should have loved you best.
Save him we will, but not for me, Oulita.
I am not worthy of him, nor of you.
Nay, let me kneel to you. Could you but know
What savage thoughts I've had, you ne'er could love me.
Let me but kiss — that shudder was not wickedness, —
I do not grudge his fondness for that cheek.
I meant that I must love what he had loved,
And I do love it [*kisses her*]. We'll rest together, dear,
And early morn shall find us planning rescue.
His peril is most urgent. I did not
Betray him; nay, I saved him once. Your Marie

Was not in all things bad, — not always wicked.
Ah, could you but have known, that fatal day
My heedless passion threatened you with stripes —
[*Puts her hand before her eyes.*
I am ashamed to look at you, and say
The base word stripes, — could you have known how tenderly
I felt to you, never so much before,
And how I roamed and roamed about in agony,
Contriving some excuse to make you ask
Your pardon, and none came, you must, you would
Have pitied me.
Down at your feet I could have humbly knelt,
Imploring you to kneel at mine, Oulita;
Indeed I could. But then my odious pride
Stiffened my soul again.

OULITA.

But more, you say,
Than ever, then, you loved your own Oulita.

PRINCESS.

What is the worth of my love that could do
So little battle with my pride?

OULITA.

We poor ones,
Who from our infancy are curbed and bent,
And bounded in, know little of the pangs
The great endure in mastering their pride
Long-seated, deep-engrained.

PRINCESS.

Generous Oulita,
Always some foolish, fond excuse for me,
I almost feel I love the Count the more
For being wise and great enough to love thee,
Discerning thy rare qualities beneath
The sorry mask of serfdom —
The world would scarce believe its mocking eyes
If it could see two women loving madly
One man, and yet the fonder of each other.
Is it not so, Oulita?

OULITA.

Dearest, it is.

PRINCESS.

Not *dearest*, I must tell the Count if you
Say that fond word to any other soul.

[OULITA *hides her head on the* PRINCESS'S *breast. They embrace — they kneel before the image in the corner of the room. The curtain falls.*

Thus the noble womanhood of the Princess's nature asserts itself: and thus the Fourth Act ends.

At the beginning of the Fifth Act, the Count, awaking from a fearful dream, finds Oulita's letter, telling him she has fled to save him from ruin, and begging that he would never let it be known that he had aided her in her escape. Even as he reads it, Grübner and his men are upon him. The Count retains his firmness, but tells Grübner that he is beaten. He is carried away, to be placed before the Czar.

And now, in Prince Lanskof's house, Oulita meets the Small Wise Man, and claims his promise to provide her poison. He gives her what, rubbed upon the lips, will in three minutes cause death; but he speaks as follows: —

Promise me this. Before
You use this fatal gift of mine, bring back —
Bring clearly back — to a calm mind, the days
When first your mother's smile was dear, when first
She trusted to your care your little brother,
And anxiously the little nurse upheld
The child, as you both strayed beside the stream —
I've often wandered there — which marked your garden,
To you a world of waters; then your father,
The ponderous man, laid his large hand upon
Your head, saying you were his wise Oulita —
Then think, was this the end for which they toiled,
And if, on thinking thus, you can resolve
In one rash moment to obliterate
What they so prized — why then God's blessing on you.
I can say nothing more.

We are next carried to the palace, where we find the Emperor and Grübner in conversation. We find that the Count is already on his way into Siberian exile; but the Emperor, who loves him, bitterly laments that there is no loophole for pardoning him. Grübner goes, and then a serf almost forces her way into the imperial presence. It is Oulita, now resolute in despair. A noble scene follows, which we regret we cannot find space to extract. She boldly tells the Emperor that greater men than the Count have loved where they should not; she justifies the Count against the charge of arson and murder; says Mitchka fell in fair fight; and appealing to the Emperor closely, declares that if the Countess whom he loved were sentenced to be scourged, and he burnt down a city to save her, she would not think less of the Czar. The Czar thinks she wishes to follow the Count; but is astonished when he learns that what she wishes is that he should wed the Princess. The Emperor grasps at the idea: says all might then be hushed; but adds that neither Princess nor Count would consent. But the poor Princess, the gentle woman at last, has come with Oulita in a page's dress; and when the Emperor asks her if she will marry the Count, reminding her at the same time of her own slighted affection and her father's wrongs, she replies humbly that she will, and not seek his love, nor ask him to live with her. The Emperor instantly signs a pardon, and tells them to hasten with it along the road to Siberia. Still he fears that the Count, however much he loves liberty, will hardly make a marriage serve as a means of safety. But he bids them God speed, and says at least they may try.

Then we are at a village on the road to Siberia.

We hear in the distance the "Song of the Exiles;" and a train of exiles enters, among whom is the Count. Ermolaï is there, kindly attending his fallen master; and the Count eagerly asks him of Oulita. There enter Oulita, the Princess veiled, and the Small Wise Man. They look anxiously among the prisoners, and at length recognize the Count. The Count sees Oulita, and bursts into a joyful speech, assuring her that the evil dreaded so much dwindles when it haps at last. She tells the Count of the conditional pardon she bears, and entreats him to marry the Princess. He declares that he is incapable of such baseness. Oulita then brings the Small Wise Man, hoping that his reasonings may move the Count: but the Count states the case to him; and he declares the Count is right. The Count then speaks to Oulita; says he will yet return and claim her:—

> If not, I have a loving memory always by me,
> Something to think of when I sit beside
> My hut, amidst the unheeded falling snow,
> Of evenings, when my sorry work is done.
> Better so sit, so thinking, than in palaces —
> A thought of inextinguishable baseness
> Fast clinging round the soul.

Then he asks Oulita if she had often thought of him —

> Once only, Edgar;—
> But that thought lasted long.

And still entreating him to wed the Princess, and so save himself for usefulness and honor, she applies the poison to her lips, and dies as she joins their hands. Poor Oulita judged that by thus unselfishly sacrificing herself, she would make the Count feel himself free.

It was a useless sacrifice. He tells the Princess he loves her now, for her true love for the dead; but he has no heart to offer. No word says the Princess, her haughty spirit quite cowed and broken ; Ermolaï receives his master's last request to bury Oulita where she died, and to mark her grave; and as the sad song of the exiles is resumed, the Count, seemingly stunned beyond present sense of his utter desolation, kisses Oulita's face, and resumes his march towards Siberia. Ah, the agony and wildness of grief will be upon him to-morrow ! And by the fair serf's corpse, in whose sad lot and noblest heart we have grown to feel an interest so profound, there sits, with covered face, the Small Wise Man ; — a jester to smile at no more, but a figure of overwhelming pathos.

L'honneur oblige ! How hard some men would find it to understand the invisible restraints that drove the Count into exile, while fortune, fame, and power were beckoning him back if he would but come ! And how hard, too, to understand Oulita's noble self-devotion ; and the self-devotion of the Princess, scarcely less complete !

And now, as we draw our notice of the tragedy to a close, we turn over the pages once more : and, as at every opening of the volume, our eye falls upon some beautiful felicity of expression, some lifelike incident that almost startles by the every-day reality it gives the story, some thought so deep, gentle, and kind, wherein the author's own mind speaks to his reader, — we feel how far such an abstract as our space enables us to give, falls short of the effect which would be produced by the perusal of the play itself on the heart of every generous man and gentle woman. We do not think that our nerves are shattered into a morbid facility of emotion, and the hand that writes these lines is not a woman's ;

yet we should hardly like to tell how often the tear has started as we read this book, — how many hours it kept sleep away, — or even how often and how long we have paused and mused with the finger in the half-closed volume. We do not pretend to much acquaintance with stage-craft; and it is possible enough that the very thoughtfulness which makes *Oulita* so fascinating to the solitary scholar, might detract from its power of popular effect were it represented on the stage. For ourselves, we do not think it would. There is incident rapid and stirring enough to keep attention ever on the stretch: and the reflections are such that while arresting the thoughtful reader who can follow the track along which they point, they will touch the mind and heart of average humanity. Of course, if *Hamlet* were published at the present day, many critics would call it dull and heavy, and many theatrical managers would not risk its presentation on their boards. And the variety of rhythm and cadence, the occasional abruptness and deviation from common metrical rules, which render the versification of a vigorous drama such as some judges would call unmusical, seem to our mind a beauty and an excellence in verse which is meant to be spoken and heard, rather than to be read; which represents real and passing life; which is put in the mouth of many diverse characters; and which is to be listened to without intermission for two or three successive hours. *Smoothness*, in Pope's use of the word, would pall and disgust by so long continuance. And only great variety of metrical character — even the occurrence of occasional discords — can furnish the similitude of life. When one goes to the Opera, one must be content to leave common sense at the door, and to take for granted that all that passes shall go on the basis of an extreme conventionality. But in the case of a tragedy, if the writing and the presentation be worthy, the spectator should forget that he is not looking at reality. The author of *Oulita* has kept this in view. Yet while remembering that unvaried melody of rhythm would result in satiety and tediousness, no one knows better how to add the charm of music to thoughts with which it accords. Very beautifully, in the lines which follow, have we Mr. Thackeray's ever-recurring philosophy of the affections, even in the trimness of modern life : —

> So dear that in the memory she remains,
> Like an old love, who would, indeed, have been
> Our only love, but died; and all the past
> Is full of her untried perfections, while
> Amidst the unknown recesses of our hearts
> Enthroned she sits, in tenderest mist of thought,
> Like the soft brilliancy of autumn haze,
> Seen at the setting of the sun.

CHAPTER XIV.

SOME TALK ABOUT SCOTCH PECULIARITIES.

BEING AN EPISTLE TO THE EDITOR OF "FRASER'S MAGAZINE," FROM HIS FRIEND, CHARLES ARDERSIER-MACDONALD, ESQ., OF CRAIG-HOULAKIM, NEAR WHISTLE-BINKIE, N. B.

WHEN I was a Country Parson, my dear friend the Editor of a certain eminent magazine came one autumn to pay me a visit. Among my most valued neighbors was a certain country squire, whom (for various reasons) I shall call Mr. Macdonald of Craig-Houlakim. When the Editor and Mr. Macdonald met, it appeared that they were old college friends, though they had died out of acquaintance for some years. The meeting was a very pleasant one: and the Editor was much amused by Mr. Macdonald's description of some of our Scotch institutions. Mr. Macdonald promised to give the Editor an account in writing of some of these: and thus originated the following letter. I may say, that in the main, I concur in the views it sets out: though they seem to me expressed with a little too much vehemence. And let me add, that Mr. Macdonald did not reside in my parish: so you will not find in his letter any reference to me.

My Dear Editor, — When you paid us a visit last autumn, and renewed so pleasantly an old college acquaintance which "change of place and change of folk" had interrupted for eight or ten years, you were wont, in your usual saturnine vein, to laugh at the completeness with which I had fallen into Scotch ways of thinking and acting. I have indeed become so familiar with the usages of my adopted country, that I see nothing very wonderful now in things which utterly astonished you, and which indeed had a similar effect upon myself when I was a freshly-imported Saxon. *Quantum mutatus ab illo*, I know you thought, who ten years since walked in your company the quadrangles of Oxford, bent upon those classical studies which (owing entirely to the bad arrangements of the University) failed to get me so distinguished a degree as my sisters and my grandmother thought I deserved, — not a little given to Puseyite notions in church matters, and in a state of total ignorance as to Scotch affairs. But time (as philosophers have on several occasions observed) works wonders. It is not yet ten years since the death of a distant and eccentric relative, whom I had never seen, made me the possessor of this property, in a district of Scotland which, I think, yields to none in beauty and interest. It is less than that time since I resolved to patch up this quaint old baronial dwelling, and make it my head-quarters for the greater part of the year. And I dare say you were surprised to find me so completely transformed into the Scotch country squire, — walking you after breakfast daily to the stables, and boring you with long stories about the hocks and pasterns of my horses; not a little vain of my turnips; quite proud of my shaggy little bullocks (finer animals than deer, I always maintain); and full of statistics about the yearly growth of my young plantations, and the girth of the noble old oaks and horse-chestnuts on the lawn. But I am sure you were much more surprised to find that I had settled down into a douce elder of the Kirk, — quite *au fait* in Scotch ecclesiastical polity, much interested in matters parochial, and loud in praise of Professor Robertson and the Endowment Scheme; and though still a warmly-attached member of the Church of England, yet a good Presbyterian when in Scotland, and quite persuaded that in all essential points the Church of England and the Kirk of Scotland are thoroughly at one. I have been fortunate in my parish clergyman, whom you met more than once while here, and whom you found, I dare say, quite different from the violent, Covenating, true-blue Knoxite you probably expected. You found him, I am sure, quite of our way of thinking in regard to most things sacred and civil: quite anxious to have his church as ecclesiastical in appearance as even Mr. Beckett Denison would wish; quite friendly to the introduction of an organ; not hostile to the restoration of the Liturgy; and, indeed, not so much shocked as he ought to have been when you and I speculated as to the probable time that must elapse before the peaceable reception of episcopal government. Let me add to these points of æsthetic nature that, like most of his brethren, he goes through all his parochial duties with great assiduity, and conducts the church-service of each Sunday with a propriety which would be excellent even on your side of the Tweed. When you went with me to the parish church, you were somewhat shocked at seeing the country-people coming in with their hats on, and rushing out as though the place were on fire, the instant the last "Amen" was spoken; and I did not expect that you would like the bare and bald ritual of the Kirk as much as your own beautiful service. Still, in the carefully-prepared prayers you heard, there was nothing of that rambling rigmarole of extemporaneous extravagance which makes one long for a Liturgy to keep people to common sense. And as for the sermon you heard from Mr. Smith, I think that, save for its not being read, and for a shade more warmth of manner in the delivery of it, it was very much such as your excellent rector gives you every Sunday morning. And though I am not much delighted with some of Lord Palmerston's recent ecclesiastical appointments, and cannot understand why such men as Mr. Melvill and Mr. Chenevix Trench are not raised to the episcopal bench in the abundance of recent vacancies, still I have grown so much of a Presbyterian in feeling, that I am pleased to find a Scotchman, brought up in the Scotch Kirk, made your metropolitan bishop. Dr. Tait has, I believe, two brothers who are elders of the Kirk; one of them, Sheriff Tait, being a prominent speaker in the General Assembly.

The change has come upon me by degrees; and really, till you were here in September, I was hardly aware how far, by familiarity with Scotch modes of thinking and acting, I had grown into a development which must seem strange in an old friend's eyes. As you know, I go little to England: my wife and weans (the latter of whom often loudly express their hope that you will soon come back again) are a tie to home; and one great pleasure of a country life is, that every day of the year, winter as well as summer, brings with it something to interest one. Horses, cows, pigs, dogs, pheasants, wheat, potatoes, newly-planted trees and evergreens, are a constant source of occupation : there is always a host of little changes and improvements going on about a country-place, which there is a pleasure in overseeing. Yet one need not grow a mere clod, like some of my thick-headed neighbors whom you met, who had never heard of Mr. Thackeray or of *Fraser's Magazine*, and who thought that Mr. Ruskin was a slang name for the Emperor of Russia. My daily hours of work in my library make me enjoy all the more a scamper on horseback, a stroll to the home-farm, or a walk through the young plantations. And notwithstanding your pity for me, cut off, as you thought, from the world of intellect, I assure you, my dear Editor, when you told me of all your toils and cares, pleasant and elevating as they may be, I thought it would be well for you, mentally and physically, to spend six months at Craig-Houlakim, where your pulse would get to beat more leisurely, where the flame of life would burn away less fast, and, like wise old Walton, you might "study to be quiet." And I put it to you, as an intelligent being, if my own personal appearance did not, by its healthy animalism, say a great deal for this calm mode of life. I don't think I am any stupider than I used to be when we were companions long ago; but am I not twice as strong, twice as active — ay, and twice as rosy, though I never drink whiskey-toddy?

There is no doubt of it, my dear fellow, that Scotland and England are very different countries, after all. I do not know what may be the particular train of reflection which is started in the mind of people in general by witnessing the departure of the Scotch mail-train from Euston-square at nine P. M.; but for myself, the thought which always impresses me is, what opposite states of things that train forms a link between. The carriage which bears the little board on its side, with LONDON AND EDINBURGH, will in the next few hours run not merely out of one country into another, with another climate and scenery; but also into another race of men, another religion, another church, another law, another way of thinking upon all conceivable subjects. Scotland and England, in short, are quite different countries. Many things which are quite familiar in each, are unknown in the other. And though between the educated classes of the two countries there is now much similarity, still it will be long before electric wires and express trains shall assimilate Pall-Mall and Prince's-street, St. Giles's and the Goosedubs.

It has always been an interesting thing to me to witness the departure of the great trains for the North. My feeling is, that the dignity and poetry of a railway train are in direct proportion to the distance it has to run. Who cares about the departure of a Greenwich train, that will reach its journey's end in ten minutes? It is quite different with one that, after quitting the brightly-lighted and bustling station, is to go on and on, hour after hour through the long dark night, score after score of miles through the wide blank country, and between the lights of fifty sleeping towns. By the side of the broad smooth platform is the long row of low dark carriages, so snug-looking internally with their warm lamp-light, their thick blue cushions, their heaps of wraps of all kinds. There is a crowd of passengers hurrying to and fro; a rapid whirl of barrows of luggage; a display of men and women in every variety of dress which has the association of warmth. At length we are all stowed in our places; rugs are folded over knees, travelling caps are endued, reviews and newspapers are cut up; and the train is off, gliding with a fluent motion through the dark. For an hour or two passengers read, and even talk a little; then gradually drop off into a sleep, which is disturbed at intervals through the night by the glare and thunder of some passing engine, fearfully snorting and panting, or by the chilly rush of raw air as the guard opens the door to ask a sight of the tickets at some large station on the road. Thus we sweep through the rich heart of England: along the valley of the Trent — through Staffordshire — through crowded Lancashire; and at length waken to full consciousness among the Cumberland hills, where the passing train sends the sheep scampering, and startles the hare from her resting-place. Then comes the comfortable though hurried breakfast in that most baronial refreshment-room at Carlisle; a few miles further on we cross the little river Sark, enter Dumfries-shire, and are in Scotland. Wild hills yet, which give the new-comer a dreary impression, and a very unfair one, of the country he has entered; ninety or a hundred miles are rapidly skimmed over; and at the end of twelve or thirteen hours from Euston-square, we hear a howling of Embra' or Gleska, as the case may be, and we emerge from the carriage to which we had grown quite attached, and find ourselves in a new world. No educated Englishman needs to be told nowadays that Scotchmen do not wear tartan, — that the figures one sees at the doors of tobacco-shops in London have no prototypes in the North, — that a kilt is seen just as frequently in Regent-street as on the Calton-hill, and that those persons who describe themselves when in England as THE MAC TODDY or THE MAC LOSKY, know rather better than to make fools of themselves by assuming such designations when at home. Still we have things among us here which you know nothing about; and I am going to give you some idea of one or two of our "peculiar institutions." I have before my eyes the recent fate of Mr. Macaulay, when he recorded certain unpalatable truths in regard to Scotland, his "respected mither." But what I say shall be said in all good-nature; and I do not believe that the sensible portion of my adopted compatriots forms such a *genus irritabile* as you might fancy from reading about the doings of the Society for maintaining Scottish Rights.

Do you remember one morning when you were here, the post-bag yielding a Glasgow newspaper, which having glanced at I pitched with indignation into the fire? The reason was, that it contained a long report of a proceeding which no acquaintance with it will ever make tolerable to me, or indeed make anything but revolting and disgusting: I mean what is called a *Congregational Soirée* in the City Hall at Glasgow. Such things are very common among the dissenters; and I am sorry to say they are not quite unknown in the church. There are some congregations consisting exclusively of the lower orders, whose ministers maintain a certain popularity by dint of roaring and ranting, and every kind of wretched claptrap which appeals to the mob. And these men find it expedient to have a *soirée* (pronounced *surree*, with a strong accent on the latter syllable) annually. I need not tell you that the more dignified and respectable among the clergy utterly abhor such things. I could no more fancy my excellent friend, Dr. Muir of Edinburgh, spouting nonsense on a platform to excite the laughter of maid-servants, than I could picture the Archbishop of Canterbury preaching while standing on his head. But let me try to give you some idea of what the thing is.

I have had occasion once or twice to see the City Hall at Glasgow. Whenever the freedom of the city is given to any eminent man, the ceremony takes place there, the Lord Provost making a speech on the occasion. It is a large ugly building, in a street called the Candleriggs, which runs out of the Trongate, the main artery of Glasgow traffic. It is very large, holding some three or four thousand people. It is simply a huge square room, with a flat ceiling. Galleries surround it on three sides: on the fourth side is a large platform, backed by a fine organ. It has a cheerful appearance, being painted throughout in white and gold. This Hall is used for all kinds of purposes; the Corporation, very shabbily I think, making a profit by letting it out to any one who may want it. There the Wizard of the North was wont for many a day to perform his tricks: there did Mr. Barnum exhibit Tom Thumb: there have Jenny Lind and Grisi sung: there does Jullien yearly give a course of concerts: there has Kossuth spoken, and there Mr. Macaulay, Lord Elgin, the Duke of Argyle, Mr. Dickens, and a greater man than all, Sir Archibald Alison: there has Mr. George Thompson howled: there has the Anti-State-Church Association made itself ridiculous: there next day have the friends of the Kirk rallied by thousands; and on the day after, the advocates of the Democratic and Social Republic: there have been held cattle-show dinners and Crimean banquets; and there *soirées* in honor of all sorts and conditions of men, from Mrs. Beecher Stowe down to Mr. Stiggins (who became a dissenting minister in Whistlebinkie after his historic kicking by the senior Mr. Weller): and after this pleasing variety of engagements during the week, the Hall is let for divine service on Sunday. There hath the Rev.

Dr. Bahoo wept, and the Rev. Mr. Spurgeon bellowed: there hath a young scamp of ten years old preached to a congregation of thousands; and thence hath the Rev. Mr. McQuack retired with a collection of £3 15*s.* 2¾*d.* for the mission to send flannel waistcoats and moral pocket-handkerchiefs to the uninstructed Howowows.

The first announcement of the approaching festival is an advertisement in the Glasgow newspapers that a Congregational Soirée of St. Gideon's Church will be held in the City Hall upon a certain evening: The Rev. Dr. Bahoo, M. A., D. D., LL.D., in the chair. Addresses will be delivered by the Rev. Melchisedec Howler, the Rev. Jeremy Diddler (Missionary to Borrioboolagha), the Rev. Roaring Buckie (of Yellington-cum-Bellow), the Rev. Soapy Sneaky (domestic chaplain to the Hon. Scapegrace Blackleg), and the Rev. Mountybanke Buffune. By the kind permission of Col. Blazes, the band of the gallant 969th will attend. Tickets, including a paper of sweeties, a cooky, two figs, and five cups of tea, price, eight pence each. N. B. — A collection at the door, *to prevent confusion.*

The proceedings begin at six o'clock upon the appointed evening, by which hour the people are seated at long tables arranged in the Hall, displaying a large assortment of tea-cups of many varied patterns. Each person on entering has received a paper-bag, containing the promised cooky (you would call it a penny-bun), the figs, and the sweeties. The platform is covered with men, the leading individuals of the congregation, and the speakers of the evening. *That* is Mr. Soapy Sneaky, with the long lank hair, the blue spectacles, and the diabolical squint. That fat, round little man is Dr. Bahoo, already affected to tears by the contemplation of so many tea-cups, and by the reflection that they will all be broken within the next hundred years. That is Melchisedec Howler, with tremendously-developed jaws and a bull-neck, but hardly any perceptible forehead. And that is Mr. Buckie, with the apoplectic face, and corpulent figure. First, a Psalm is sung; then a long prayer is offered. The band of the 969th then plays a polka. Next greasy men go round, and pour tea of uninviting appearance out of large kettles into the numberless tea-cups. The men on the platform partake of the same cheering beverage. A great clatter of crockery is heard: many of the guests, ere they have finished their fifth cup (they are breakfast-cups) become visibly distended: most of the children find it expedient to stand up. Tea being over, the military band plays the "March of the Cameron Men," or "Bonnie Dundee," amid great shouting and stamping. The Rev. Dr. Bahoo, the minister of the congregation, then gets up and makes a speech in the nature of a sermon, with a few jokes thrown in. The reverend gentleman gets much excited. He frequently weeps during his speech, and in a little laughs again. He tells the people how hawppee he is to see them awl: how many additional seats have been let in St. Gideon's Church during the past year: how many scores of Sawba schule teachers and Sawba scholars are connected with the congregation. A Psalm is then sung by the people: a polka follows: then there is a pause to allow the figs to be eaten. Then the Rev. Melchisedec Howler addresses the meeting. He shouts and stamps: he bellows out his ungrammatical fustian with perfect confidence. Happy man, he is so great a fool that he has not the faintest suspicion that he is a fool at all. Streams of perspiration flow down his face. In leaving the Hall, you will hear the general remark among the enlightened audience, "Wasna' yon gran'?" "Oh, but he *swat extraordinar.*" The meeting goes on for three or four hours, with the same strange jumble of prayers and polkas, religion and buffoonery, tears of penitence and roars of laughter. At length, about ten or eleven at night, after three cheers for the chairman, the benediction is pronounced, and the festival is ended.

Well, my dear Editor, is not that a peculiar institution, with a vengeance? I assure you I am not exaggerating or caricaturing, in my description of the hateful exhibition. Anything more irreverent and revolting than what I have myself witnessed (for I went out of curiosity to two or three such scenes) cannot be. I have seen clergymen say and do things at them which were just as degrading as if they had shaved their heads, painted their faces with ochre, put on a spangled dress, and tumbled head over heels. I have stated that the more staid and reputable clergy utterly eschew such meetings: most of the ministers who appear at them are men prepared to have recourse to the very lowest and most contemptible means in order to gain a wretched popularity with the least intelligent of the community. Don't you feel that Dr. Bahoo and Mr. Howler would preach standing on their heads, if *that* would draw a crowd to the scene of their buffooneries? Don't you feel that they would severally sing *Hot codlins* from the pulpit, rather than see the boxes deserted and the pit empty? They are simply tenth-rate melodramatic actors; and I will speak of them as such.

Now for another Scotch peculiarity.

I remember well your look of amazement when, one

day as we drove past a whitewashed barn a few miles off, I said to you, "That is the parish church of Timmerstane-parva." You thought at first that I wished to practise on your credulity, in return for certain wicked mystifications which you practised upon me in our college days. But I spoke in sober sadness. We have abundance of churches in Scotland which no mortal would ever guess were churches; buildings without one trace of Christian character; whitewashed barns externally, with a belfry at one end; and internally, just four walls and a flat roof, with a higgledy-piggledy of rickety pews, and a rude box at one end to serve for a pulpit. Now I have no doubt that you thought all this was the remaining leaven of the sour Puritan spirit: and that you supposed that the mass of the Scotch people really think that God is most likely to be worshipped in sincerity between walls green with damp and streaming with moisture, and under a flat ceiling whence large pieces of plaster are wont to detach themselves during divine service. You were quite mistaken if you took up any such impression. There are one or two bigoted sects which have inherited the spirit of the Covenanters, among which a good deal of stupid prejudice still lingers; and the people of these sects would very probably prefer Timmerstane Kirk to York Minster. But I am sure the well-filled pews you saw in our parish church testify that Scotch people will come very willingly to a decent church when they can find one; and if you knew what frantic efforts the dissenting congregations in large towns make to imitate our cathedrals in cheap lath-and-plaster Gothic, you would be convinced that it is no preference for shabbiness and dirt on the part of the people that keeps numbers of Scotch kirks the disreputable places they are. No, my dear Editor; I wish to reveal to you, and through you to your countless readers, including so great a portion of the intelligence and refinement of England, what is the real blight of Scotch church architecture. It is, in brief, the abominable, mean, dirty, and contemptible shabbiness and parsimony of a great many of the *heritors* of Scotland. But what are the *heritors*, you will say, and what have they to do with the churches? I will tell you all about it.

The heritors of a parish are the proprietors of land within it. They are bound by law to build and maintain the church and parsonage. They likewise pay the stipend of the clergyman. Now, of course, when they or their fathers bought their estates, they got them for so much less in consideration of these circumstances. The primary charge upon all the land of Scotland is the Church Establishment; and in rendering its due to the church, the heritors are simply fulfilling the condition on which they hold their property, — doing what it would be dishonest not to do; and they are, manifestly, no more entitled to take credit for maintaining the church and clergyman, than the farmer is entitled to flap his wings and cry aloud, "I am a virtuous man; I am a hero in morality; I actually pay my landlord his rent!" Now many heritors forget all this: they fancy that the church is a burden upon them; and they endeavor by every shabby dodge to render that burden as light as possible. You see I don't spare the class to which I myself belong: as a general rule, in all church matters, we are about as mean a set as you can find in Europe. Very many of us are dipped in debt, and are struggling to maintain an appearance quite beyond our means. I have in my mind's eye at this moment at least a score of men who are the very ideal of Mr. Thackeray's *Country Snob.* We really have not a sixpence to spare; and we must save all we can off the Kirk. And the rascally barns which in so many places do duty as parish churches, testify to our shabbiness and that of our fathers. No doubt there are many noble exceptions to what I have been saying. Here and there one finds a really beautiful and ecclesiastical church, testifying to the liberality of Mr. Stirling of Keir, Mr. Tyndall Bruce of Falkland, or Colonel Cathcart of Craigengillan. And the Duke of Buccleugh, a nobleman in the best sense of the phrase, is a splendid instance of liberality in all church matters. A writer in *The Times* told us lately that we country gentlemen of Scotland were such a race of snobs, that if the duke became a Mormon, we should all believe in Joe Smith too. I have no doubt a great many of us would. But you won't find us imitating that eminent personage when the act to be imitated consists in putting our hand in our pocket. No: we are independent men, who think for ourselves when it comes to *that!* And an especial evil is, that at a meeting of the heritors of a parish, each person has an equal voice. A man with ten thousand a year has one vote only, and so has the proprietor of a pigsty. Neighboring proprietors don't like to come to loggerheads, and divisions are avoided at such meetings. And so, as the weakest link in a chain is the limit of its strength, the shabbiest heritor at a meeting is generally the limit of its liberality.

I have been reading with great interest and pleasure Mr. Beckett Denison's *Lectures on Church-building.* If that accomplished gentleman would pay me a visit, I think I could astonish him. I could show him men, passably intelligent on other topics, who in the matter of church-building utterly gainsay and deny those elementary principles which appear to Mr. Denison and myself as indisputable as any axiom in morals. I will back a meeting of Scotch heritors against any collection of men anywhere in the world, for dense ignorance, dogged obstinacy, and comfortable self-conceit. I should imagine the feelings of a man driving a large flock of refractory pigs to market, must be much what mine were when I first set to work to persuade my brother heritors of this parish to build the handsome church you saw here. I don't believe that Lord Clarendon needed more diplomatic skill to manage matters at the Paris Congress, than was requisite to talk over some of the miserable little scrubs of small proprietors into common sense. The upshot was, that Sir —— —— and I agreed to bear the entire expense, provided the matter were left to our own management. About two thirds of the parish belong to us; the remainder being parcelled out among some five-and-forty heritors. We paid the share of these men in addition to our own; and though they were not involved in the work to the extent of a sixpence, they still cast every vexatious annoyance in our way.

Let me try to give you an idea of a meeting of heritors. It is held in the church. About ten minutes before the appointed hour, we see three or four blue-nosed pragmatical-looking old fellows approaching, arrayed in long brown great-coats of remote antiquity, each man wearing a shocking bad hat. These are some of the smaller heritors, each possessor of a few bare acres of moor-land in some wild part of the parish. They are certainly Dissenters, probably Cameronians; and quite ready at a word to smite the prophets of Baal, as they would call your amiable bishop or your good rector.

They look around in a hostile and perverse manner, and snuff the air like wild asses' colts. A little after comes a man with a red pimply face, a hoarse voice, and a bullying manner. He is the *factor* of some proprietor who is ashamed to do dirty work himself, but does not object to having it done for him. Then comes a little withered anatomy of a man, a retired Manchester tradesman, who has bought a few fields, planted them with hoaks and hashes, and built there an Ouse from his own design, a great work of hart. Half-a-dozen more blue-nosed small heritors, two or three more factors, and one or two gentlemen, complete the meeting. Suppose they are examining the drawings of the new kirk. Oh, rare are their critical remarks.

"Aw doant see ony need for a speere," says one low fellow. "Whawt 's that croass doin' aboove the gahble?" says another; "we're no gangin' to hawve a rawg o' papistry in this pawrish." "If that's the way to build a church," says a pig-headed blockhead who never saw a decent church in his life, "I know nothing aboot church-building." Sober truth the creature utters; but he fancies he is talking sarcastically. Something is said of an open roof. "Wha ever saw a roof like thawt?" says one of the blue-nosed men; "thawt's jist like maw barrrn." A Cameronian elder says, in a discordant whine, "Goad is to be wurshupped in spurrit and in trewth: whawt house will ye big unto him? Habakkuk thirteenth and fifth." "Stained glass," says a pert little shopkeeper from Whistlebinkie, "is essentially Popish and Antichrist." Finally a burst of coarse laughter follows the witticism, from an individual with a strong smell of whiskey, — "If Mr. Macdoanald wants the kirk sae fine, let him pye for it himself. Aw heer he was bred at

Ooxfurd; maybe he wants us a' to turn prelatists. He had better gang awa' bawk to Inglan' wi' his papish notions." At this juncture the honorable proprietor's utterance becomes indistinct, and in a little a loud snoring proclaims that he is asleep. While the discussion is going on, some of the heritors are spitting emulously at a pew door about a dozen feet off. They generally hit it, with a dexterity resulting from long practice.

What wonder if educated men and gentlemen avoid such meetings? And thus, unhappily, the management of matters falls into the hands of some blowsy village demagogue, whose impertinence has driven the squire or baronet of the parish away; or of two or three of the withered old Cameronians with the long brown greatcoats.

The Scotch are not a demonstrative race. I do not believe that among our laboring class here in the country, there is any want of real heart and feeling; but there is a great awkwardness and stiffness in the expression of it. People here do not give utterance to their emotion like your volatile Frenchman: they have not words to say what they feel; and they would be ashamed (*blaté*, in their own phrase) to use these words if they had them. I have had a touching instance of this within the last few days. Do you remember our taking a walk together one beautiful afternoon to the cottage of one of my people, a poor fellow who was dying of consumption? You sat upon a stile, I recollect, and read a proof, while I went in and sat with him for a few minutes. It seemed to cheer him a little to have a visit from the laird, and I often went to see him. After you left us he sank gradually, — it was just the old story of that hopeless malady,

— till at last, after a few days in bed, he died. I hate all cant and false pretence; but there was earnest reality in the simple faith which made my humble friend's last hours so calm and hopeful. When he felt himself dying he sent for me, and I went and stayed beside him for several hours. The clergyman's house was some miles off; and apart from private regard, it was a part of my duty as an elder of the kirk to go and pray as well as I could with the poor fellow. He was only thirty-two, but he had been married eight or nine years, and he had four little children. After lying silent for a while, he said he would like to see them again; and his wife brought them to his bedside. I know well that no dying father ever felt a more hearty affection for the little things he was leaving behind, or a more sincere desire for their welfare after he had left them. He was not so weak but that he could speak quite distinctly; and I thought that he would try and say something to them in the way of a parting advice, were it only to bid them be good children, and be kind and obedient to their mother. Yet all he did was just to shake each of the three elder children by the hand, and to say *Gude-day.* As for the youngest, a wee thing of two years old, he said to it, "Will you gie me a bit kiss?" and the mother lifted up the wondering child to do so. "Say Ta-ta to your feyther," she said. "Ta-ta," said the poor little boy, in a loud, cheerful voice, and then ran out of the cottage to play with some companions.

The story, I feel, is nothing to tell; but the little scene affected me much. I believe I have told you the exact words that were said; and then the dying man turned away his face and closed his eyes, and I saw many tears running down his thin cheeks. I knew it was the very abundance of that poor man's heart that choked his utterance, and brought down his last farewell to a commonplace greeting like that with which he might have parted from a neighbor for a few hours. *Gude-day* was his farewell for ever! He felt that he had so very much to say, that he did not know where to begin it; and so his weary heart shrank from the task, and he said almost nothing. I thought how your friend Mr. Tennyson could have interpreted that *Gude-day*. How much of unutterable affection — how much of good advice and fatherly warning — how much of prayer for them to the great Father of the orphans — was implied in poor David's *Gude-day!*

I read a paragraph in *The Times*, a few weeks since, in which it was stated that the late Bishop of London had informed a certain congregation, which had the choice of its clergyman, that he would not upon any account permit a succession of candidates for the living to preach in the parish church. I think the Bishop was right. There is something most degrading to the clerical character, and inconsistent with the nature of preaching, in the practice of persons "holding forth" to a congregation to let the people see how well they can do it, the congregation meanwhile sitting in a critical and judicial capacity. And I lament to tell you that what is a very rare and exceptional thing in England, is a very common thing in Scotland — the practice of *hearing candidates*, as it is termed. You are aware that, at different periods, a great row has been made in this country about the existence of church patronage; the people always agitating to get the selection of their ministers put in their own hands. In one shape or another, this agitation has been the source of all the secessions from the Scotch Kirk. Ever since the great secession in 1843, most patrons have been anxious to make popular appointments, for fear of driving the people away from church to some of the multitudinous neighboring conventicles; and instead of directly presenting a clergyman to a vacant benefice, they have in some way consulted the wishes of the parishioners. In the case of the parish in which I reside, and of which I possess the patronage, I did not take this course. I took every pains to find a clergyman who should be a good preacher, a scholar, and a gentleman; and then I presented him without consulting the people in any way. I knew thoroughly that, had I given them their choice, I should simply have been devolving my privilege of appointing a minister upon Smout the baker, Swipes the publican, and Muttonhead the butcher. *They* would, to a certainty, have directed the judgment of the humbler parishioners; and I conceived myself to be a more competent judge of clerical qualifications than these gentlemen. And though the people grumbled a little at first, their good sense and Mr. Smith's faithfulness triumphed in the long run, and he is now extremely popular with all classes. I did not choose to allow Smout, Swipes, and Muttonhead to give me for a parish clergyman some bellowing boor, whom I should have been ashamed to ask to meet my friends at my table.

When a patron is more desirous of immediate popularity than I was, he follows one of two courses: he appoints three or four individuals, each of whom he thinks suitable for the cure, and allows the people to select one of these; or he says to the parishioners, "You may nominate three clergymen, and I shall take my choice of these." The former course, which is called "giving a leet," is the more usual, I believe. In either case, a preaching-match follows, and the people select by comparative trial. In the case of some town churches, where the congregations have the entire matter in their own hands, with no patron to keep them within reasonable limits, forty or fifty candidates have sometimes been heard. Then, by a process of elimination, that number is reduced to two or three; these two or three are asked to preach a second time; and, finally, the election is completed, amid all the degrading circumstances which attend most contested elections. Don't crow over us, my dear Oliver, for I see that you have lately had in London a similar discreditable course of procedure.

Each of the competing candidates of course does his best to make a favorable impression. With congregations of the lower orders the victory lies with him who possesses the strongest lungs and the emptiest head. It is a great stroke in preaching as a candidate to repeat the sermon entirely from memory; a successful claptrap is to shut the Bible with a bang immediately after giving out the text. It very generally happens that the upshot is the division of the parishioners into two violently opposed parties; the educated and respectable people declaring for some preacher of cultivated mind and gentleman-like manner, and the lower classes for some huge, raw-boned, yelling, and perspiring animal, with intense vulgarity in his every tone and gesture, whom they regard as one of themselves. After some weeks of excitement and diplomacy, something like unanimity is generally arrived at; the patron generally holding it *in terrorem* over the people, that if they do not agree within a given time, he will appoint a minister without consulting them. The *hearing-candidate* system has a most degrading effect upon those preachers who seek to get preferment by it. It tempts directly to every coarse expedient for pulpit effect, and every sneaky means to gain the private good-will of the rabble. Still the system works in practice a shade better than might be anticipated *à priori*; and though sometimes permanent splits result, the minority going off to the Dissenting meeting-house, yet this is far from being the general rule. I need not tell you that no clergyman of any standing would "preach as a candidate" for any living. Candidate preachers are for the most part drawn from the class of newly-fledged licentiates; and from that species of much-perspiring, loud-howling, flabby-faced, and big-jawed preachers, who formed the dunces of the philosophy-classes at college, and who now constitute the parliamentary train of the Kirk.

I have been so little in England of late years, that I do not know whether the institution which I am about to describe is a Scotch peculiarity, or whether it exists on your side of the border: I mean what may be called the *testimonial nuisance.* There is hardly anybody left in this country who has not had a snuff-box, watch and chain, purse of sovereigns, tea-kettle, claret-jug, book-case, gig-whip, saddle and bridle, pony, horse, cow, pig, dog-cart, set of harness, timepiece, Matthew Henry's *Commentary on the Scriptures,* load of meal, cart of potatoes, pig's face, German-silver pencil-case, everlasting gold pen, pulpit-gown and cassock, case of mathematical instruments, tea-tray, set of teacups, dozen of teaspoons, dozen of shirts, dozen of pocket handkerchiefs, or dozen of flannel waistcoats, presented to him by a circle of friends and admirers, and the presentation chronicled at great length in the local newspaper. Country gentlemen, clergymen, railway guards, drivers of stage-coaches, gamekeepers, shepherds, local poetasters, farmers, newspaper reporters, keepers of public-houses, schoolmasters, turnpike-gatekeepers, railway signal-men, stokers of coasting steamers, are among the people most frequently honored in this way. When a testimonial is presented to a man in the humbler walks of life, it is usually followed by a supper, concerning which the *Whistlebinkie Gazette* never fails to record that the arrangements reflected the utmost credit on mine host of the Blue Boar; the evening was spent most harmoniously, Mr. Ronald McCracken favoring the company with his favorite song, "Jenny dang the weaver;" and at a late hour all parties went home, "happy to meet, sorry to part, and happy to meet again." Whenever a new minister comes to any parish, on the day of his induction he is presented with a superb pulpit gown (made by Messrs. Roderick, Doo, and Co., our enterprising fellow-townsmen), and a pulpit Bible and psalm-book (purchased at the establishment of Mr. McLamroch, bookseller, 91, High-street). On going away, he receives a timepiece or silver salver, (furnished, we understand, by Messrs. Waxy and Jollikin, Chronometer-makers, Saltergate); and if a poor man, perhaps a purse of sovereigns (the purse made by the fair fingers of Miss Jemima McCorkle, daughter of the much esteemed surgeon of that name). The handsome gift (we invariably learn) was presented in a few brief but pithy remarks by Mr. James McWilliam, farmer in Cleugh-Lochacher; and the reverend gentleman, who appeared much overcome by his feelings, made an affecting and suitable reply. Occasionally we find it recorded that the tenantry on the estate of Netherwoodie and Clanjamfry proceeded to the Mansion House, and presented Skipness Alexander Skipness, Esq., their esteemed landlord, with his portrait, drawn in the first style of art by Cosmo Saunders, Esq., R. S. A. They likewise presented an elegant cairngorm brooch to Mrs. Skipness; a whip to Master Sholto Skipness Skipness; and a humming top to Master Reginald Comyne Skipness, the latter gentleman aged one year and eight months. Mr. Skipness, much affected (recipients of testimonials in this country are always much affected), made a suitable reply. He felt his merits were greatly over-estimated. If indeed it were true that he had been the first to introduce into the county an improved breed of pigs, he had his reward in the whisperings of an approving conscience. Turnips had for years occupied much of his attention; nor had cheese passed without many serious thoughts. Onions and carrots, he might say, had rarely been absent from his mind. Still, much remained to be done. There was no limit to the fat which might be carried by the Clanjamfry breed of cattle; and whatever might be the feeling of others, he, for one, would always connect the gimmers and hogs of this district with the future prosperity of the country. The tenantry were then entertained at the hospitable board of Netherwoodie, and left at a late hour, having spent an evening which will long be cherished as a green spot in memory's waste.

Do you remember one morning glancing over the *Whistlebinkie Guardian*, and reckoning up thirty-eight testimonials which had been presented in the preceding week to different individuals in the county? I doubt not that, in your simplicity, you fancied that this district contained an immense number of deserving characters, surrounded by a most generous public. Quite a mistake. Most of the recipients deserved nothing particular: most of the subscribers were lugged into giving sorely against their will. Let me explain to you the philosophy of the matter. A, let us say, wants a testimonial for himself. It would not do, however, to endeavor directly to get one up. A therefore goes to B, and proposes to get up a testimonial to C. Now C never did anything remarkable in all his life; and B does not want to give him anything. But it would be a most invidious thing to refuse to subscribe: and so, for fear of giving offence, B, D, E, F, G, and H, severally put down their shilling or their pound, as the case may be: the present is given; the supper or dinner comes off; and the *Gazette* and *Guardian* report the proceedings. In a few months C, who has been made aware who it was that set his own testimonial on foot, feels himself called upon to get up one to A. Then B gets up one to D; D reciprocates; and so on all round. Thus, you see, the balance of property in the district is not disturbed; for each man gets as much as he gives. Neither are people's relative positions and estimations altered; for no man is distinguished above his neighbor. The secret vanity of each individual is gratified: a kindly spirit is maintained in the neighborhood; and in the long run the truth is not prejudiced, for these testimonials come to be valued at pretty nearly what they are worth.

The mention of *testimonials* reminds me of another Scotch peculiarity, about which I may tell you something. All sorts of people in this country are fond of making what they call a collection of *testimonials* or *certificates*, setting forth their qualifications and merits. They apply to any one who may be in a prominent position, whether he knows much of them or not; and receive a sheet of note-paper inscribed with the most outrageous and exaggerated compliments. Each person who is asked to give a certificate considers what good qualities the man ought to have in order to be fit for the place he is aiming at, or what good qualities the man would like to be thought to possess; and incontinently sets his signature to a declaration that the man does possess the very highest degree of all these good qualities. A really profligate disregard of truth prevails in Scotland as to this matter. One constantly finds men, even of established reputation, asserting in written testimonials what, if you ask them their real opinion in private, they will confess to you is absurd and untrue. We all understand that in newspaper reports all sermons are eloquent and impressive, all landlords are liberal, all county members are unweared in their attention to their duties, all professors are learned, all divines are pious, all magistrates are worthy, all military men are gallant, all royal dukes are illustrious. We all understand what such statements are worth; nor does any man but the most verdant care a straw for the critical notices of the *Whistlebinkie Gazette*, which assure us that Mr. Snooks, the local poet, is a much greater man than Mr. Tennyson; and that Mr. Green, our talented young townsman, has already surpassed Turner as a landscape-painter. I don't suppose that you are much elevated when the *Guardian* of our county town declares, at the beginning of a month, that "*Fraser* holds on its way with a ringing and jubilant wildness and manliness of fierceness and terror," — whatever all that may mean, which I confess I don't know. But the Scotch system of exaggerated and (in short) false declarations, made by grave divines and high-spirited gentlemen, as to the qualifications of Smith, Jones, and Robinson, ought to be put down. It deceives and misleads: it is calculated and, I believe, *intended* to deceive and mislead. I feel strongly on the subject, for I take a warm interest in the schools of this parish; and when I first came here, I was most thoroughly taken in by the flaming characters which several teachers brought, who afterwards proved shamefully incompetent. A lad of very deficient intellect and education, and quite devoid of common sense, applying for a teacher's place, comes with a long array of testimonials from clergymen and professors, which, if true, would prove him a prodigy of talent, industry, amiability, and all other virtues under heaven. An extremely bad preacher and wretched scholar, applying for a living (I had no end of such applications when this parish was vacant), brings with him testimonials which tend to show that the human race cannot be expected to produce many such wonders in a single century. The result of all this is, that written testimonials now mostly go for nothing — at least, with people of any experience. They are sometimes even regarded with suspicion. If a teacher in a parish school becomes a candidate for another parish school, and brings with him a very high certificate from the heritors and clergyman of the parish where he is at present, the fear is that they have given him this strong recommendation in order to get rid of him.

A story is told *apropos* of this. A teacher came to the parish of X, bringing an immensely strong certificate from the parish of Y, in which he was at present settled. On the strength of this certificate, the heritors of X elected him to their vacant school. It should be mentioned that the parishes of X and Y are many miles apart. The teacher began his work at X, and speedily proved worth nothing — a lazy, stupid, useless incubus on the parish.

One of the heritors of X met a heritor of Y, and inquired, with some indignation, what on earth the heritors of Y meant by giving such a flaming certificate to an utterly incapable teacher? "Why," said Mr. Y, with great coolness, "We gave that certificate to get you to take him off our hands; and, let me tell you, you people of X will have to give him a far higher character before you will get rid of him!"

I do not vouch for the story's truth: and I believe that good-nature, and unwillingness to give pain by a refusal, are the origin of most of these undeserved panegyrics. When a poor fellow asks you to give a certificate of fitness for some place for which you know he is not fit, but which he has yet set his heart on, it is hard to say no. The temptation is strong to stretch a point in order to say a good word for him; or at any rate to write a few sentences which, without meaning anything, sound as though they meant something in his praise.

And now, my dear fellow, I dare say you are wearied of all this gossip about our Scotch Peculiarities. I have a vast deal more to say, but I think I had better stop for the present. I hope soon to see you here again. It is curious how arbitrarily the memory singles out little incidents and keeps them vividly alive, when worthier things have perished. When I look back upon your late visit to us, I am ashamed to say that the thing which comes out in strongest relief is, not any of your wise and witty sayings, not any of your philosophical reflections, not any of the grand or beautiful scenes on which we looked together. None of these: but I see you yet, with a doubtful expression on your usually serene face, eating a plate of oatmeal porridge, and assuring my wife that you liked it. Well I knew that in your secret soul you would rather have read the very dullest article in the Balaam-box.

Believe me,

Ever your sincere friend,

C. A. M.

Craig-Houlakim,
November 24th, 1856

CONCLUSION.

HESE were the kind of thoughts that passed through my mind in the leisure hours of various months in town. The hours, indeed, in which I have been free from the pressure of duty, were short; and they were not many: yet, by regular use, one may turn even these to some account. All kinds of hours, morning and evening, of every day of the week except Saturday and Sunday, have gone to the production of these pages. I have not an evergreen now, though I have planted so many; nor am I the possessor of a single tree of any kind. And when I go and visit the pleasant homes of certain friendly country parsons, I feel my loss; and I sigh a little for the days that are gone. And so these pages have not been thought out amid the sunshiny and breezy places where I wrote certain other pages which possibly you have read. Many of them were thought out by a city fireside; some of them in solitary half-hour walks on quiet winter evenings in a certain broad gas-lit street, remarkable for that absence of passers-by which is characteristic of many of the streets of this beautiful city. But especially I remember many restful hours, happily combining duty with leisure, which are within the reach of every unambitious Scotch clergyman. I mean the hours

which on one day in each month he may spend in attending the Presbytery to which he belongs. The Presbytery, possibly you do not know, is a court of the Scotch Church; consisting of the clergymen of a number of adjoining parishes, with a lay member from each parish besides. This court exercises over a certain district of country the authority which in England is exercised by a Bishop. It is the duty of every member to be present: so that while attending its sittings you have a pleasant sense that you are in the way of your duty. The business of this Ecclesiastical Court is of deep interest to those who feel a deep interest in it. And a weighty responsibility rests with those members of it whose experience and administrative ability are such as entitle them and fit them to lead their brethren. But a good many of the clergy, especially of the younger clergy, have no vocation that way: and the very eloquent and remarkably long speeches which are often made, would be somewhat wearisome if you tried to listen to them. But if you do not try to listen to them, unless at some specially interesting juncture, or when some one is speaking whose words carry special weight, you may have many hours of leisure there; and think of material for various chapters like those you have been reading. I have found my hours at the Presbytery very favorable to contemplation, as well as a delightful rest to body and mind. You are in the path of duty: and yet you feel that your insignificance makes your responsibility quite inappreciable. You do your work, we may hope, as a parish clergyman, diligently and not unsuccessfully. But as an ecclesiastical lawyer and legislator, in all probability, your influence is very properly at zero. You have entire confidence that the affairs of the district are being managed by wise and good men, who are your seniors in age and your superiors in wisdom. So you may enjoy a day of rest: and of rest happily combined with duty. I have a very great veneration and affection for the Church of England: but I do not think that grand Establishment affords her clergy any season, recurring regularly and not unfrequently, during which they may feel that they are attending to their clerical duty, while yet they are quite free from any sense of responsibility, and from any feeling that they are doing anything whatever.

And so I commend these chapters to the kindly reader, hoping that they are not the last.

THE END.

CAMBRIDGE: PRINTED BY H. O. HOUGHTON.

www.ingramcontent.com/pod-product-compliance
Lightning Source LLC
LaVergne TN
LVHW021138110826
845150LV00005B/1060
9781425549046